Envisioning Sustainabilities

Envisioning Sustainabilities:

Towards an Anthropology of Sustainability

Edited by

Fiona Murphy and Pierre McDonagh

**Cambridge
Scholars**
Publishing

Envisioning Sustainabilities: Towards an Anthropology of Sustainability

Edited by Fiona Murphy and Pierre McDonagh

This book first published 2016

Cambridge Scholars Publishing

Lady Stephenson Library, Newcastle upon Tyne, NE6 2PA, UK

British Library Cataloguing in Publication Data
A catalogue record for this book is available from the British Library

ISBN (10): 1-4438-9537-7
ISBN (13): 978-1-4438-9537-8

TABLE OF CONTENTS

LIST OF TABLES

LIST OF FIGURES

Fig 4.1 Sustainability within the project with regard to landscape ecology, hydrology, and anthropology

Fig.5-1. People gathered for a collective bread-making event at the first Bread House community center in Gabrovo, Bulgaria

Fig 5-2. Bread puppets expressing the vision and hopes of the traumatized women in Plovdiv for a better future life, in a home where the aroma of hot bread is a marker of peace and love.

Fig.5-3. Julian, a young man with Down Syndrome, like many others found accepting environment and friends around the wood-fired oven and kneading table. People of all ages and all walks of life mixed without any unease, as if this is the most natural thing, and perhaps it is when the right conditions are at place.

Fig.5-4. Students from the different classes at a high-school in Nova Zagora get united by their Director and vision to build a communal wood-fired oven, which becomes a focus of multiple inter-generational and inter-cultural gatherings– a perfect case of "cross-sensorial learning".

Fig. 5-5. A young woman war-veteran in Massachusetts (USA), suffering mental trauma after the fights in Afghanistan, participates with enthusiasm in the baking after her initial skepticism – bread reminds her of her grandmother.

Fig 5-6 young men from Harlem, visibly a gang member, also joins and become like a child around the dough, joking that is better than the financial "dough".

Fig. 5-7. The Mobile Bread House built by students from Princeton University (NJ), regularly traveling to low-income neighborhoods to engage people in breaking bread and talk about non-violence and values.

ACKNOWLEDGEMENTS

This book is a result of collective energies and conversations following a panel entitled 'Towards an anthropology of sustainability'. The idea for the initial panel emerged through conversations between co-editors Fiona Murphy and Pierre McDonagh and was developed in full through the IUAES. The book bears the imprint of a number of institutions- Dublin City University where the two co-editors first came together and following this the University of Bath and Queens University Belfast. Our thanks go to the authors of the individual contributions in this book. Two of the panel participants were unable to submit. We would also like to thank the individuals from marketing and anthropology disciplines who gave of their time to act as peer reviewers for our individual chapters. Prof. Pat Breterton author of our closing reflection took immense time out of his own schedule to read, reflect and engage with the various contributions in this book and for that we are grateful. Finally we would like to thank CSP. Thanks to Andy Prothero for her cover photo. We hope this book will speak to a range of individuals working in different academic disciplines and applied contexts. The importance of a social scientific reading of sustainability can not be understated Post-Brexit and we sincerely hope this book goes some of the way to stress the importance of this relationship.

FM and PM, July 2016

INTRODUCTION

FIONA MURPHY AND PIERRE MCDONAGH

> We owe it to ourselves and to our interlocutors to say loudly that we have
> seen alternative visions of humankind–indeed more than any academic
> discipline–and that we know that this one . . . that constructs economic
> growth as the ultimate human value . . . may not be the most respectful of
> the planet we share, nor indeed the most accurate nor the most practical.
> We also owe it to ourselves to say that it is not the most beautiful nor the
> most optimistic.
> —Michel-Rolph Trouillot, *Global Transformations* 2003:139.

The guiding inspiration of this book is to explore the important
contribution that social scientific research on sustainability can make to
sustainability science- as a whole. The contributors in this book are in the
main anthropologists-with one contribution from a political scientist and
one from a sociologist. Our contributors work in both academic and
applied contexts, thereby bringing with them a wealth of diverse
geographic, practical and theoretical expertise. The two co-editors come
from both an anthropological and critical marketing background, thus
positioning the collection in an interdisciplinary frame. Sustainability, the
key focus of this collection, is a concept with a diverse array of meanings,
anchored most firmly within issues connected to the natural environment.
Within its widespread application in the world of business, governmental
policy and the development world: its underlying principles and
definitions often prove nebulous and sometimes even conflicting; it is
reduced to the social, ecological and economic as a triple bottom line in
business circles. In the current climate of global crisis and indeed,
recovery, the question of how sustainable lifestyles, communities, and
businesses can be characterized is at the root of much debate. If, as
Charles Redman (2011) has recently proclaimed, anthropology should be
seen as key to the development of sustainable science, then how should
anthropology respond to this provocation?

This collection thus interrogates the evolution of '*sustainability
imaginaries*' in contexts as varied as urban planning, community gardens,
bread-making, sustainable food movements in Italy, applied projects such

as water projects in Bangladesh, and disaster studies (such as our example from Bulgaria on foot and mouth disease). Anthropology, and especially ethnography, are particularly well placed to proffer an understanding of the changing role of sustainability practices. An anthropology of sustainability, we believe, may well collapse facile divisions between academic and applied contexts, as well as, in this age of silo busting, facilitate greater dialogue between disciplines, for sustainability as a topic of study can only be an interdisciplinary one.

For its part, anthropology has a very long relationship with thinking about the environment accompanied by a rich literature (too numerous to list here) which, has led easily to the development of an anthropology of sustainability. A large number of anthropological monographs addressing the challenge of (in particular) environmental sustainability (see Milton 2002; Tsing 2005) exist. A rich history of practical, applied work on sustainability also exists within anthropology as a number of the contributors in this volume attest to.

In moving towards 'an anthropology of sustainability' (AoS), the contributors herein mark out a space to reconsider how ethnography can be an important tool on the path to understanding patterns and discourses of sustainability. Throughout this volume, various contributors map out some of the debates around the changing nature of ethnographic practice and attempt to reconceive its relationship to the study of sustainability. This kind of engagement is certainly not easy or assured, and there are complexities in conducting any 'ethnography of sustainability,' which our contributors highlight. It is notable too that this volume should be read in conjunction with the myriad of work already collated in the area of ecological or environmental anthropology.

What is to be learned then from the many encounters contained in this book? AoS seeks to contribute in manifold ways to the larger sustainability project, both academic and applied. Given notions of materialism, belief, perception, and values are at the core of the sustainability vision, anthropology as a discipline is particularly well placed to explore the challenges encountered by the sustainability movement. Further, applied anthropology, we submit, can and should be central to the implementation of many of these ideas. With such a project in mind, the editors of this book organised a panel at the 2013 International Union of Anthropological and Ethnological Sciences (IUAES) conference at the University of Manchester. Our panel entitled 'Towards an Anthropology of Sustainability,' gathered together a range of voices interested in contributing to a discussion on the relationship between the social sciences and sustainability studies. Our aims were modest, we were seeking simply to implement a more grounded and focused conversation on the value of anthropology, and more broadly, the social sciences in making real, valuable and practical contributions to what is one of the most urgent issues of contemporary times-the sustainability crisis. Our questions were simple and posed in exact terms. We wanted to very specifically investigate what anthropology offers to an interdisciplinary study of sustainability? In sum, what methods, concepts and applications work best in various research and field contexts- and how these engagements challenge anthropology as a discipline and the social sciences as a field of thought. We saw our panel as contributing to and checking the burgeoning body of interdisciplinary work examining the impact of anthropologies of sustainability on environmental injustices and the everyday of the contemporary world in the context of the climate change crisis. Further, this collection addresses the old divides between applied and academic anthropology in important ways (see- in particular- Suzanne Hanchett- this volume).

One aim in this book is to give a taste of the kind of work going on and the impressions this work is making, indeed, to do otherwise would be an encyclopedic endeavor- beyond the scope of this project. In this respect, the contributions in this volume combine to form a kind of "self-conscious ethnography" (Burton 2005:6) of sustainability in diverse geographical contexts. We want to stress that we are in some ways looking to anthropology to provide at least some answers to the urgent issues of climate change and community building during the reign of austerity. We accomplish this by asking specific scholars to delineate both their research practices as well as how they envision the relationship of anthropology to sustainability studies. For AoS to have value in the larger study of sustainability, it must learn to respond to the puzzles and pressures that climate change and economic crisis engender. The question of temporality also figures within this –addressing climate change is an urgent issue, one that requires speed and clarity, ethnographic research often takes long periods of time in order to get it 'right.'

What we present in this book is then a set of questions to stimulate further reflections on what kind of role AoS can play. In a globalised Europe, where crisis has become deeply anchored in discourses of loss, failure, and indeed, nostalgia, little research has been conducted on how sustainability practices (across different sectors) have been challenged or altered by economic austerity. While a general sense of disenchantment and malaise is part of the current zeitgeist, so too is the theme of recovery and sustainable lifestyles. Many of the chapters in this panel were researched and written in a moment when austerity policies figured large in public experience and debate. Amongst these debates, questions of well-being (societal and individual), of what constitutes a 'good life' (Skidelsky and Skidelsky 2012) and how this can be achieved, and environmental-sustainability politics figure large. A number of the contributions reflect these debates capturing thus an important moment in European cultural history and politics.

A rush to theorize the relations between anthropology and sustainability might ultimately lead to an overstatement of how such an engagement can lead to addressing some of the most urgent issues attached to climate change. We therefore see this collection as the opening up of an important conversation, embracing the knowledge of how collaboration and interdisciplinarity are key to the future of both anthropology and sustainability studies. This opening up is still required to avoid premature evaluation of the challenges at hand. Zizek (2011) has declared humanity is in denial as it lives in the 'end times,' which one would expect should propel anthropology into action. The chapters contained herein evince the view that sustainability issues exist across a broad range of societal issues as diverse as bread-making projects and urban planning. Herein, we provide an account of the complexities of ethnographic research practice, on the scale and application of AoS, and finally, how an anthropology of sustainability can in some ways be constructed as a moral anthropology. Finally, we give a brief account of how the chapters figure within the larger conversation to which we contribute. We note the chapters cannot necessarily be organised according to all of the themes we deal with here-rather they overlap and interconnect in myriad ways.

Mapping the Field of 'Sustainabilities'

One of the earliest definitions of sustainable development originated in the UN Bruntland commission, in a report called *Our Common Future* in 1987. It defined sustainable development as-"Sustainable development is development that meets the needs of the present without compromising the ability of future generations to meet their own needs". A number of the chapters in this collection engage with or debate the Bruntland commission's definition. While it is a definition widely lauded, many have critiqued these earlier visions of sustainability as eliding the importance of the social and over-emphasising the role of economic development. Of late, McDonagh Dobsha and Prothero (2012), elucidate the evolution towards Sustainable Consumption & Production (SC&P), which offers a more rounded understanding of the challenge. SC&P is taken from the United Nations Environment Programme (2009:8) to be, "the use of services and related products, which respond to basic needs and bring a better quality of life while minimizing the use of natural resources and toxic materials as well as the emissions of waste pollutants over the life cycle of the service product so as not to jeopardize the needs of further generations". We see from this collection that we have moved very far away from earlier definitions with the role of the social, society, and everyday life-worlds playing a much more profound role similar to the UNEP definition for SC&P.

A vision of 'sustainability' and sustainable behaviour is widely utilised in both the corporate and consumer's imaginary in a European and indeed, global context. Sustainability has become, we suggest, the connective tissue between ideas of responsibility, rationality, value, and ethics, all embedded in broader concerns for the future of the world in which we live. These concerns amongst others are embedded in the chapters in this book. Sustainability, as McDonough and Braungart (2010), posit is indeed the latest manifestation of a modernity seeking new modalities of competitive advantage and forms of economic growth through the demand for green technologies, green finance and other kinds of green products. Sustainability exists as a new paradigm for economic expansion (or sustainable capitalism). Corporations have become concerned with notions of sustainability models, with large companies such as INTEL and IBM recently launching 'sustainable' or 'smart' cities projects in London and Dublin. In some regions attempts have been made to reconfigure conflicting and complimentary voices in sustainability discourse (see SustaiNext EU 2012, where industry and education joined with policy makers and environmental non-government organisations to debate what is to be done to enable a green economy). Whether it is possible to see some domain of shared logic within these sustainability projects and networks, remains an important question, which we argue, ethnography as method and anthropology as analysis, is particularly well placed to answer. Our contributors debate the layered multivalent nature of the 'sustainability project' across diverse geographic regions, thus making an important statement on the existence of multiple 'sustainabilities'. This echoes earlier critiques in sociology on the meaning of nature (see Murphy 1994; 1995) and also early attempts to map the complexity of Green Organisations and Management (see McDonagh and Prothero 1997).

How we begin to map out and understand the intersecting lineaments of sustainability and anthropology's role within this is an important challenge, one we begin to address in this collection. The backdrop to these debates is a humanity and literature steeped in conflict, some of which views sustainability projects as part of a larger movement towards reflexive modernization in late-modern risk society (Beck 1992), a rational

response to globalization and a growing body of knowledge about the
"consequences of modernity" (Giddens 1990). Kilbourne, McDonagh, and
Prothero (1997) bring this further with their claims that ideas of
sustainable consumption prove a challenge to the dominant social
paradigm. Other scholars construct sustainability discourse as a reflection
and acceptance of neoliberal, market based policies, which engenders little
more than 'elitist environmental submarkets and lifestyles' (Paavola 2001:
244). As such the literature is permeated with an enduring suspicion which
both masks and reveals the dynamics of power and responsibility
embedded in sustainability projects, whether at individual, community,
corporate or governmental level. This seeming ambiguity embedded
within the project or projects of sustainability is undoubtedly a source of
cleavage for the ethnographer attempting to address sustainability
measures. Ambiguity serves a purpose when polysemy and competing
views of reality are to be embraced to envision new or untapped potential
for ideas, ideals, tragic historic events or disaster. We therefore position
this collection as a space attempting to converse with these ambiguities in
such a way as to argue the case for a solid sub-discipline such as an
anthropology of sustainability.

Constructing an Ethnography of 'Sustainabilities'

The challenges of conducting any 'ethnography of sustainability' are dealt
with by a number of contributors in this volume (see especially- McCabe
and Woodcraft- this volume). Conducting and writing any ethnography of
'sustainabilities' is then a particular craft wherein the nexus between
personal, ethical, moral, academic and applied viewpoints inheres. Many
of the contributors in this book deploy a range of methods, some
advocating for a mixed methods approach due to the scale of sustainability
projects. Other contributors draw on the 'auto-ethnographic' to think
through sustainability (see especially- chapter five). Researching
sustainability from an anthropological perspective calls for, to some
degree, a rethinking of traditional ethnographic methods.

The creative tensions in the project of ethnography and more widely,
anthropology have been well documented (Marcus 1998; 1995; Marcus
and Fischer 2009; Vered Amit 2000). Fieldwork and how we conceive of
ethnography has greatly evolved, wrought by new research contexts and
changing realities and definitions of ethnography. While fetishised both
within and outside the discipline of anthropology (see especially its
increased use in corporate settings), ethnography, we argue, as a contact
zone or sustained encounter with modalities of worldviews, value systems,

and beliefs (the list is long) is a methodology that can provide key insights into the issue of sustainability. If a 'sustainability conscience' (and indeed, values, motives) is located somewhere in the interstices of the everyday, then this is where ethnography operates best, uncovering and engaging with the unseen, the unacknowledged, the yet to come, and wedding it to the known, the presumed and the taken for granted in order to create new forms of understanding. Since sustainability discourses exist across a range of varied spaces, they are forged with different kinds of emphases, wherein we find differing ethics and politics at play. The chapters in this book also provide important comparative material in understanding how variant sustainability policies and politics manifest and have impact.

Sustainability as a term and mode of being seems to find itself reinterpreted at any given moment across these sometimes-conflicting spheres. Whether then it exists in the form of soteriology (the technology will save us) (in the movement towards smart and sustainable cities), or as a form of market environmentalism (in the space of CSR and trading policies), or in the community garden, where individuals attempt to evolve a world compatible with their green conscience (aspirations of slow food, reasserting the local), ethnography is a useful methodological being to shift between these layers. In a world where international organizations such as Amnesty International and the UN have instituted very specific programs addressing issues around a narrower vision of sustainable consumerism, we need to be cognizant of what kind of political action is being encouraged and where within this space the issue of responsibility lies. If we adhere to Lipsitz's (1998) argument that this focus on consumerism resituates and commoditizes political action, thereby allowing state devolution of responsibility, and more autonomy for industry in managing environmental impact and their sustainability measures, then alongside individual consumers, we need to address larger structural issues (see Kilbourne et al. 1997).

Ethnography and Anthropology as important research and analytical tools bring great value to the investigation and development of sustainability science. Indeed, Charles Redman (2011) points to this by positing that anthropology and its methods can be hugely helpful in developing a more coherent sustainability science, in both an academic and applied sense. He is also quick to point out that engaging with the very current issue of sustainability will reflect back on the development and positioning of anthropology within the broader context of academia. Redman's conviction emerges out of a belief that anthropology through its long relationship to notions of value and belief should allow us to find a route to combine value and science. He argues:

We all get, as anthropologists, that it takes lots of different ways to understand why people do what they do and what they're like. The past, the present, the biology, the language—we've always understood that a variety of lines of evidence can help enrich our understanding of something. This is a sustainability message too. We can't just invent a new hybrid car and not worry about who can use it and who can't. We can't just put a solar panel on a roof and think that we've saved the world. We need to look at it from all different directions and the impacts. Anthropology is a natural for that. In sustainability, what we have to get across is that there are not only multiple lines of information that we need to incorporate, but there are multiple ways of knowing the same information (Redman 2011: 1).

What Redman and other anthropologists (see Minnegal 2004) are debating (for both applied and academic anthropologies) is the need to move beyond the simple statement that anthropology has a lot to offer sustainability science (or indeed a number of other research contexts) and to begin to engage with what are and continue to be the barriers to communicating ethnographic discoveries and anthropological analyses to different disciplines and audiences. In a collection of papers on this very topic entitled *Sustainable Environments-Communities: Potential dialogues between anthropologists, scientists and managers (2004)* a number of anthropologists working in the area of sustainability and environmental management in Australian contexts argue to varying degrees that the anthropologist must find a meta language with which to communicate anthropological insights (see Minnegal 2004). Equally, anthropologists must employ the tools of anthropology itself to learn how to communicate with and to the science world (see Minnegal 2004). For some scholars then, anthropologists must learn to be translators, the conduit between oppositional worldviews (see Minnegal 2004), and yet others see the anthropologist as an initiator –as providing the catalyst for different kinds of exchanges between local people, communities, scientists and broader society (see Minnegal 2004). In sum, then, we believe that the ethnographer is well placed to facilitate a rapprochement between different disciplines and worldviews, one that through collaboration and co-creation can engender a space to further important conversations. It is within these debates that a notion of rethinking the scale and form of ethnography crystallizes, indeed, a larger debate well beyond the scope of this particular collection.

We believe (categorically) that AoS requires a *tempo adagio* fashioned through a reimagining of the scale and scope of ethnographic practice. Confronted (and stifled) by a surfeit of 'speed,' the sustainability movement requires the emergence of a repository of socio- cultural/

political/economic and scientific interconnections, which can be embedded in the weave of individual lives and social worlds. What this means for an ethnographic examination of this process, is a *more* not less complex form of research practice. This is, however, an ethnographic practice that is in the same moment confronted by the urgency with which we need to address some of the more pressing problems attached to 'sustainability,' in particular climate change.

In *Designs for an Anthropology of the Contemporary*, Faubion et al. (2008) point to a number of ethnographies such as work by Kim Fortun (2001), Adriana Petryna (2002), and Anna Tsing (2005) as examples of texts that are reflective of a 'new ethnography' confronted by assemblages (Deleuze and Guattari 1997) and unwieldy structures of temporality. Tsing writes:

> In these times of heightened attention to the space and scale of human undertakings, economic projects cannot limit themselves to conjuring at different scales-they must conjure the scales themselves. In a sense, a project that makes us imagine globality in order to see how it might succeed is one kind of 'scale making project;' similarly projects that make us imagine locality, or space of regions or nations, in order to see their success are also scale-making projects. In a world of multiple, divergent claims about scales, including multiple divergent globalism, those global worlds that most affect us are those that manage tentatively productive linkages with other scale making projects. (Tsing 2005: 36)

Alongside Tsing, we argue for AoS that is in fact a 'scale making project,' one that espouses the multiplicity, hybridity, and indeed, uncertainty of sustainability discourses and forms. Pivotal to this should be an understanding that sustainability projects are also scale-making projects in and of themselves. So, in accessing them as research objects we are also accessing the politics of sustainability scales as they are imagined and practiced. Imaginaries of sustainability or 'sustainabilities,' while divergent, often have at their core (and as a point of intersection), an ambition to make universal or global the desire for 'sustainability.' This is one of Anna Tsing's concerns within her theory of 'scale making,' how to imprint particular scales in universal form for people inhabiting different kinds of scales. When different scales engage and negotiate with one another, the force of 'friction' is attenuated and some form of consensus is arrived at.

Hanchett's chapter asks us to reconsider concepts such as "social sustainability," "sustainable livelihoods," "vulnerability," and "resilience" while Tzaneva reflects on the disaster of foot and mouth disease for Bulgarian culture in terms of 'coping' and 'adapting' while McCabe talks of sustainability through a lens constructed from local meaning, history and social relations in New York and Belfast. Corcoran also charts the upsurge of Urban Agriculture across Europe and questions how this can serve the common good while Savova recalls collective bread making in Bulgaria. Such works underscore the need to acknowledge that it will be increasingly difficult to effect one singular notion of sustainability across regions of the globe.

While there is a wide theorization of the notion of scale making in geography (see for example Richard Howitt 1993), we have yet to fully embrace this idea within new attempts to redefine ethnographic practice. Embracing the politics of scale within ethnographic practice challenges not only how we conceive of ethnography but also how we do ethnography. Traditionally imagined as a lone researcher, the ethnographer worked in a particular setting on a singular topic and translated such work into a single authored ethnography. If we are to engage the notion of scale making in a world where (as with the work of Tsing 2007) the temporalities of our projects 'threaten to outrun' us (Faubion et al 2008)), then we have to shift into a more collaborative space, where working as part of a research team allows us to engage the politics of scale. An ethnography of 'sustainabilities,' then, with its attendant complexities calls on us to critically engage (as a scale making exercise) the permutations and formations of what Tsing (2007) calls 'encounters across difference.' A number of the authors in this book implicitly recognize this fact-working on large scale comparative research projects- which attempt to grasp the workings of sustainability at different scales. The work of Mary Corcoran on community gardens (see chapter nine) is an excellent example of this.

In a world where Ikea is building its own sustainable town, where INTEL and IBM have ambitious, smart and sustainable city projects; where policy experts, leading scholars, and industry specialists struggle to mark out a terrain for sustainability models and policies, the challenge of an ethnography of sustainability is to speak between fields of experience and domains of knowledge. Ethnography can accommodate different scales of experience, scales that are brought into being, 'proposed practiced, and evaded' (Tsing 2005: 58). Further, it is just such a project that ethnographers themselves must engage, moving from our local area of expertise through national frames to the globally scaled projects such as those funded by the European Union.

An Anthropology of Sustainability as Moral Optimism?

Michel Rolph Trouillet claims that:

> At the end of the day, in this age where futures are murky and utopias mere reminders of a lost innocence, we need to fall back on the moral optimism that has been anthropology's greatest –yet underscored-appeal…We need to assume this optimism because the alternatives are lousy, and because anthropology is the best venue through which the West can show an undying faith in the richness and variability of human kind. (2003:139).

Herein, we construct AoS as a form of moral optimism, this is not to say that this is not a critical anthropology, but rather one that foregrounds a humanistic approach to sustainability in a putative risk society. So what is it that AoS constructed as a form of moral optimism can offer sustainability science? We suggest, as do the many of these chapters, that AoS anchored in moral optimism recasts sustainability science, as one which embraces human behaviour in its entirety, in order to fully progress the visions and end goals of the sustainability project. While not a panacea to the challenges of sustainability, it certainly extends the depth and breadth of sustainability science beyond its current incarnation. In a time where economic crisis, austerity, environmental disasters and climate change have generated such global disaffection-can such AoS bring about and encourage societal hope through scholarly and policy application? What kinds of societal hope can be generated if we make a claim to moral optimism in a context where sustainability imaginaries are really only partial, fragmented, and certainly not fully connected- as evidenced by the chapters in this book. Anna Tsing reminds us that, "Hope is most important when things are going badly in the world; in the face of almost certain destruction, hope is a Gramscian optimism of the will. Such "unrealistic" hope begins in considering the possibility that tiny cracks might yet break open the dam"(2005:267). AoS, as our contributors evince in their varying analyses, thus confronts how everyday settings and approaches to sustainability are being recast by human actors. Not without conflict, these evolutions of sustainability point to the uncertainty embedded in how sustainability 'actors' are producing and executing sustainability projects. Nonetheless, this is a fully human recasting of sustainability, one which our social scientific readings in this volume attest to as being wholly embracing of the complexity of sustainability.

***

Among the chapters that follow we find a lively debate on the conditions of possibility for a conversation between AoS and sustainability science. At the centre of the debate we find a project coeval with anthropological thinking. It is not our intention here to give a summary of each chapter; rather, we offer some signposts by tracing how each contributor builds their relationship to sustainability studies.

At the end of this volume, Professor Pat Brereton of the School of Communications, Dublin City University joins us to give a detailed analysis of the chapters through a reflection which can be read after or in conjunction with the various sections of this collection. A fascinatingly varied picture of the relationship between sustainability and anthropology emerges in this volume as each author sustains a different kind of relationship to the project of sustainability. These relationships seem to be shaped not only by the kind of intellectual puzzles that might arise in a scholar's study as he reflects on how sustainability is imagined and engaged with but by a deep inhabiting of the ethnographic project. Two of our contributors come from political science and sociology, and the remainder anthropology, but all evoke the rich texture of the everyday in their analyses of sustainability. Many of the contributors evince ethnographic sensibilities formed through deep immersion in fieldwork or their own lives. Each of the chapters allows for the interplay of the textures, tones, and voices of sustainability actors, thus their originality lies in the deepening of our understanding of how anthropology can contribute to sustainability science. Many of the themes in the chapters overlap, so while we have demarcated significant sections, the essays all interrelate in quite significant ways.

The first section of this book is entitled *New Modalities of Sustainability* and opens with a chapter by Suzanne Hanchett called *'Social Dynamics and Sustainability: Some Anthropological Insights.'* This chapter is an excellent frame for the book as a whole presenting an insightful reading of the evolution and relationship of sustainability studies to anthropology, and more broadly, the social sciences. Further to this, Hanchett shows how such AoS can be rigorously applied in a challenging setting such as a water resources management project in Bangladesh. Next, we hear from Gregor Claus, whose chapter *'Why we need a different socio-economic system for a just, sustainable society: Sustainability as an implication of Social justice,'* is a chapter that also offers a well-rounded unpacking of how sustainability thinking has evolved. Claus brings his own position to this asking the reader to consider the usefulness of Rawl's theory in thinking through how we can achieve a just and sustainable society. His premise is one that unfolds well with the ethnographic rigour of the chapters and analyses that follow. The final chapter in this section entitled *'Emerging Spheres of Resonance: "Clandestinely Genuine" Food Networks and the Challenges of Governing Sustainability in Italy'* by Alexander Koensler brings a strong ethnographic close to this section. Through the window of ethnographic research conducted on the changing relationship to sustainability and food production and ownership in Italy, he marks out a space to consider how successful grassroots political mobilization around food production can truly be.

Our next section *'Sustainability in Practice'* highlights how effective applied sustainability projects anchored in the social sciences can be. As such, the chapters in this section showcase some of our key intentions in putting this edited collection together, and particularly, in how AoS can infuse the practicalities and implementation of real world sustainability projects in all sorts of contexts. The opening chapter in this section is by Anja Salzer (et al.) entitled *'Transforming Sustainability into action: Challenges of an interdisciplinary project with multi-ethnic actors in the South Caucasus/Georgia,'* this piece outlines the life of an interdisciplinary project on "Biodiversity and Sustainable Management of Mountain Grassland in the Javakheti Highland, South Caucasus, Georgia." Much of our argument herein is centred on the call for a functional sustainability to move towards a true interdisciplinarity, and Salzer et al. show the challenges of doing just this. The chapter indicates the difficulties of translating these ideals into an authentically applied project while emphasising the urgency of needing to reflect and devise solutions to these very issues-this too is central to the concerns of this edited collection. The second chapter in this section is entitled, *'BREAD: Bridging Resources for Ecological and Art-Based Development is enlivened by the presence of the auto-ethnographic'* by Savova. Savova writes with heart about a project that is deeply personal, one with important professional and applied outputs. This is a chapter that interweaves the personal, the ethnographic, the theoretical, and the applied with aplomb. Speaking about developing a project focused on bread-making as a form of community building, this chapter shows firmly how ecological and arts-based development projects can truly contribute to bridging gaps of many kinds, and this is a sustainability project imagined as a form of reconciliation. The final chapter in this section is by Elya Tzaneva –entitled-*'Bulgarian Traditional Ecological Knowledge as Adaptive Strategy,'* it focuses on the outbreak of Foot and Mouth Disease in South East Bulgaria in 2010 and 2011. This chapter shows how anthropological readings of sustainability can greatly contribute to our understandings of disaster situations and their engendering of individual and collective trauma. Tzaneva as such through an anthropological lens brings voice to the humanity behind a disaster such as Foot and Mouth disease.

The final section of this book entitled *Towards an Urban Sustainability* emphasises the urgent need to consider the place of sustainability projects in an increasingly urbanised world. In a world victim to widespread global economic crisis, growing unemployment and poverty levels, sustainability can present real solutions to enriching the everyday lives of people subject to such conditions. Community gardens, sustainable architecture, greening the city- all present pathways to ameliorating and combatting the increasingly difficult life-worlds of people caught in the poverty trap, and the chapters in this section present illuminating arguments as to why we need to pay more attention to these projects. Rebekah McCabe's chapter *'Restoring Nature, Renewing the City: Local Narratives and Global Perspectives on Urban Sustainability,'* brings a refreshing comparative angle to this discussion, comparing two greening projects in very different contexts-Belfast and New York. McCabe's chapter moves seamlessly from state-led discussions on sustainability to the ways in which community activists interpret and implement sustainability- all within a strong ethnographic frame. The poeticism and perils of sustainable place making figure large in McCabe's chapter which brings us neatly to Saffron Woodcraft's chapter entitled *'Urban Translators: The role of anthropologists in sustainable urban planning'*. Woodcraft's focus is on the need for anthropologists to pay better attention to the spatial aspects of sustainable urban planning by introducing anthropological critique to develop more efficiently (indeed, more wholly) a social sustainability. Woodcraft thus echoes our call to heed what applied anthropological sustainability projects might bring to this overall goal. The final chapter in this section is Mary Corcoran's *'Rurs in urbs (re-visted): European urban agriculture in the age of austerity.'* Corcoran a sociologist using visual and ethnographic methods and working on a large EU project on community gardens brings a fitting close to our book by drawing out the significance of the growth of community gardening right across Europe to the backdrop of economic crisis and austerity. What is core in Corcoran's chapter is her claim that urban regeneration right across Europe is opening new spaces of potential in the public realm- Corcoran's claims are ultimately the claims of this book- that sustainability projects can be crucial to sustaining communities in times of dire need.

As editors of this volume, we alongside our contributors, hope you enjoy what we see as the beginning of an important conversation on what we believe to be a significant, impactful sub-discipline within anthropology – an anthropology of sustainability.

References

Amit-Talai, Vered. *Constructing the Field: Ethnographic Fieldwork in the Contemporary World.* London and New York: Routledge, 2000.

Beck, Ulrich. *Risk Society: Towards a New Modernity.* New Delhi: Sage, 1992.

Beck, Ulrich, Giddens, Anthony, and Lash, Scott. *Reflexive modernization: Politics, Tradition and Aesthetics in the Modern Social Order.* California: Stanford University Press, 1994.

Brosius, J. Peter. Analyses and Interventions: Anthropological Engagements with Environmentalism. *Current Anthropology* 40 (3) (1999): 277-309.

Bodley, John H. *Anthropology and Contemporary Human Problems.* Altamira Press: Lanham, MD, 2008.

Brundtland, Gru, Mansour Khalid, Susanna Agnelli, Sali Al-Athel, Bernard Chidzero, Lamina Fadika, Volker Hauff et al. "Our Common Future (\'Brundtland report\')." (1987).

Burton, Antoinette. ed. *Archive Stories: Facts, Fictions, and the Writing of History.* Durham, NC: Duke UP, 2005.

Faubion, Johannes, Rabinow, Paul, Marcus, George and Tobias, Rees. *Designs for an Anthropology of the Contemporary.* Durham: Duke University Press, 2008.

Faubion, Johannes and George, Marcus. *Fieldwork is not what it used to be: learning anthropology's method in a time of transition.* UK: Cornell University, 2009.

Fortun, Kim. *Advocacy After Bhopal: Environmentalism, Disaster, New Global Orders.* Chicago: University of Chicago Press, 2001.

Guyot, Jodi. Anthropology as Key to Sustainability Science: An Interview with Charles Redman. *Anthropology News* 52 (4) (2011): 12.

Handwerker, W. Penn. *Quick Ethnography: A Guide to Rapid Multi-Method Research.* Walnut Creek, CA: AltaMira Press, 2002.

Hannen, Nora and Richard, Wilk. eds. *The Environment in Anthropology: A Reader in Ecology, Culture, and Sustainable Living.* New York University Press: New York, NY, 2006.

Heather Lazrus and Carol, Farbotko. "The first climate refugees? Contesting global narratives of climate change in Tuvalu". *Global Environmental Change* 22 (2012): 382-390.

Howitt, Richard. ""A world in a grain of sand": towards a reconceptualisation of geographical scale". *Australian Geographer* 24 (1) (1993): 33-44.

Kilbourne, William, McDonagh, Pierre, and Andrea, Prothero. "The possibility of Sustainable Consumption in Global Policy and the Environment". *Journal of Macromarketing*, 22 (2) (2002): 156.

Kilbourne, William, McDonagh, Pierre, and Andrea, Prothero. "Sustainable Consumption and Quality of Life: A Macromarketing Challenge to the Dominant Social Paradigm". *Journal of Macromarketing*, 17 (1) (1997): 4-24.

Lipsitz, George. "Consumer spending as state project: Yesterday's solutions and today's problems." *Getting and Spending: European and American Consumer Societies in the Twentieth Century* (1998): 138.

Marcus, George. *Para-Sites: A Casebook against Cynical Reason.* Chicago: University of Chicago Press, 2000.

Marcus, George. *Ethnography through Thick and Thin* Princeton: Princeton University Press, 1998.

—. Ethnography in/of the World System: the Emergence of Multi-sited Ethnography *Annual Review of Anthropology* 24 (1995):95-117.

McDonagh Pierre and Andrea, Prothero. *Green Management: A Reader*, Dryden Press, 1997.

McDonagh, Pierre, Susan Dobscha, and Andrea Prothero. "Sustainable Consumption and Production." *Transformative consumer research for personal and collective well-being* (2012): 267.

McDonagh Pierre and Andrea, Prothero. "Sustainability marketing research: past, present and future", *Journal of Marketing Management*, 30:11-12 (2014), 1186-1219

McDonough, William, and Michael, Braungart. *Cradle to Cradle: Remaking the way we make things.* MacMillan, 2010.

Murphy, Raymond. "The sociological construction of science without nature."*Sociology* 28, no. 4 (1994): 957-974.

Murphy, Raymond. "Sociology as if nature did not matter: an ecological critique." *British Journal of Sociology* (1995): 688-707.

Milton Kay. *Loving nature: Towards an ecology of emotion.* London and New York: Routledge, 2002.

Minnegal, Monica. "Sustainable Environments, Sustainable Communities." Proceedings of a symposium, University of Melbourne, 2004.

Petryna, Adriana. *Life Exposed: Biological Citizens after Chernobyl.* Princeton: Princeton University Press, 2002.

Paavola, Jouni. "Towards Sustainable Consumption: Economics and Ethical Concerns for the Environment in Consumer Choice." *Review of Social Economy* 59 (2) (2001): 228-248.

Sharpe, Diana Rosemary. "1 5. The relevance of ethnography to international business research." *Handbook of qualitative research methods for international business* (2004): 306.

Skidelsky, Robert. And Edward, Skidelsky. *How Much is Enough? The Love of Money, and the Case for the Good Life.* UK: Allen Lane June, 2012.

Trouillet, Michel. *Global Transformations.* US: Palgrave Macmillan, 2003.

Tsing, Anna. *Friction: An Ethnography of Global Connection.* Princeton, N.J.: Princeton University Press, 2005.

Prothero, Andrea and Pierre McDonagh "Introduction to the Special Issue: Sustainability as Megatrend II", *Journal of Macromarketing* 35: 1, (2015) 7-10 DOI: 10.1177/0276146714556818

United Nations Environment Programme "Frequently asked questions: The Marrakech Process: Towards a 10 year framework of programmes on sustainable consumption and production." Paris: 2009 Author. Retrieved October 20, 2010, from http://www.unep.fr/scp/publications/details.asp?id=DTI/1177/PA%20

Žižek, Slavoj. *Living in the end times.* London: Verso, 2011.

PART I:

NEW MODALITIES OF SUSTAINABILITY

CHAPTER ONE

SOCIAL DYNAMICS AND SUSTAINABILITY: SOME ANTHROPOLOGICAL INSIGHTS

SUZANNE HANCHETT

Sustainability and Development

Environmentalists since the 1962 publication of Rachel Carson's *Silent Spring* have persuaded many that ignoring the environmental consequences of human actions will lead to tragic consequences for humanity and the environment alike. One source defines a sustainable way of life as being one which "…recognizes that all Earth's resources are finite and that there are limits to the growth of all living systems. These limits are finally dictated by the finite size of the Earth and the finite input of energy from the sun" (Button 1988:446, Campbell entry, cited by McManus 1996:50).

In the 1980s- the sustainability concept- though vaguely defined-gained new life and broad acceptance beyond environmentalist circles. There is, however, considerable disagreement about how to achieve a sustainable way of life, or indeed even about what that might mean. Definitions of "sustainability" have a wide variation. Environmental and social justice advocates, governments, and multi-national corporations, "Everyone it seems is making some claim to sustainability" (Partridge 2005). Merle Jacob (1994) describes sustainability as a "metaphysical principle." Within its general meaning of "continuity through time," she points out that sustainability has different meanings in different contexts. Phil McManus identifies nine groups claiming this goal. Economists, Anarchists, Eco-feminists, Eco-Marxists, and others have framed their theories and action goals in the supposed light of this word's many possible meanings (McManus 1996).

The 1987 Brundtland report, *Our Common Future*, was the source of this flurry of activity and image management. The document expanded the focus of discourse from general "sustainability" to the more controversial notion of *"sustainable development,"* which is understood by some as purely a pathway to economic development. The Brundtland report's declared goal, however, is to create harmony between three pillars, "Economy, Society, and Environment" – in moving the sustainability development agenda forward to a point where we can "[meet] the needs of the present without compromising the ability of future generations to meet their own needs" (WCED 1987).

Promoting "sustainability" and "sustainable development" was a positive move- one which created "a new social project," a new normative standard guiding change (Robinson 2004, cited by Partridge 2005). Ambiguities of meaning allows for wide acceptance. This is despite important differences among adherents with differing degrees of sincerity and conflicting social goals. Within the cacophony of definitions lies an important, over-arching goal- to devise solutions to some of the most pressing problems now facing humanity. Problems such as climate change, air and water pollution, and depletion of critical resources are primary among them. No company, organisation, or government wants to be perceived as not caring about such problems.

The United Nations in 2013-2014 has been promoting discourse on new definitions and understandings of "sustainability" – and their policy implications -- by sponsoring a series of inclusive discussions intended to forge international agreement on a new set of "sustainable development goals" (SDGs). These are expected to replace the currently used Millennium Development Goals, which will mature in 2015.

Sustainability and Society

A natural entry point for anthropologists and other social scientists is in the "Society" part of the Economy-Society-Environment scheme. This aspect of the sustainability framework was initially less well developed than the other two pillars, but by now there are a number of useful statements about the ways that society connects to sustainability.[1] Some explore the social dimension itself, while others emphasise the connections between the three pillars. Some comments and analyses are general and theoretical- while others draw on research in a broad range of subject areas.

M. Priscilla Stone (2003) identifies three issues central to an "anthropological sustainability," namely persistence, innovation, and responses to stresses and shocks. Arguing for a fluid and flexible approach to the subject, she stresses the "central role of social systems in enhancing sustainability" (Stone 2003:95). She also points out that, "Sustainability is interpreted quite differently by different disciplines":

In discussing sustainable agriculture, Conway and Barbier (1990:39-43) outline the differing interpretations it is given by agriculturalists, who stress food self-sufficiency; environmentalists, who are concerned with stewardship of natural resources; economists, who stress efficiency over time; and sociologists or anthropologists, who seek to preserve traditional cultures, values and institutions (Stone 2003:96).

A Canadian sociologist, Margrit Eichler, has tried to "reconceptualize sustainability" by identifying four pertinent aspects of the human system. The four parts she mentions are Economy, Governance, Society, and Culture. The dynamics or "imperatives" of each aspect- she points out- have distinct environmental consequences. Kevin Murphy's (2012) literature review on the topic of "the social pillar" of sustainable development highlights four concepts, that can link social development processes to environmental conservation goals. He argues that policy makers should focus on goals promoting equity, environmental awareness, inclusive participation, and social cohesion.

Social Sustainability

The "social sustainability" concept is a potentially useful way of articulating the need for human systems to adapt and reform in ways that will ensure the long-term viability of the human species. Juliette Koning summarises the potentially enormous scope of this concept:

> From a social science perspective, "sustainability addresses the question of how societies can shape their modes of change" and refers to "the viability of socially shaped relationships between society and nature over longer periods of time" (Becker, Jahn and Stiess 1999:4). As such the field is defined as basically social, "addressing virtually the entire process by which societies manage the material conditions of their reproduction, including the social, economic, political and cultural principles that guide the distribution of environmental resources." (*Ibid.*) In this change is a central element and sustainability thus includes both "sustaining a particular resilient state and adjusting to changing internal and external conditions" (Köhn and Gowdy 2001:3) (Koning 2002:66-67).

Koning's paper goes on to identify key concepts needing definition- especially "social capital," and proposes ways to measure and monitor "social sustainability."

Emma Partridge, an Australian political scientist, has proposed a working definition of "social sustainability," one that reflects a broad consensus on what should be included under this rubric. "Social

Looking at Sustainability in lens of finance is questionable!!
Process of Interconnectivity

sustainability," she says, occurs when formal and informal social processes, systems, structures and relationships "actively support the capacity of current and future generations to create healthy and livable communities" (Partridge 2005). Akin to other scholars addressing this topic, Partridge argues that it is unfair and unjust to deprive future generations. Also needing further consideration are equity concerns within the present generation. Because total social systems must support new practices- participatory decision-making must be part of the change process, she argues.[2]

Koning argues that because "generalized urbanization is part of the process of economic globalization and the information revolution," the social sustainability concept must expand to include urban life. Chapters from Mary Corcoran, Rebecca McCabe and Saffron Woodcraft in this volume relate directly to her observation that:

> Globalization ... new risks and uncertainties, new social forms and inequalities, and wide-ranging urbanization form the context for discussing sustainable development and social sustainability (Koning 2002:66).

One pertinent body of literature concerns "sustainable livelihoods." Ian Scoones, drawing on the work of Robert Chambers, Gordon Conway, and others, describes the Institute for Development Studies' working definition:

> A livelihood comprises the capabilities, assets (including both material and social resources) and activities required for a means of living. A livelihood is sustainable when it can cope with and recover from stresses and shocks, maintain or enhance its capabilities and assets, while not undermining the natural resource base (Scoones 1998:5).

Those pursuing sustainable livelihoods, according to this analysis, work with four types of "capital" (assets), namely natural resources, financial capital, human capital, and social capital. The livelihoods literature thus links society to environment, as well as to the monetary economy. It carefully describes what is known about the interplay of numerous factors that do or do not lead to long-term viability of human populations, whether at small or large scale:

> Rather than focusing solely on conventional interventions (transfer of technologies, skills etc.) the sustainable livelihoods approach emphasises getting the institutional and organisational setting right, with emphasis on both formal and informal mechanisms (Scoones 1998:14).

Anthropological discussions of disaster also connect to sustainability issues. This body of work deserves close attention as humanity confronts climate change. Core concepts resemble those of the sustainable livelihoods group in highlighting (a) the fundamental influence of social structure and culture on human adaptation and coping strategies, and (b) the importance of resilience and vulnerability. Anthony Oliver-Smith argues that disasters "occur in societies. They do not occur in nature." More precisely, he continues, disasters "emerge from societal environmental relations and the institutionalized forms those relations take" (Oliver-Smith 1999: 28). Oliver-Smith and other disaster researchers work from the assumption that "disasters are as deeply embedded in the social structure and culture of a society as they are in an environment. In a sense," he continues, "a disaster is symptomatic of the condition of a society's total adaptational strategy within its social, economic, modified, and built environments" (Oliver-Smith 1999: 24). These observations lead us to "reconsider questions of the adaptive fitness of all societies," he argues. The common anthropological assumptions regarding environmental adaptation need reconsideration, he claims, as the present global situation creates "levels of environmental stress and vulnerability to hazards [that are] are being exacerbated by political, economic, and social forces." This situation calls into question "the long-term sustainability, or, to put it another way, the adaptive fitness of industrial societies" (Oliver-Smith 1999; see also Hastrup 2009).

Priscilla Stone claims that anthropological research often lacks "a dynamic view" and asks whether concepts such as culture, traditional values, core institutions, and ideologies continue to be useful. This and other commentaries (especially the sustainable livelihoods work) proceed to answer the question by emphasising the importance of people's own perceptions of their situations- along with "the role of cultural and social assets" in supporting human survival – "the bundle of institutions often referred to as the moral economy" (Stone 2003:96).

Themes in Socially Oriented Commentaries

Socially oriented writings on sustainability have raised important questions that challenge some assumptions underlying current, widely accepted policies and approaches to problem-solving. One persistent theme is the relationship between society and economy, specifically the monetized, globalized economic system. Social theorists and researchers constantly emphasise the point that, as Scoones puts it, "value" often is defined in ways that have nothing to do with money. Quoting Robert Chambers

(1997a), Scoones argues that allowing people themselves to define their most important goals and standards of well-being "may result in a range of sustainable livelihood outcome criteria, including diverse factors such as self-esteem, security, happiness, stress, vulnerability, power, exclusion, as well as more conventionally measured material concerns." This is an important contribution to the international sustainability policy discussion, where economists' voices are strong and often dominant.

A second theme – actually a pair of themes- that arises is resilience or vulnerability. Anthropological case studies, including some in this book, have analysed numerous situations in which human groups confront hazardous stresses, shocks, and disasters. These can be physical (tsunami, drought, and so on) or financial. The global economy in this connection has the capacity to disrupt, even destroy, human well-being, as in the case of abrupt withdrawal of monetary supports in Greece or Portugal. As many events have demonstrated by now (the 2010 earthquake in Haiti and Hurricane Katrina in Louisiana, for example), poverty and other social vulnerabilities greatly increase the likelihood that a "hazard" or risk situation will become a "disaster." As such "resilience occurs when resources are sufficiently strong to buffer or counteract the effects of a stressor such that a return to functioning, adapted to the altered environment, occurs" (Sherrieb and Norris 2009:72).

A third theme has to do with participatory planning. Since the 1960s "participation" has been a constant theme in social development and community development. Numerous writers and practitioners have used this concept to promote involvement of affected people in planning or implementing programs and projects that concern them. This has been done with varying degrees of sincerity, of course, but the principle of "participation" is widely recognized as a positive one in the world of planned change. The concept has been integrated into social thinking relating to sustainability as a way to promote equity.

Participation, as it turns out, is not always an equitable process. Social status differences interfere with the ideal of democratic involvement that the principle implies. Powerful individuals and groups can dominate a participatory planning process, rendering outcomes less equitable than the ideal implies. These drawbacks have not discredited the practice, but they do raise concerns.

Trial and Error in Socially Sustainable Water Management: Three Examples

Social analysis can help to supplement and refine the formalised and necessarily simplified concepts used by policy makers and development agencies. Water issues are among the most sensitive and difficult challenges facing humanity in this era of climate change. Large-scale efforts to deal with these challenges are always going to be imperfect- but social analysis can help by identifying crucial factors potentially leading to success or failure. A useful, common sense observation has been made by the environmentalist and writer, Jonathon Porritt (1998):

> You can dress up all sorts of useful things at the local level in the trappings of sustainable development, but unless those useful things are rooted in and permanently nurtured by their host communities they simply won't deliver ... long term environmental or social dividends....

The notion of "social sustainability" implies (and recommends) a two-way influence in the society-environment relationship. First, any proposed changes in the environment or its use should influence all concerned social groups (in both present and future generations), however diverse in culture, power position, or economic status, in an equitable manner. Secondly, human systems themselves should change in ways that will protect long-term environmental sustainability, *i.e.*, long-term survival of a population and the natural resources on which it depends.

Integrated Water Resources Management: A Critique. One sphere in which "participation" ideals and problems may collide is in the widely accepted practice known as Integrated Water Resource Management (IWRM). This innovative and ambitious approach involves bringing together multiple "stakeholders" (nation states, other government entities, organisations, businesses, social/ethnic groups, and so on) to coordinate planning for water resources on which all depend. The United Nations explains IWRM in the following way:

> IWRM is an empirical concept which was built up from the on-the-ground experience of practitioners. Although many parts of the concept have been around for several decades - in fact since the first global water conference in Mar del Plata in 1977 - it was not until after Agenda 21 and the World Summit on Sustainable Development in 1992 in Rio that the concept was made the object of extensive discussions as to what it means in practice. The Global Water Partnership's definition of IWRM is widely accepted. It states: "IWRM is a process which promotes the co-ordinated development and management of water, land and related resources, in order to maximize

the resultant economic and social welfare in an equitable manner without compromising the sustainability of vital ecosystems" (UNDESA 2014).

Critiques of IWRM by social researchers, especially anthropologists, raise important questions that deserve attention. The issues are summarised in a 2010 review article by Benjamin Orlove and Steven Caton, who refer to the work of Ken Conca and others. The reviewers claim that, "Integrated water resource management (IWRM) has become the new and, many would claim, the hegemonic paradigm for discussing, legitimizing, and implementing policies regarding the management of the world's water resources, subsuming within it the notion of 1970s and 1980s development discourses." Ken Conca's (2005) observation on IWRM is that it "has shifted discussion about rivers toward environmental concerns, [but] it has not been able to manage the intense social controversies around big dams and the privatization of water" (Gareau and Crow 2006).

Orlove and Caton (2010) raise important questions about "participation" in IWRM by critiquing the concept of the "stakeholder." They point out that participants in watershed councils represent many types of interests and status groups. Urging IWRM proponents to avoid a "simplistic view of ecological citizenship," they observe that, "Stakeholders may engage in exclusionary practices while caring deeply about areas far from the ones in which they live."

A further criticism of IWRM has to do with recognising local or indigenous landscape categories and boundaries. The basic unit of an IWRM process is a "watershed," or a basin (river basin, for example) in which water sources are interconnected. Watersheds may extend across national or other political boundaries. In many parts of the world now there are watershed councils that are generally "nonprofit participatory organizations that seek environmental quality and sustainable development" (several examples can be found, they point out, in the semiarid region of northeastern Brazil). This review introduces a "few words of caution about the term watershed."

> The conceptual boundaries that humans use reflect cultural systems as well as the natural world, so it gives us as anthropologists pause to hear that an administrative unit has an *a priori* material or natural existence. Other environmental and ecological categories, such as "forest" and "wetland," include both natural and social elements, given the complex nature of their characteristics and boundaries. Watersheds may be simpler, more straightforward units than forests and wetlands, but they are not entirely and unproblematically present in nature.... [W]atersheds are not always the well-bounded management units that water managers and others often assume them to be (Orlove and Canton 2010).

We will now consider two Bangladesh examples relating to planned change. They concern domestic water supplies. One example, relating to the introduction of a new technology, shows a positive outcome when viewed in terms of social sustainability.[3] The other example has to do with a specific village's efforts to organise safe water by installing a "pond sand filter." The second case is a failure associated with social decisions and economic factors. It demonstrates a lack of "social sustainability."

Bangladesh Case Study No. 1.

This generally positive case demonstrates the way that a useful new idea can take hold and become part of social reproduction processes. This case has to do with introducing hand-pumped tube wells (borehole wells) in Bangladesh rural and peri-urban areas by an 18-district Dutch-funded project in the 1990s.[4] Gender equity was a strong focus, and gender training was an important part of the project. Local women got training and tool-kits, so that they could repair the hand-operated pumps that were provided through the project. This was a controversial aspect of the project. A great many local men objected on various grounds. A few said this could not succeed because women's brains were too small, making it impossible for the poor things to work with wrenches and screwdrivers. When we organised follow-up focus group discussions, however, we learned that women in one area were not only repairing their tube well pumps, they also were teaching other women how to do so. A few of their men had changed their minds and decided not to object. This we took as a positive sign that the training and tools were what would now be called "socially sustainable."

Bangladesh Case Study No. 2.

In sanitation and domestic water supply projects – a principal focus of our applied studies – technology is an important part of the social sustainability story. New technology is introduced and promoted for its public health benefit. People's willingness and ability to continue using this technology (a toilet, a well, or a water filter), are signs of social sustainability. Such items are installed in human communities, and their use, non-use, and maintenance (as in Case Study No. 1) are decided in a social context. They may be mechanically functional- but social and economic considerations determine their ultimate effectiveness. Case No. 2 was a village-level failure of social sustainability.

We first encountered this situation in 2006 while doing an evaluation study on behalf of UNICEF.[5] We were studying the public's reaction to the serious problem of arsenic in drinking water and the effectiveness of various mitigation efforts. In one village, some women, with support from a UNICEF-funded NGO, had organised themselves and their men to get arsenic-free water from a large, local water body by using a well-built and easily maintained "pond sand filter." Echoing the familiar "care for future generations" theme of the sustainability discourse, one elderly woman proudly announced that she had persuaded her husband to support this activity for the sake of the long-term health of their grandchildren. They were proud to inform us that people from neighbouring villages were starting to use the filtered water- as a woman of a nearby area recently had died of arsenic-related causes.[6]

Returning to the same village in 2009, three years later, however, we found the filter in disrepair. The pond was once again being used for a highly profitable fish culture, which makes the water non-potable, even if it is filtered, because chicken manure is used to feed fish. The richest households had purchased expensive, in-home arsenic-removal filters. The same women who had spoken so proudly during our first visit were angry and disappointed at having to return to drinking "arsenic water." A good beginning is only that, as this example shows. It should never be assumed that a social change actually has occurred without long-term (perhaps very long-term) follow-up and analysis. Careful field investigations are needed to monitor the social dynamics leading to success or failure.

The pond sand filter is a useful technology, which often fails for social reasons. Water bodies mostly are owned by groups of cousins who have inherited them. When tube wells were introduced, providing convenient and microbe-free drinking water, ponds formerly used for drinking water were turned over to lucrative fish culture. When the tube well water turned out to be unsafe, some co-owners were reluctant to give up fish culture income and refused to return to the use of pond water for drinking. Since a water body is indivisible, such decisions affect all owners/users. Out of more than 25 visited, we have identified just two successful pond sand filter cases (*i.e.*, continuing to be used, as far as we know). Neither of them is installed in a jointly-owned water body.

Conclusions

The preceding case studies and general discussion show, among other things, that technically oriented and science-driven donors and their local counterparts need social information- if their planned changes are to take root. Ethnographic and other types of "qualitative" information often provide the only opportunities that such scientists and policy makers have to hear people's voices and learn about actual lives affected by their policies and projects. Social information on perceptions and social constraints can provide a valuable balance to economic information. A statement about anthropological work on water resources management by Orlove and Caton applies to policy-related research in other sectors as well:

> As for the valuation of water, what is meant by a basic right or a commodity is hardly questioned, as if these matters were settled long ago in philosophical and scientific discourses and need not be revisited in settings where these concepts are highly contested or do not hold sway. Anthropology has an important role to play in keeping these questions open rather than to consign the discipline to the study of how the "natives" value and use water locally. That said, the meanings and values placed on water by its users and the contestations over these among those same users (along class, gender, and ethnic lines, as well as urban versus rural divides) will fundamentally affect how water can be managed at the watershed in the first place, and here anthropology has an obvious and perhaps singular contribution to make to the understanding of water's valuation (Orlove and Caton 2010).

There are at least five perspectives that anthropologists' research and theory can contribute to the sustainability discussion. (1) One is a holistic perspective, which can help to explore connections between disparate parts of a scheme such as the economy-society-environment model. Kirsten Hastrup asserts the value of anthropology's approach: "...The idea of holism upon which anthropology builds gives us a certain authority to address the critical importance of the assumption of an inextricable link between the physical and the social world" (Hastrup 2009:26-27). (2) We also have some unique techniques for understanding social dynamics in both organisations and in small-scale communities. These techniques can be applied to life in formal or informal organisations. (3) Our familiarity with Indigenous languages and world views – and the translation skills to help get them recognised, respected, possibly even used (Ross *et al.* 2011) – have lead us to document the enormous variety and complexity of humanity's environmental adaptation modes.[7] (4) Our training in qualitative analysis prepares us to use the flexible approaches to social problem solving which sustainability problems require (Guyot 2011; Redclift 1999). (5) We have practical fieldwork skills that can support new ways of involving socially excluded groups, women, and the poor, thus advancing the equity agenda implicit in the "social sustainability" concept.

These fieldwork skills are invaluable assets for strong monitoring and evaluation studies that can help by (a) identifying and strengthening positive programme results, or (b) using mistakes as learning opportunities.

While anthropologists have much to offer, sustainability related research and planning should always be inter-disciplinary. Some sustainability problems are outside of our usual expertise. Equally needed are the knowledge and skills of those with backgrounds in sociology, geography, environmental studies, public health, political science, public administration, and economics (of the non-neoliberal varieties). When working on water and other environmental issues, close collaboration with natural scientists and engineers is inevitable. Integrating the theories and research of academic and applied/practicing anthropologists also poses challenges. There are practising and applied anthropologists working in all sorts of public and private sector organisations. They have the experience and expertise suited to a wide variety of practical matters, but unless they teach, they are not well connected to academic networks (Hanchett 1994, 1999).

Research oriented professionals need to recognise that political forces are more likely to determine humanity's future path than are scientific efforts. As Hastrup has wisely said of climate change, the political challenges surrounding "this uniquely global and thus far intractable environmental problem" are far more daunting than the scientific ones (2009:26-27). Governance is an urgent concern, as several documents point out; and public and private sectors both need to agree to work in new and more coordinated ways if sustainability is to be achieved. More regulation is needed. Political will must improve (SDSN 2013). How is all this ever going to come about? Becker, Jahn, and Stiess argue that it would be good for social scientists to "examine the policy context in which environmental targets are formulated, and to develop ways of making the implications of environmental policies visible, including related tensions and conflicts, so that these can be resolved or ameliorated through democratic politics" (Becker et al. 1999:10).

With some closer collaboration among ourselves and with colleagues in other fields, anthropologists can provide helpful insights to guide policy makers and development agencies committed to sustainable development. These insights can support visions of harmony between Economy, Society, and Environment, moving humanity toward actions that can "[meet] the needs of the present without compromising the ability of future generations to meet their own needs" (WCED 1987).

References

Becker, Egon, Thomas Jahn, and Immanuel Stiess. "Exploring Uncommon Ground: Sustainability and the Social Sciences." In *Sustainability and the Social Sciences: A Cross-disciplinary Approach to Integrating Environmental Considerations into Theoretical Reorientation*, edited by Egon Becker and Thomas Jahn, 1-22. Paris: UNESCO, Frankfurt am Main: ISOE, London and New York: Zed Books, 1999 .

Becker, Egon, and Thomas Jahn, eds. *Sustainability and the Social Sciences: A Cross-disciplinary Approach to Integrating Environmental Considerations into Theoretical Reorientation.* Paris: UNESCO, Frankfurt am Main: ISOE, London and New York: Zed Books, 1999.

Button, John. *Dictionary of Green Ideas*. London: Routledge, 1988.

Carson, Rachel. *Silent Spring*. Boston and New York: Houghton Mifflin Harcourt, 2002.

Chambers, Robert. "Responsible Well-being -- A Personal Agenda for Development." *World Development* 25 (1997a):1743-1745.

—. *Whose Reality Counts? Putting the First Last.* London: Intermediate Technology Publications, 1997b.

Chambers, Robert, and Gordon, Conway. "Sustainable Rural Livelihoods: Practical Concepts for the 21st Century." *IDS Discussion Paper* No. 296. Brighton, UK: Institute for Development Studies, 1992.

Chambers, Robert. "Sustainable Livelihoods, Environment and Development: Putting Poor Rural People First." *IDS Discussion Paper* No. 240. Brighton, UK: Institute for Development Studies, 1987.

Christie, Ian, and Diane Warburton. *From Here to Sustainability; Politics in the Real World.* London and Sterling, VA: Earthscan, 2001.

Conca, Ken. *Governing Water: Contentious Transnational Politics and Global Institution Building.* Cambridge, Massachusetts: MIT Press, 2005.

Conway, Gordon R., and Edward Barbier. *After the Green Revolution: Sustainable Agriculture for Development.* London: Earthscan, 1990.

Eichler, Magrit. "Sustainability from a Feminist Sociological Perspective: A Framework for Disciplinary Reorientation." In *Sustainability and the Social Sciences: A Cross-disciplinary Approach to Integrating Environmental Considerations into Theoretical Reorientation*, edited by Egon Becker and Thomas Jahn, 182-206. Paris: UNESCO, Frankfurt am Main: ISOE, London and New York: Zed Books, 1999.

Gareau, Brian J., and Ben Crow. "Book Review: Ken Conca, *Governing Water.*" *International Environmental Agreements: Politics, Law and Economics* 6 (2006), No.1.

Guyot, Jodi. "Anthropology as Key to Sustainability Science: An Interview with Charles Redman." *Anthropology News,* April 2011:12.

Hanchett, Suzanne. "Commentary: International Perspectives on Academic, Applied, and Practicing Anthropology." *Practicing Anthropology* 16 (1994):2,39.

—. "Anthropology and Development: the 1998 ICAES Discussion." *Practicing Anthropology* 21 (1999):44-48.

Hanchett, Suzanne, and Tofazzel Hossain Monju. "The Bangladesh Arsenic Mitigation and Water Supply Project: A Public Administration and Public Health Failure." Paper presented at the annual meetings of the American Anthropological Association, 2009. Available online: http://www.planningalternatives.com/id31.html

Hanchett, Suzanne, Tofazzel Hossain Monju, Kazi Rozana Akhter, Shireen Akhter, and Anwar Islam. *Water Culture in South Asia: Bangladesh Perspectives.* Pasadena, CA: Development Resources Press, 2014.

Hastrup, Kirsten. "Social Anthropology: Towards a Pragmatic Enlightenment?" *Social Anthropology* 13 (2005):133-149.

Hastrup, Kirsten. "Waterworlds: Framing the Question of Social Resilience." In *The Question of Resilience: Social Responses to Climate Change,* edited by Kirsten Hastrup, 11-30. Copenhagen: Royal Danish Academy of Sciences and Letters, Historisk-filosofiske Meddelelser 106, 2009.

Jacob, Merle. "Toward a Methodological Critique of Sustainable Development." *The Journal of Developing Areas,* January 1994, pp. 237-252.

Köhn, Jorg, and John, Gowdy. "Sustainability as a Management Concept." In *Sustainability in Action; Sectoral and Regional Case Studies,* edited by Jorg, Köhn, John, Gowdy, and Jan van der Straaten. Cheltenham: Edward Elgar Publishing, 2001.

Koning, Juliette. "Social Sustainability in a Globalizing World: Context, Theory and Methodology Explored." In *More on MOST: Proceedings of An Expert Meeting*, 63-89. The Hague: UNESCO, 2002.

Littig, Beate, and Erich Griessler. "Social Sustainability: A Catchword Between Political Pragmatism and Social Theory." *International Journal of Sustainable Development* 8 (2005):65-79.

McCabe, J. Terrence. "Toward an Anthropological Understanding of Sustainability: A Preface." *Human Organization* 62 (2003):91-92.

McManus, Phil. "Contested Terrains: Politics, Stories and Discourses of Sustainability." *Environmental Politics* 5 (1996):48-73.

Murphy, Kevin. "The Social Pillar of Sustainable Development: A Literature Review and Framework for Policy Analysis." *Sustainability: Science, Practice, & Policy* 8 (2012):15-29.

Oliver-Smith, Anthony. "'What Is a Disaster?': Anthropological Perspectives on a Persistent Question." In *The Angry Earth: Disasters in Anthropological Perspective*, edited by Anthony Oliver-Smith and Susanna Hoffman, 18-34. New York: Routledge, 1999.

—. "2013 Malinowski Award Lecture; Disaster Risk Reduction and Climate Change Adaptation: The View from Applied Anthropology." *Human Organization* 72 (2013):275-282.

Orlove, Ben, and Steven C. Caton. "Water Sustainability: Anthropological Perspectives and Prospects." *Annual Review of Anthropology* 39 (2010):401-415. Palo Alto, CA: Annual Reviews.

Partridge, Emma. "'Social Sustainability': A Useful Theoretical Framework?" Paper presented at the Australasian Political Science Association Annual Conference, Dunedin, New Zealand, 2005. Accessed in 2013: cfsites1.uts.edu.auj/isf/staff/details.cfm?StaffId=2408

Porritt, Jonathon. "Foreword." In *Community and Sustainable Development; Participation in the Future*, edited by Diane Warburton. London: Earthscan, 1998.

Redclift, Michael. "Dance with Wolves? Sustainability and the Social Sciences." In *Sustainability and the Social Sciences; A Cross-disciplinary Approach to Integrating Environmental Considerations into Theoretical Reorientation,* edited by Egon Becker and Thomas Jahn, 267-273. Paris: UNESCO, Frankfurt am Main: ISOE, London and New York: Zed Books, 1999.

Robinson, John. "Squaring the Circle? Some Thoughts on the Idea of Sustainable Development." *Ecological Economics* 48 (2004):369-384.

Ross, Anne, Kathleen Pickering Sherman, Jeffrey G. Snodgrass, Henry D. Delcore, and Richard Sherman. *Indigenous Peoples and the Collaborative Stewardship of Nature; Knowledge Binds and Institutional Conflicts.* Walnut Creek, CA: Left Coast Press, 2011.

Sachs, Ian. "Social Sustainability and Whole Development: Exploring the Dimensions of Sustainable Development." In *Sustainability and the Social Sciences: A Cross-disciplinary Approach to Integrating Environmental Considerations into Theoretical Reorientation*, edited by Egon Becker and Thomas Jahn, 1-22. Paris: UNESCO, Frankfurt am Main: ISOE, London and New York: Zed Books, 1999.

Scoones, Ian. "Sustainable Rural Livelihoods: A Framework for Analysis." *IDS Working Paper* 72. Brighton, UK: Institute of Development Studies, 1998.

Sherrieb, Kathleen, and Fran H. Norris. "Community Resilience and Health Outcomes in Mississippi Counties." In *The Question of Resilience*, edited by Kirsten Hastrup, 70-87. Copenhagen: The Royal Danish Academy of Sciences and Letters, Historisk-filosofiske Meddelelser 106, 2009.

Stone, M. Priscilla. "Is Sustainability for Development Anthropologists?" *Human Organization* 62 (2003):93-99.

Sustainable Development Solutions Network/SDSN. "An Action Agenda for Sustainable Development; Draft for Public Consultation, 7 May 2013." http://unsdsn.org/files/2013/05/130507-Action-Agenda-for-SD-Draft-for-Public-Consultation.pdf

United Nations Department of Economic and Social Affairs/UNDESA. "Integrated Water Resources Management," Accessed 2014. http://www.un.org/en/development/desa/index.html

Vallance, Suzanne, Harvey C. Perkins, and Jennifer E. Dixon. "What Is Social Sustainability? A Clarification of Concepts", *Geoforum* 42 (2011):342-348.

Warburton, Diane, ed. *Community and Sustainable Development; Participation in the Future.* London: Earthscan, 1998.

Western Australian Council of Social Service Inc./WACOSS. "Submission to the State Sustainability Consultation Paper, April 2002." www.sustainability.dpc.wa.gov.au/docs/submissions/WACOSS.pdf

World Bank. *Implementation Completion and Results Report, No. ICR 000028.* Washington, DC: The World Bank, Sustainable Development Department, Environment and Water Resources Unit, South Asia Region, 2007. (Available for download from http://www.planningalternatives.com/sitebuildercontent/sitebuilderfiles/bamwsp-icr.pdf)

World Commission on Environment and Development /WCED. *Our Common Future*, Oxford: Oxford University Press, 1987.

Notes

[1] In contrast, 'Economy' is considered to be more widely understood among those involved in the sustainability conversation. The *un*sustainable nature of many economic activities, after all, was one reason why the sustainability concept was introduced in the first place.

[2] Partridge identifies six criteria defining social sustainability: quality of life, equity, inclusion, access, a futures focus, and participatory processes. (Partridge 2005, citing WACOSS 2002) Similar arguments are offered by contributors to the edited volumes of Becker and Jahn (1999), Christie and Warburton (2001), and Warburton (1998).

[3] My teams and I have done a number of evaluation studies in Bangladesh. We did most of these using rapid appraisal research methods, focus group discussions, structured observations, case studies, and situation analyses. We have revisited some sites to follow up on interesting situations. I also have been involved in a few policy related discussions with government officers and donor representatives, but my principal work has been in the field.

[4] 18 District Towns Project, funded by the Royal Netherlands Embassy.

[5] This complex and still unsolved problem is discussed in detail in Hanchett and Hossain-Monju 2009, in World Bank 2007, and in Hanchett et al. 2014.

[6] Symptoms of arsenic poisoning include various cancers (skin, lung, bladder), neuropathy, and skin discolouration.

[7] Communicating about indigenous views with scientifically trained colleagues is a challenge that the anthropologist is likely to face in this context. Despite the strong efforts at the U.N. to give indigenous people (or uneducated people, or women, or the poor) a voice, and lofty proclamations about human rights and inclusion, science rules most projects, programs, and institutions. The advocate for indigenous points of view is not going to get much support in the day-to-day world of international development. Some exceptions are the by-now well accepted 'participatory' approaches (PRA and others), which are used extensively in the programs of non-profit organisations. (Chambers 1997b) Medical anthropologists also do a good job of straddling the science-society boundaries. There are formidable institutional constraints (career incentives, academic departments, grants).Epistemological differences also interfere with the needed interdisciplinary collaboration. We are more comfortable with 'qualitative' research methods than are most physical scientists. Within anthropology there also are serious theoretical and epistemological rifts that make some not receptive to these applied concerns and the kinds of communication required to address them.

CHAPTER TWO

WHY WE NEED A DIFFERENT SOCIO-ECONOMIC SYSTEM FOR A JUST SUSTAINABLE SOCIETY: SUSTAINABILITY AS AN IMPLICATION OF SOCIAL JUSTICE

GREGOR CLAUS

Sustainability -or indeed, unsustainability- as some might argue- is one of the biggest issues of the 21st century, being as such the common refrain for a wide variety of human societal and human-related issues; be it climate change, human population growth, ageing societies, issues of automation, mass species extinction, resource depletion or issues of social justice. But sustainability is -as is also commonly noted- an issue which is associated with a wide variety of different meanings and interpretations, depending on who is talking about it; an economist, a politician, a marketer or an environmentalist. Further, it is not unusual for the meaning that a traditional economist associates with sustainability to be fundamentally incompatible with that which a radical environmentalist understands, for whom phrases such as sustainable growth will be an oxymoron. Given this issue, I will initially refer to one of the most widely used definitions for the term, which comes from the Brundtland commission in 1987:

> Sustainable development is development that meets the needs of the present without compromising the ability of future generations to meet their own needs (Brundtland 1987).

What is mentioned less often, however, is that the report then goes on to say that, "Development involves a progressive transformation of economy and society" (Brundtland 1987). In other words the report implies as a given that sustainability and sustainable development require fundamental change or the transformation of our current socio-economic system. But why would that be the case? Can modern capitalism and the global community not be utilised and motivated to achieve sustainable growth and development? The short answer is no, they cannot. A look at the core principles of capitalism, and our modern consumer society, suggests why that is so; modern capitalism requires growth to function. Without economic growth, modern societies slide into recession and even depression, due to the need of invested capital to generate interest within a debt fuelled system of complex credit relationships. Because of this most economists talk about sustainability in the context of sustainable growth. However, the implicit assumption of indefinite growth in that concept clearly clashes with the physical realities of a planet with limited resources, as was already picked up on the 1972 report 'Limits to Growth' (despite some of the report's shortfalls). Some economists argue that it is possible to decouple growth from resource and energy consumption, but the reality of expanding consumerism in the past century -which reliably was correlated with increasing overall resource consumption- suggests otherwise, as long as one includes indirect energy use through imported goods. For the United Kingdom (UK) this meant, for example, that between 1990 and 2004, the UK reported a 6% decrease in carbon-emissions, which turned into an 11% increase when imported goods were taken into account (Druckman and Jackson 2009). In other words, as Jackson (2009) argues, while there may be some truth that there is a relative decoupling of growth and energy consumption per GDP within industrialised nations, there is no indication of the absolute decoupling needed to combat climate change (Jackson 2009:63-66). From a sustainability point of view the 'really existing' socialist societies of the 20th century hardly fared any better than modern neo-liberal capitalism does today, as they too were geared for industrialised, energy intensive production with little thought being spent on sustainability (all other faults of the systems left aside).

Nonetheless, finding a solution to the problem of sustainability will likely require a more communal than individualistic approach, as individuals acting on their own are unlikely to have the ability to change the course the global community is currently on. Some examples of these communal approaches have been explored in previous chapters of this book, be it community gardens in Ireland and across Europe, the transformation of urban space in New York and Belfast, or even something seemingly innocuous as bread-making projects in a number of contexts. However, while those examples are positive steps in the right direction, they are also relatively small scale compared with the juggernaut of the global economy. Deciding upon a course of action for creating a truly sustainable, global society will require careful foresight and (self-) critical thinking in order to avoid the pitfalls that brought down any serious alternative to modern capitalism.

Consequently, a meta-analytical approach to studying and considering past and present alternative socio-economic models is needed. In this chapter, I will be making the case that an updated version of John Rawls' *'Original Position'* might fit the bill when it comes to evaluating ideas for a just and -both economically and environmentally- sustainable society. In essence, the proposition is to use the theory of the *Original Position* as a rational, critical intellectual tool to achieve some degree of intersubjective acceptability for any new societal suggestions.

The Original Position and Veil of Ignorance outlined

Before considering how to apply some of Rawls' concepts to the issue of sustainability it is probably helpful to summarise the intentions and ideas behind Rawls' Original Position and the Veil of Ignorance in order to make clear both its benefits and -alleged- shortfalls. So what was Rawls trying to achieve with his theory of 'Justice as fairness'? When Rawls was writing his 'A theory of Justice' he was primarily driven by the desire to give a coherent counter-theory to the, at the time, dominating utilitarian approaches to political theory. He was hoping to revive parts of the old contract tradition -or what he saw as the contract tradition- and to come up with a strongly Kantian influenced framework for his political theory (Rawls 1971). He even went as far as to say that he "must disclaim any originality for the views I put forward. The leading ideas are classical and well known. My intention has been to organize them into a general framework by using certain simplifying devices so that their full force can be appreciated" (Rawls 1971). Arguably, he was, of course, not without originality altogether, given that he reorganised existing theory in an altogether new fashion and attempted to form a coherent whole that would stand up to a number of critical challenges. The central piece of this process of reorganisation being of course his Original Position and the veil of ignorance in 'A Theory of Justice', which he defines as follows:

> In justice as fairness the original position of equality corresponds to the state of nature in the traditional theory of the social contract. [...] It is understood as a purely hypothetical situation characterized so as to lead to a certain conception of justice. Among the essential features of this situation is that no one knows his place in society, his class position or social status, nor does anyone know his fortune in the distribution of

natural assets and abilities, his intelligence, strength, and the like. I shall even assume that the parties do not know their conceptions of the good or their special psychological propensities. The principles of justice are chosen behind a veil of ignorance. This ensures that no one is advantaged or disadvantaged in the choice of principles by the outcome of natural chance or the contingency of social circumstances. Since all are similarly situated and no one is able to design principles to favor his particular condition, the principles of justice are the result of a fair agreement or bargain (Rawls 1971).

This 'hypothetical situation' or thought experiment works, firstly, to counter-favour the views of one societal group over another, but more importantly forces people who engage in the thought experiment to consider all levels of society equally as they could not presume which part of society they would belong to. This works as a rational vehicle (Rawls follows the Kantian tradition of rationalists) for creating – or at least simulating- empathy for diverse living situations. In a sense, the original position can, in this way, be used to force self-interested but rational sociopaths (essentially- what economist's homo economicus is) into not only considering others but also cooperating with others for the overall benefit of everyone – themselves included. Therefore the concept would provide a solution to the challenge which Kant's society of intelligent devils poses, "each of whom is secretly inclined to exempt himself from them, to establish a constitution in such a way that, although their private intentions conflict, they check each other, with the result that their public conduct is the same as if they had no such intentions" (Kant 1795). Given the evolution of modern society towards individualism/self-isolation- any project that proposes a new societal design will likely have to face that very challenge if it wants to success, "Instead of a better society, the only thing almost everyone strives for is to better their own position – as individuals – within the existing society" (Wilkinson 2010). How does the veil of ignorance function practically? Despite the term 'veil of ignorance,' the Original Position demands a substantial knowledge of various areas of society, as one can only negate what one is aware of to start with, "Indeed, the parties are presumed to know whatever general facts affect the choice of the principles of justice" (Rawls 1971). Essentially, it is meant as a tool to abstract from individual circumstances and allow a rational discussion of principles of justice and fairness in an unbiased and constructive manner:

> To say that a certain conception of justice would be chosen in the original position is equivalent to saying that rational deliberation satisfying certain conditions and restrictions would reach a certain conclusion (Rawls 1971).

The restrictions he is interested in are primarily connected to what he considers to be coherent concepts of justice, which have to be logical, avoid contradictions, be equally applicable to everyone and all generations living under the rules, have to be public and easily comprehensible, and be truly general in scope (Rawls 1971). He thinks this type of restriction should exclude all societal conceptions that most of us today would consider inherently unjust and/or unfair, such as dictatorial systems (Rawls 1971). However, as some people -such as Nussbaum (2006) - note, Rawls shares some -in her opinion- problematic restrictions with previous contractarians. Nussbaum believes that they will lead to a treatment of - amongst others- disabled people and animals in a way that can only be described as inconsiderate/condescending, as they are excluded from active participation of the societal design within the circumstances of the Original position (Nussbaum 2006). Given the definition of the Original position, though, it should be pointed out that the only disabled people truly excluded from it would be severely mentally disabled, while anyone with mere physical disability but still capable of rational thought would not be excluded. Of course, this still leaves a considerable number of humans excluded, not to mention non-human animals. But the question of how, in truly practical ways, animals and other non-rational actors (such as infants) could be included in such a scenario as the Original position is not answered by Nussbaum, as she seeks instead to create a societal conception driven by evolving (parallel to societal development) value systems based around certain basic rights. Consequently, if one seeks a rational path for setting up just societies- Nussbaum's criticisms -given what she favours as an alternative- do not quite apply, as evolving value systems are hard to rationally plan for. That is not to say that there are no challenges in applying a rationality filter in terms of the participating parties in the Original Position, but those issues very much mirror existing practical challenges of how to treat infants and small children, and severely mentally disabled people within our current society. In other words, it seems likely that compassionate solutions within the system of justice as fairness would also likely imitate existing 'best practice' solutions.

The next basic principle Rawls stresses is the universal applicability that rules generated in the Original position need to possess - a clear nod towards Kant's categorical imperative. He states that, "Principles are to be chosen in view of the consequences of everyone's complying with them" (Rawls 1971). In other words, no system produced within the constraints of the Original Position can "be self-contradictory, or self-defeating, for everyone to act upon it. Similarly, should a principle be reasonable to

follow only when others conform to a different one, it is also
inadmissible" (Rawls 1971).

The Original position and Sustainable Societies

Following this summary of Rawls' theoretical construct let us examine
how some of his logical conditions compare with those proposed by
modern environmental thinkers for truly sustainable societies and systems.
In terms of deciding what qualifies a society as being 'sustainable' for the
purposes of that societal model I will rely on Attfield's definition of
sustainable processes. Compared with the Brundtland definition of
sustainable development it seems to more clearly capture the complexity
of discussing full sustainability as opposed to partial sustainability, which
is in truth, not sustainability at all. For Attfield, sustainable processes are
those "which are capable of being maintained indefinitely and which
undermine neither themselves, nor the segments of nature on which they
depend, nor other sustainable societies, nor the segments of nature on
which those societies depend, nor a potentially sustainable world system"
(Barry 2001). These comprehensive definitions illustrate what a complex -
on multiple levels- task one embarks on when talking about sustainable
societies. One can easily imagine a future where Europe has reached a
zero carbon-emission target, yet fails to be sustainable in reality, as it
simply shifts those emissions and general pollution resulting from
industrial production through outsourcing to other countries, mostly
located in Asia. As a matter of fact, the European Union seems to be
heading precisely in this direction, by focusing largely on service sector
employment while still consuming a disproportionately large percentage of
both raw resources and industrial output.

Contrasting Attfield's definition of sustainability with some of Rawls'
principles for just societies (derived from the Original Position) highlights
some striking similarities; both necessitate universal applicability and
exclude contradictory and self-undermining structures. But given further
consideration- both points of view can be seen as two approaches to the
two sides of the same coin, since as Talshir puts it "[...] ecological
problems deal precisely with the most existential needs of all – life, health,
sustainability and ways of life"(Barry 2001). This means that all social
systems are ultimately dependent on nature/the natural environment for
their perpetuation. In short, it will need to be coherent, rational with
universal, non-contradicting and non-self-defeating rules, consider future
generations and -implicitly- be sustainable, both economically and
environmentally. If one contrasts this with existing economic liberalism, it

is clear that one draws a short straw. Therefore, no system that does not consider sustainability at its core can possibly pass through Rawls' above mentioned side-constraint of being not self-contradictory and self-defeating. Given all the above mentioned conditions, one has to ask what type of society can actually fulfil all of the criteria for a truly just and sustainable society. Or in other words, what conditions would participants in the Original Position need to be aware of- to come up with suggestions for truly -socially and economically- sustainable societies?

At the very least, any serious societal future proofing will have to consider a number of issues. By 2050, the number of older persons - defined as 60 year's old, or indeed, older- in the world- will exceed the number of youth population for the first time in history (Un.org 2015). By the same date, the UN estimates that the world population will have reached the 9.6 billion mark, even though population growth for the whole world has now slowed down (UN News Centre 2015). Another milestone for the middle of the century will be the dramatically urbanised nature of humanity at that stage, with two thirds of all human beings being expected to live in cities with developed regions reaching urbanisation levels as highs as 85.4% (Esa.un.org 2015). Lastly, we will have to consider what automation might do to current economic models, when as much as "about 47 percent of total US employment is at risk" from automation, including such occupations as accountancies or telemarketers, which so far are purely within the human domain of work (Frey and Osborne 2013). In other words, by the middle of the century, we will be faced with a large, predominantly old and urban population, severely lacking in meaningful tasks to occupy itself with. It is very hard to imagine how our current economic model will be able to deal with these issues as they combine to form a potentially very dark societal picture. As Jackson (2009) puts it:

> Do we have a decent vision of prosperity for such a world? Is this vision credible in the face of the available evidence about ecological limits? How do we go about turning vision into reality?

And all of these issues are purely on the social side of the sustainability question, once one starts to consider environmental issues such as climate change, the boundary conditions for our future society model are further constrained. Reading the regular reports on climate change by the International Panel on Climate Change (IPCC), one cannot help but notice how climate scientists are simultaneously getting more certain (now above 97%) as to its human made origins and the increasing urgency with regards to stressing the need to take immediate radical measures to start reducing carbon emissions. The distilled knowledge of those scientists, in other words, shows that with the best available knowledge of our modern environmental and sustainability challenges, it is clear that the current globalised socio-economic system cannot be maintained without engendering grave damage to the biosphere/environment (both natural and man-made) which underlies our human existence. Given the natural societal inertia attempting to sustain the unsustainable, however, it is far from obvious how a shift of a large enough magnitude can be achieved- to at least- minimise the problems both humanity and nature will face within the next century- if current trends are left to continue. But how do these gloomy predictions for the future help us develop a model for a sustainable socio-economic model? If we add these societal side-constraints to the thought experiment of the Original Position, we should be able to narrow down the list of potential candidates for sustainable societal models, simply by eliminating those falling short of one or more of the constraints. In other words, any approach to sustainable development that does not include prescriptions for a largely urban, ageing overpopulated world under severe environmental pressure would need to be excluded. To quote Rawls:

> A theory however elegant and economical must be rejected or revised if it is untrue; likewise laws and institutions no matter how efficient and well-arranged must be reformed or abolished if they are unjust. (Rawls 1971)

And it is easy to argue that a lack of care and protection of the environment we inhabit, as well as not protecting our societies from growing levels of inequality, is at the least unjust for future generations, which Rawls thinks are implicitly owed consideration within his idea of cooperation over time (Rawls 1993). Of course, this will exclude neoliberal approaches to arranging our economy and society, but as mentioned in the introduction it will also exclude any economic model based -even indirectly- on economic growth. As Jackson clearly shows, using the so-called Ehrlich equation calculating human impact on the planet, for as long as we have a growing global population, coupled with on average increasing levels of affluence, the amount of technological progress and efficiency (carbon intensity) that we have historically experienced will always fall short of limiting human impact on the planet. Jackson points out that between 1990 and 2007 carbon intensities have declined on average by 0.7 per cent per year while population grew by 1.3 per cent and average per capita income has increased by 1.4 per cent each year. Meaning that efficiency did neither compensate for the growth in population or incomes, never mind combined:

Instead, carbon dioxide emissions have grown on average by 1.3 + 1.4 − 0.7 = 2 [Ehrlich equation] per cent per year, leading over 17 years to an almost 40 per cent increase in emissions (Jackson 2009).

This compares especially unfavourably when considering that to achieve the IPCC goal of CO2 levels no higher than 450 parts per million (ppm) for the year 2050 we will need to decrease emissions by an average annual rate of 5% (Jackson 2009). This means that given the UN-predicted population increase rate for the next 35 years (up to 9.6 billion), technological efficiency increases of the energy intensity of economic growth will fall far short of enabling a decrease in global emissions. Furthermore, it seems that the Ehrlich equation when applied to C02 emissions implies that not even a steady state economy without any growth would help limit emissions, but that rather the only option for achieving the IPCC climate goals will lie in a path of de-growth, or a shrinking of our currently unsustainable economies. Given that a zero growth economy is anathema to the vast majority of even progressive economists, the idea of de-growth will be hard to sell. As Murray Bookchin puts it, "Capitalism can no more be "persuaded" to limit growth than a human being can be "persuaded" to stop breathing" (Wilkinson and Picket 2010). However, if one considers a Price Waterhouse Coopers (PWC) study to be reliable, reducing global Carbon emissions by 50% by 2050 will cost about 3% of annual, global GDP leading up to 2050 (Guardian 2008). This proves that costs for reduction of emissions will exceed annual growth rates of the recent post-crisis years (Data.world bank.org 2015). That is before one considers the ambitious EU targets for CO2 reductions by 2050 of 80-95% compared with 1990 (Ec.europa.eu 2015). This would seem to imply that government funded tackling of climate change in the developed world will have to far exceed growth rates, which in turn would require either increased borrowing or prioritisation of decarbonisation of economies over other government run services such as health and education. This will happen if we continue to rely on orthodox economics.

Engaging in a thought experiment such as the original position is about identifying new solutions to complex issues such as social justice and sustainability. Go together they must if one believes Wilkinson and Picket (2010) who state, "It looks not only as if the two are complementary, but also that governments may be unable to make big enough cuts in carbon emissions without also reducing inequality" (Wilkinson and Picket 2010). Luckily, their statistical research seems to also indicate that high quality of life, development and a large carbon footprint are by no means necessarily intertwined, even if only one country currently exists that brings together a low carbon footprint, with a high score on the Human Development Index maintained by the UN; Cuba (Wilkinson and Picket 2010). While Cuba is by no means a paragon of democracy, it, nonetheless, can act as a show case for what might be required for a transition -even if it was a forced one- in this instance- to a low carbon future that maintains and improves quality of life. Many of the solutions practised by inventive Cubans -often against initial government resistance- could be applied in developed nations around the world, be it urban community gardens, a refocusing on public transport, decentralisation of services and education, and finally, first class accessible healthcare (compare The Power of Community: How Cuba Survived Peak Oil 2006). However, it also shows that change of this magnitude does not come on its own, as virtually none of these positive paradigm shifts would likely have happened, if not for the external pressures created by both the collapse of oil imports from the former Soviet Union when it ceased to exist in 1991 and the ongoing US embargo of most goods to and from Cuba. As Jackson shows, our current socio-economic thinking is locked into what he calls the "iron cage" of consumerism, which is characterised by a severe lack of macro-economic models that do not rely on growth, but rather are designed for functioning at a steady state, i.e. without growth (Jackson 2009). As he says:

> Economics – and macro-economics in particular – is ecologically illiterate. [...]We have no model for how common macro-economic 'aggregates' (production, consumption, investment, trade, capital stock, public spending, labour, money supply and so on) behave when capital doesn't accumulate (Jackson 2009).

Getting us out of that iron cage is where the true challenges lie. In recent years, more high ranking business leaders and politicians have started to truly appreciate the need to get away from a carbon-emission intensive economy, but while there is a call for green investment, there is no challenge to the growth agenda (Courtice 2015 and Harvey 2015). Instead, businesses started to focus on the idea of green growth, which is as flawed as any growth driven economy in the long term, as any kind of growth will eventually encounter the physical limits that exist in the real world. In essence, what we face is the issue that current macro-economic thinking is driven by world-removed mathematical formulae for the calculation of GDP and growth, which is fundamentally incapable of considering the conditions which make human economies possible to start with, be that household work (ironically given the origins of the word economy in the concept of *oikonomia*), environmental conditions sustaining human life, or the fact of limited availability of resources (compare

Jackson 2009). As we are now starting to encounter the consequences of that from humanity removed method of organising the economy, it might be time to (re-)consider ways of organising the economy from the bottom up with human values and sustainability at its heart.

The Original Position as an Intellectual Tool for considering Socio-economic Models

Now that we have outlined both the problems of our current consumerist societies and identified some of the conditions that have to be considered in creating more sustainable societies, it is time to have a look at the Original Position once more, with an eye to evaluating whether those societal concepts would function for the kind of new macro-economic system we clearly seem to be in need of. So let us imagine a group of rational human beings without any concept of their gender, age and mental or physical capabilities coming together to discuss how a just and sustainable society should be arranged for everyone's benefit and with the well-being of future generations in mind. They are fully aware of political and economic theories, history, the natural sciences, availability of resources and the state of the environment. Given those conditions, which socio-economic system would they then favour? - knowing that they might have to live in the worst conditions of what that system might have to offer. Primed with these considerations, it should be possible to have a somewhat neutral reflection on the systems that could fit the constraints thrown up by environmental constraints (while also bearing in mind human social needs and desires for social justice). As most philosophical concepts are best explored through practical experiments, let us have a look at one possible concept for a fairer future society, the so-called "Resource based economy" (RBE) (Sando 2015).

Both concepts turn modern economic systems and their assumptions on their head. They design a rationalistic economic system based on what is there, and not on what is desired. The RBE would, according to its inventor Jacque Fresco, be a rational system of arranging the economy around the idea that the earth and its resources are a finite system (Freso 2015). To act upon this assumption, the RBE then does very much what its name suggests, it attempts to anchor the economy to the limited resources that are available to humanity, be that water, arable land, metals and mineral energy sources, but also considers constraints such as space, time and environmental systems (Mujezinovic 2015). This contrasts starkly with current growth based economic systems that start out with the implicit assumption of the possibility of limitless growth, and indirectly, therefore, limitless resource consumption. In the RBE, the approach would require for resources to be surveyed on a global scale, and then treated as a common property for all of humanity. Based on this information, the available resources would then be shared out fairly across the globe, in the most efficient way possible, with available technology based on principles of sustainability. It would be a moneyless, global economy based on rational principles alone, with the aim of avoiding disruptions to human life and well-being that the current growth dependent, resource-and environmentally ignorant monetary economy -with its frequent crises- necessarily entails. As Mujezinovic points out, "market prices do not measure externalities, and companies can actually gain competitive advantages by externalising costs and passing them on to society in the form of pollution, increased job insecurity, potentially harmful products, etc. The *real* cost, not in money, but in the effect on individuals, society and the environment, is *hidden* by the market price" (Mujezinovic 2015). In contrast to capitalism, with its singular focus on the profit motive for supposedly everyone's benefit, the RBE would approach resources and production from a flexible, multi-dimensional perspective, that rationally considers the myriad of values that might be affected by the production of any given item we consume. Issues of complexities would therefore not be solved by an "invisible hand", but rather by taking into consideration, on a case by case basis, specific circumstances of any production process in any given locality, possibly by using appropriate ordinal scales to rank priorities, assisted by computerised decision procedures to create consistency and to ensure best practice is followed (Mujezinovic 2015). Now let us analyse this proposed global economic system through the lens of the Original Position, to evaluate if it would meet its criteria in terms of social justice and sustainability.

The first point that stands out here is the fact that the RBE has - similarly to capitalism indeed- a universal ambition, in that it aspires to be a global system of resource distribution. Unlike capitalism, however, Fresco argues that a resource based economy can only properly function as intended if it is implemented on a global scale, as the argument goes that anything else would lead to wealth inequality, and therefore, conflict (Fresco 2015). This is nonetheless not a draw back as the RBE as part of its rational approach demands sustainability, which as was indicated in the earlier definition ultimately necessitates a global approach as well. With regards to social justice the system is essentially deliberately designed to produce the most equitable and just society possible given the available resources and taking sustainability and the well-being of future generations into account. It is essentially supposed to be a framework for enabling the kind of lives we wish we could have if it were not for supposed economic necessity. And it is meant to be flexible in its approach to specific circumstances (Mujezinovic 2015), meaning it should not be yet another dystopian attempt to make all human beings perfect copies, the totalitarian misunderstanding of equality. Essentially it is meant to enable us for the first time to use organised societal complexity to achieve the full potential of the human intellect, instead of having intellect serve nothing but the wish-fulfilment machine that is consumerism.

In essence this would seem to be an example of what a society designed from within the Original position might look like. However, there are a number of possible societies that might fill the same criteria that are the constraints of this thought experiment, such as, for example the socialist utopia described in Bellamy's "Looking Backward" (Bellamy 1888). Therefore, in effect, a secondary step will be required once an extensive list of candidate societal systems has been compiled, which prove to be potentially just and sustainable. This crucial secondary step will need to be the question of transition from the world as it is now- to propose new societal set up. In other words, the second question would have to be-what is the probability of humanity being able to bring about this new state of being in a peaceful manner? The condition of any transition being peaceful is a crucial one, if one is to avoid the totalitarian outcomes that were the result of the attempted transition into communism, the last model that attempted to challenge the predominance of capitalist economic systems.

Conclusion

In conclusion, this chapter explores the possibility of using a consequently thought out version of Rawls' Original Position as a tool for critical analysis with regards to societal models concerned with both social justice and sustainability. It showed how the Original Position -with all its implications- already has a requirement for not just social justice, but also sustainability. As was illustrated, modern consumerist societies clearly fall short on both accounts of sustainability and social justice, given current ongoing levels of environmental degradation and inequality. Arguably, alternative local societal approaches would fare better on both points, however, the Original position should help filter out those options that might function locally on a small scale, but cannot be applied on the global scale needed to successfully combat issues such as climate change, growing, ageing populations and international wealth inequality. Lastly, the chapter provided-in the form of the RBE- an example of a societal model that seemingly would pass through the filter of the Original Position successfully, but which might nonetheless be unlikely to be implemented, due to its distance from the status quo, throwing up the issue of socio-economic transitions and transformations which will require further research and analysis.

References

Barry, John and Mark J. L. Wissenburg (eds) *Sustaining Liberal Democracy: Ecological Challenges and Opportunities*. Basingstoke: Palgrave. 2001.

Bell, Derek. 'How can Political Liberals be Environmentalists?', *Political Studies*: 2002 Vol 50. 703-724.

Bellamy, Edward. *Looking backward from 2000 to 1887*. Champaign, Ill.: Project Gutenberg. 1996.

Courtice, Polly. Climate change: how can we move beyond the committed few?. *The Guardian*. [online], January 27, 2015. Accessed 27 Jan. 2015
http://www.theguardian.com/sustainable-business/2015/jan/27/
sustainable-green-growth-collaboration-business

Data.worldbank.org. *GDP growth (annual %) | Data | Graph*. [online], 2015. Accessed 26 Jan. 2015.
http://data.worldbank.org/indicator/NY.GDP.MKTP.KD.ZG/countries
?display=graph

Dobson, Andrew. 'Foreword' in John Barry and Mark Wissenburg (eds) *Sustaining Liberal Democracy: Ecological Challenges and Opportunities*. Basingstoke: Palgrave, 2001.

Druckman, Angela and Tim Jackson. 'The carbon footprint of UK households 1990–2004: A socio-economically disaggregated, quasi-multi-regional input-output model'. *Ecological Economics* 68 (7): 2066–2077. 2009.

Ec.europa.eu. *EU action on climate - European Commission*. [online]. 2015. Accessed 26 Jan. 2015.
http://ec.europa.eu/clima/policies/brief/eu/

Esa.un.org. *United Nations - Population Division*. [online].2015. Accessed 25 Jan. 2015. http://esa.un.org/unpd/wup/Highlights/

Fresco, Jacque. *The Venus Project - Resource based economy*. [video]. 2015. Accessed 31 Jan. 2015.
https://www.youtube.com/watch?v=PIMy0QBSQWo

Frey, Carl B. and Michael A. Osborne. The Future of Employment: How susceptible are jobs to computerisation. *Oxford Martin School seminar.* [online]. 2013. Accessed 25 Jan. 2015. http://www.oxfordmartin.ox.ac.uk/downloads/academic/The_Future_of_Employment.pdf

Guardian. Climate change: Time for deeds not words to reach emissions target, PwC study warns. [online]. July 03, 2008. Accessed 26 Jan. 2015 http://www.theguardian.com/environment/2008/jul/03/carbonemissions. climatechange

Harvey, Fiona. Prince Charles: global pact on climate change could be Magna Carta for Earth. *Guardian.* [online]. January 26, 2015. Accessed 27 Jan. 2015 http://www.theguardian.com/uk-news/2015/jan/26/prince-charles-global-pact-climate-change-magna-carta-earth

Jackson, Tim . *Prosperity without Growth: Economics for a Finite Planet* [Kindle Edition]. Routledge; 1 edition. 2009.

Kant, Immanuel. *Perpetual Peace: A Philosophical Sketch.* 1795. Accessed on 31.03.2014 https://www.mtholyoke.edu/acad/intrel/kant/kant1.htm

Mujezinovic, Davor. *Economic Calculation in a Resource Based Economy – A Defence.* [online] THE RESOURCE BASED sharing ECONOMY. 2015. Accessed 30 Jan. 2015 http://www.theresourcebasedeconomy.com/2015/01/economic-calculation-in-a-resource-based-economy-a-defence/

Nussbaum, Martha. *Frontiers of Justice: Disability, Nationality, Species Membership.* Harvard University Press. 2006.

Rawls, John. A Theory of Justice. Revised edition. Oxford: Oxford University Press. 1971.

Rawls, John. Political Liberalism. New York: Columbia University Press. 1993.

—. Justice as Fairness: a Restatement. Cambridge MA: Harvard University Press. 2001.

Sandø, Harald. *The Resource Based Economy.* [online]. 2015. Accessed 27 Jan. 2015. http://www.theresourcebasedeconomy.com/

The Economist. The future of jobs - The onrushing wave. [online]. January 18, 2014. Accessed 25 Jan. 2015. http://www.economist.com/news/briefing/21594264-previous-technological-innovation-has-always-delivered-more-long-run-employment-not-less

Faith, Morgan. *The Power of Community: How Cuba Survived Peak Oil.* [video] USA. 2006.

UN News Centre. *World population projected to reach 9.6 billion by 2050 – UN report.* [online] 2015. Accessed 25 Jan. 2015
http://www.un.org/apps/news/story.asp?NewsID=45165#.VLP8mNKs Xy0 Un.org. *World Population Ageing.* [online] 2015. Accessed 25 Jan. 2015
http://www.un.org/esa/population/publications/worldageing19502050
Wilkinson, Richard and Kate Pickett. *The Spirit Level: Why Equality is Better for Everyone.* Penguin [Kindle Edition]. 2010.

Chapter Three

The Emerging Spheres of Resonance: "Clandestinely Genuine" Food Networks and the Challenges of Governing Sustainability in Italy

Alexander Koensler

The Power of Standardization

When K. arrives at the village, he stops at the old bridge. He then looks up to where "the castle" should be, but perceives only an apparent emptiness, darkness. He is overcome with the feeling that he is somehow lost. With reference to the apparent emptiness of power, Franz Kafka (2009) thus begins his book *The Castle*. The story remains, throughout the book, one of a search to penetrate into the unreachable, fugitive, abstract emptiness of a power-governance conundrum that remains ever present. Such glimmers of how power is experienced in the wake of the Habsburgerian bureaucracy by Kafka might also serve as a metaphor for the theme of how policy regulations, including those for sustainable food and agriculture, are experienced by many independent small-scale farmers. The evolution of food governance is increasingly characterized by a proliferation of apparently objective procedures of evaluation, standardization and certification, including those who demonstrate sustainable ways of production. K's experiences of alienated, depersonalized power bring us into the heart of a debate over food sovereignty and the right to certify. Despite the growing sophistication of regulations for sustainable food and agriculture, the sense of lost control over the quality of food products has become a powerful symbol of the alienating aspects of globalisation.

This chapter aims to contribute to a more detailed understanding of these dynamics through a case study of a novel form of political mobilization in a rural context. Based on ongoing ethnographic fieldwork in Umbria, Central Italy[1], I started to document the rapid growth of the movement "Genuinely Clandestine" (GC) out of a range of dispersed pre-existing consumer-producer groups (*Gruppi d'acquisto solidali*, GAS) and eco-anarchistic networks. Founded in 2012, GC contests the efficacy and practicality of the current regime of EU regulations for sustainable agriculture and hygienic food processing.[2] As an emerging network, it unites small-scale independent growers who oppose the EU-driven regulations of food certification, - considered to be driven by global agribusiness interests. In 2013, I started to follow systematically these developments in the peripheral region of Umbria, an area with a long history of rural activism which has traditionally attracted not only farmers who experiment with methods of advanced organic agriculture, but also eco-anarchic and permaculture communes, as well as eco-villages related to "bioregional" or "deep ecology"-movements. Throughout Italy, CG has recently succeeded to promote different types of so-called "participatory self-certifications" of "genuine" food products, direct marketing and public demonstrations. From this perspective, the attempt to guarantee sustainability through standardized policy approaches remains contested and subverted by those who actually would be expected to benefit from such policies. In contrast to the ethical consumerism of local food networks such as the Slow Food movement, this rapidly growing network acts provocatively in grey legal spaces. Why and how are some farmers drawn into the activities of the network? What potential does this movement have to cause the re-thinking of policies for sustainability standards?

Sustainable Food Networks and Governance

Over the past decade, food studies have pursued new directions. A growing body of research examines practices of resistance against the global agribusiness, including the emergence of local food activism (Counihan and Siniscalchi 2014; Lvkoe 2011; Nonini 2013).[3] A growing realm of ethnographic research highlights the array of farmers' practices of resistance against certifications (Gladwin and Trueman 1989; Papa 2002).[4] Some authors have analysed the role of ethical food activism such as the Slow Food movement in lifestyle changes (Leitch 2013), creating a debate about important methodological issues in social anthropology regarding the understanding of community and networks (Parkins and Craig 2006; Pink 2008). This body of research is also beginning to make a major contribution to how global political issues are considered through food, in contrast to a more positivist strand that considers eating and culture as an issue of research in itself. This is evident, for example, in *The Oxford Handbook of Food History* (Pilcher 2012), which focuses on an encyclopaedic approach attempting to list knowledge. A similar approach of rather limited analytic depth can be found in the extensive writing on specific foods in circumscribed local contexts (Munn 1992; Ohnuki-Tierney 1994; Albala 2012). In addition, a body of anthropological research has begun to investigate challenges and contestations to the food system, treating them as struggles over global social justice (Counihan and Van Esterik 2013; Counihan and Siniscalchi 2014). However, the relation between food and political dynamics is often considered as an assemblage of localist practices (Nonini 2013: 267; Papa 2002), framed in terms of ethical consumerism (Guthman 2013; Levkoe 2011) or individual agency (Gladwin and Truman 1989; Wu and Cheung 2002). In other words, a systematic understanding of practices of resistance against the standardization policies in the realm of food production is still missing.

Although offering a welcome contribution to the existing literature on local food chains, the bulk of the literature on local food networks often celebrates ethical activism and individual agency, overshadowing more political dynamics related to governance and food policies. Following Bourdieu's (2015) analysis of resistance as an instrument to understand the evolution of contemporary governance, I attempt to investigate the issues around sustainable and organic certifications as an analytical prism for the positive and productive aspects of power (Foucault in: Dreyfus, Rabinow and Foucault 1983: 209). In this sense, the rise of farmer's activism that attempts to re-invent food certifications in democratic and participatory terms offers a catalyst for the understanding of changing social relations within the evolution of contemporary governance. In a world where power relations are hidden behind objective procedures of unquestionable standardization, resistance and activism, food certification has become a prism through which to understand power relations, "locate their position, find out their points of applications and the methods used" (Foucault 1982: 209).

Ethnographic studies of government policies such as certification are part of a broader shift of anthropological knowledge towards an interest in the functioning of institutions in complex societies (Marcus 1999; Fischer 1999; Rabinow 2008). In their seminal work on the anthropology of policy, Shore and Wright (1997) demonstrate how "policy" has become an important instrument in the organisation of contemporary societies. This interest has been developed in line with ethnographies of the ways in which political power is played out in specific contexts, a cornerstone of political anthropology (Wolf 2001; Paley 2001; Lewellen 2003).[5] Some studies of the anthropology of policy have also shifted attention to how policies are productive, performative and contested (Müller 2011; Zinn 2011). In other words, through this anthropological "eye" cast on the way in which policies are implemented allows one to examine otherwise hidden social relations and realities.

This body of research can offer a new perspective on the ways food safety policies are implemented into the dynamics of contemporary food governance. For example, in the so-called "horse-meat scandal" in 2013, foods advertised as containing beef were found to contain undeclared or improperly declared horse meat - as much as 100 per cent of the meat content in some cases.[6] A first report by the House of Commons Select Committee on Environment, Food and Rural Affairs on the incident was not critical of UK or Irish producers.[7] Only afterwards did the UK government call for an "independent" and "objective" investigation on the website of the Food Standards Authority.[8] The report outlines how instrumentalised relations in food production also leads to some curious, if not fascinating issues. A 'stand-alone' cold-store (e.g. on an industrial estate) will be subject to checks by the local authority. Such cold-stores are assumed to be lower risk than manufacturing or processing plants for inspection purposes, and so may be subject to infrequent inspections. Inspections that do take place also present practical difficulties when attempting to detect fraud; they may be announced, and are not usually fraud-aware. Both local authorities and so-called "private sector audits" are generally more concerned with food hygiene and safety than with fraud. However, the report concludes, "fortunately, consumers in the UK have access to perhaps the safest food in the world. Major scientific advancements are being made to help minimise risks to the food chain." What might be true for "safety," in the strict sense of the term, might not be true for food quality and its sustainability. Thus, by defining and reframing public concerns in terms of "safety" rather than "quality", policy committees shape the way reality is perceived, presenting subjective political choices as rational and objective. In short, the value of an anthropological perspective on policy lies in its ability to unmask how policies create an apparently neutral world of meaning and are a "type of power and embodiment of instrumental reason" (Wedel, Shore, Feldman and Lathop 2005: 37).

The Limits of Governing Sustainability

Alternative food exchange networks are widely associated with "ethical consumerism", niche markets which are situated outside the sphere of dominant relations. At first glance, they seem to offer a solution to what are perceived as the limits, dangers and damage of the industrial agribusiness. However, as ethical niche markets, mainstream food activism does not engage actively with structures of governance and policy. The rather unique case of the emerging network "Clandestinely Genuine" (*Genuino Clandestino*, in Italian) in Italy indicates a different approach. The movement was originally created in 2010 as an ironic "anti-logo" to commercialised organic food labels in organic markets in Bologna. On one occasion, problems arose when not all independent small-scale farmers who participated in the market could prove they adhered to standards for official organic and hygienic certifications. The farmers in question, however, claimed to adhere to higher standards than the current labels for organic food and were forced to produce their products "clandestinely", in legally grey or informal spaces. The common opinion understood that current hygienic standards and the complicated and expensive rules for organic certifications intentionally favoured large industrial producers. In a similar vein, the procedures to obtain organic labels were considered incorrect due to the high fee that had to be paid to third-party certifying bodies as a sufficient condition to obtain organic labels. The broad consensus of this opinion transformed rapidly into a campaign for the "grassroots-certification" practices of small farmers.

For members of the "Clandestinely Genuine" (CG) network, participatory self-certification follows a set of rules and conventions that are democratically and locally set in consumer-producer assemblies. For example, they involve visits of consumers to farms or production units, the drafting of documents that represent the product, and the final approval in consumer-producer relations. As an open challenge to bureaucratic regulations in 2014, CG expanded to a national and international network present throughout central and northern Italy-with separate local markets, food cooperatives and political events. In contrast to past forms of individual forms of resistance or ethical activism, the innovative potential of CG derives from its ability to drastically rethink the way we exchange food, to re-appropriate the right to certify and to set quality standards. Thus, CG engages actively with the power structures of governance rather than eluding or silently subverting them. Importantly, the GC network also distinguishes itself from elite-driven local food networks that target the upper classes, a point frequently criticized by research into the subject (Nonini 2013). Independent small-scale farmers who sell their products can offer low prices since they skip intermediate steps. Interestingly, this engagement can assume different political stances. In some regions, local groups of CG intersect and overlap with other farmer-movements, such as the reformist movement "Small-scale Farmer's Agriculture" (*Agricoltura Contadina*, in Italian). This movement proposes a reformulation of current legislation in favour of local, small-scale productions that valorise the environment and create non-market relations. Rather than "clandestine", activists believe that legislative reform could change power dynamics in their favour. However, CG activists are more sceptical and believe that the interests of the agribusiness lobby, or generally of capitalist structures, would prevent such a reformist approach.

In my fieldwork, I have chosen to work with farmers who live in the mountains and hills of Umbria in Central Italy, because this is a region that traditionally has attracted alternative farming experiments. Its remote hillsides and valleys have long been considered as ideal places for alternative farming by activists of Eco and communal movements. Here, the idea of "participatory self-certifications" spread in 2012-13 from the more organised branches of the network in Northern Italy, such as Emilia Romagna. In Umbria, the first small-scale independent food producers who took up the ideas of "Clandestinely Genuine" have been those who are part of movements of urban citizens who moved into the countryside in order to become self-sufficient alternative farmers in the eighties. However, some of these are afraid to join the movement due to the provocative legal challenges. They prefer not to participate in "illegal" activities and to risk the confiscation of their self-certified, "clandestine" cheese or bread. These experiences illustrate the role of ethnography as an instrument to unearth unexpected elements or, as William James is quoted as stating in Willis and Trondman's (2010: 395) *Manifesto for Ethnography*, "experience, as we know, has ways of boiling over, and making us correct our present formulas". The richness, ambiguity and even contradictory nature of social reality constitutes a heuristic resource to understand what is at stake. In a wider sense, this form of relational thinking as a scientific practice is also central to Pierre Bourdieu's (1990, 1991) sociology and theory of practice, which constantly criticises the "realism" or "substantialism" of knowledge and calls for an attempt to go beyond ordinary, first-hand experiences.

Tony

In this methodological attempt to follow relations around activism- rather than studying activism in itself and to transcend the obvious experiences of mobilization- a certain complex "ambiguity" of activism emerges towards the political goals of the national GC network. There is, for instance, Tony.[9] His story exemplifies the shifting and sometimes contradictory aspects of political engagements considered within GC's wider web of social relations. Tony is a man who made the most of his wealth in the eighties- in the city of Perugia, running a popular pub with three terraces, as he proudly notes. When the profits decreased and he became more inclined towards a more relaxed life, he bought an abandoned farm in the mountains. On his Facebook page, he calls this "Free Collelumesco", an allusion to a semi-independent entity in which state authority has little space. One of his preferred products is a wine called "Red Clandestine," which he sells at markets and political events. With his wife, he also bakes traditional cakes (*crostate*), with organic wheat and marmalade provided by their neighbours. On his Facebook page, he uploads regular pictures taken during the production of his products. At markets and festivals, he likes to celebrate, talk and dance-despite his age. In interviews, he demonstrates attachment to the idea of a "market place," conceived as a place of social exchange beyond profit and instrumental relations.

In GC markets, ordinary consumers are considered as co-producers who are invited to participate in the production process, and to share food, knowledge and some local products. Tony's talkative, even festive approach to the markets remains at the forefront here. "Participating in markets", he claims, "gives me a sense of my work". However, things are not always so peaceful. At one of the markets that I attended regularly, producers and co-producers would share their lunch – and Tony contributed with his wine. On one occasion, towards the end of the lunch, conversation turned to one participant who had temporary financial difficulties and some participants considered possibilities to help him out, either with money or labour. When someone mentioned that the year prior, Tony was helped out after some difficulties, a discussion started on whether this was a similar or a different situation. Tony became increasingly angry at this and he interrupted the discussion vehemently. This event illustrates the role of deep personal involvement in this space-far beyond instrumentalised market-relations. It also indicates the complex role of such political engagements, which shift between material constraints, solidarity and the wider political goals of CG.

Angela

Another enlightening example of the centrality of human relations over profit from my ethnographic research is provided by the story of Angela. When she lost her job two years ago, she recovered the uncultivated land belonging to her father up in the mountains, about a two-hour drive from her home. From her savings, she bought a used tractor and some equipment and started producing wheat and lentils and some sheep milk. In the first year, she invested a great effort in obtaining certifications for her products. She paid 1600 Euros per year just for permission to sell her lentils, and had to take them to an officially recognised cleaning facility situated a three-hour drive away from her fields. During the second year she met with other farmers and started to sell her milk to a friend who made cheese without official certification. At markets, Angela can be found selling both her legal lentils and the clandestine cheese. Initially, she participated in the local Slow Food Presidia meetings, but remained disappointed by the rules of the presidia. For example, the price of lentils was fixed at 4.50 Euro and she found it more convenient to sell them at 3.50. She says, "I like to be honest and why should I earn more than I need. At Slow Food they told me I was thinking like a consumer and not a business person". As these words show, Angela is proud to think as a "consumer" and focus less on profits. In an almost Zen-like attitude, many activists seem to succeed in overcoming many constraints of profit-making through engaging in non-market relations- rather than at a later stage- allowing (indirectly) higher profits. In the case of Angela, her "social" approach to selling lentils widened her range of consumers and strengthened their trust in her and her products. What is interesting in both cases is the emphasis on social relations and the opposition to economic logics in the statements of both small-scale farmers, the one who does it in order to make a living and the one who sells his wine in order to keep abreast with friends. Exchange of food is transformed into a way of developing human relationships, based on trust and creativity.

"Spheres of Resonance"

Despite several ambiguities, the value of these "non-market" relations, in both the experiences of Tony and Angela, are at the basis of dynamics that establish new forms of "trust" between producers and consumers (often re-labelled as co-producers within CG circuits). This emphasis on trust and the recovery of social relations is evident in the organizational structures of CG assemblies, markets and meetings. At Clandestinely Genuine markets, producers are keen to spend a surprisingly lengthy time with buyers, explaining the processes of production and making friends. Moreover, relations are organized horizontally- rather than in a hierarchical manner- as in the procedures of certification through external authoritative experts. Within the GC network, participatory self-certification works not on the basis of objective guidelines or structured descriptions, but rather relationally. What you find is a list of voices of people. For example, in a document published on a blog focusing on how these certifications work, Laura says, "To propose meetings and workshops at the farm, this might be one of the ideas on how to create contacts". In another significant passage, Carlo says, "The path of participatory self-certification leads mainly to a human relationship, a relationship of trust: it represents a welcome to the community of consumption, from the moment you begin to share the day, the week, the year: to be born forces a relationship of mutual trust".

These rather short extracts aim to demonstrate the innovative attempts of CG to recover horizontal and trustful social relations in food chains, thereby opening up the possibility to rethink food governance in unexpected ways. The concept of "spheres of resonance," as developed in the work of Hartmut Rosa (2012), offers a possibility to better understand the emphasis on personal relations in CG's approach to sustainability. Inspired by the interest of the Frankfurt School in understanding alienation in contemporary capitalism, Rosa examines how the increased sense of alienation in contemporary societies derives from the need of finance capitalism to economize, accelerate, measure and standardize human relations.[10] In this line of argumentation, the proliferation of these instrumental relations also de-politicizes issues of public concern, ultimately threating democracy. Rosa contrasts these instrumentalised relations as a means of governance with humanistic "relations of resonance", inspired by Charles Taylor (1994), which are based on experiences of fullness, similar to the experience of a good song, a prayer or a dance. In other words, social acceleration leads directly to a loss of "resonance" in human relations. For example, listening to a delightful song, our heart and soul is touched in a way that resonates with the piece. In other words, the song "resonates" throughout our body and spirit in an emotional experience that is based on trust. As subjects, we feel a sense of being in the world through such relations of resonance. This type of relation is for Rosa a, "relation of resonance," in contrast to empty, causal, and instrumentalised relations, as in the case of filling out a form, the completion of so-called To-Do-Lists (before we actually start to do what we want), and so on. In industrialized agribusiness, the exchange of food remains organized over such instrumentalised relations, not only in supermarkets. The process of food production itself is also increasingly regulated not through relations of resonance and trust, but on formalized and automated processes of certification and standardization. Farmers do not know who consume their products, but experience depersonalized relations towards big intermediate traders. By contrast, the motivations of people like Tony or Angela to engage in the alternative networks of Clandestinely Genuine are motivated through various practices and experiments to recover the direct personal relations of trust between consumers and producers.

Conclusion

In *The Castle*, Kafka's figure K remains ambivalent. K never succeeds in his struggle to reach out to meet the aristocratic elite of the castle. Kafka did not finish the book and as such, we cannot ever know the ultimate fate of K. This book remains a fragment. It might well be said that the invisibility of the aristocratic elite in Kafka can be seen as a precursor of the contemporary reconfiguration of social relations, as evident in the establishment of authority through objective certifications. The limits of these relations are demonstrated forcefully in the experiences of people like Tony and Angela- who challenge the right to certify. As a novel form of re-appropriation of the "right to certify", the practices of activists and independent small-scale farmers who engage with the Genuinely Clandestine network have broader and more profound political implications than well-known ethical consumer activism. The attempts of this network to rethink instrumentalised relations as enacted in de-personalized food certification cannot be explained in terms of ethical consumerism or the emergence of new and specialized niche markets. By contrast, the Clandestinely Genuine network has the ability to penetrate and challenge a cornerstone of contemporary power- it constitutes a broader model that can be used to rethink the kernel of the articulation of contemporary power, certification and standardization.

Thus, the "ethnographic eye" offers a critique of the way in which mainstream policies of sustainability are implemented. Emerging and experimental forms of activism such as the CG network point to the *status nascendi* of forms of mobilization that cannot be confined or contained in institutional definitions of governance of sustainability. Unnamed figures make their appearance beyond the expectations of instrumentalised practices of governance. According to Engin Isin, "it is unidentified ...not because it is invisible, but because we have not recognized it. It is inarticulable" (Isin 2009: 367). These unnamed and experimental forms remind us of the subversive beginnings of organic agriculture itself. In sum, an anthropology of sustainability rooted in the ethnographic praxis of uncovering emerging figures of mobilization might destabilise the certainty of some policies of sustainability, but reveal those yet unnamed dynamics that are often at the forefront of new development.

References

Albala, Ken. *Routledge international handbook of food studies.* 1st ed. ed. London; New York: Routledge, 2012.

Bourdieu, P. *In Other Words: Essays Towards a Reflexive Sociology.* Cambridge: Polity Press, 1990.

Bourdieu, Pierre. *Language and Symbolic Power.* Cambridge, Mass.: Harvard University Press, 1991.

Bourdieu, Paul. *On the State.* London: Polity, 2015.

Counihan, Carol, and Valeria Siniscalchi. *Food Activism: Agency, Democracy and Economy.* London: Bloomsbury, 2014.

Counihan, Carol, and Paul Van Esterik. *Food and Culture: A Reader.* London: Routledge, 2013.

Dreyfus, Hubert L., Paul Rabinow, and M. Foucault. *Michel Foucault: Beyond Structuralism and Hermeneutics.* Chicago: University of Chicago Press, 1983.

Fischer, Michael M. J. "Emergent Forms of Life: Anthropologies of Late or Postmodernities." *Annual Review of Anthropology* 28 (1999): 455-78.

Foucault, Michel. *Microfisica del potere.* raccolta. Torino: Einaudi, 1977.

Gladwin, Christina H., and Kathleen Truman, ed. *Food and farm: current debates and policies.* Lanham, MD: University Press of America; Society for Economic Anthropology, 1989. Print.

Guthman, Julie. "Fast Food/Organic Food: Reflexive Tastes and the Making of "Yuppie Chow"." *Food and Culture: A Reader.* Ed. Counihan, C., and P. Van Esterik. London: Routledge, 2013. 496-510.

Herzfeld, Michael. *The Social Production of Indifference. Exploring the Symbolic Roots of Western Bureaucracy.* Chicago: University of Chicago Press, 1992.

Isin, Engin. "Theorizing acts of citizenship " *Acts of Citizenship.* Eds. Isin, Engin F and Greg M Nielsen. London: Palgrave Macmillan, 2008. 15–43.

Kafka, Franz, Anna Bell, and Robert Robertson. *The Castle.* OUP Oxford, 2009.

Leitch, Alison. "Slow Food and the Politics of "Virtous Globalization"." *In Food and Culture: A Reader, edited by C. Counihan, and P. Van Esterik, 496-510. London: Routledge.* Eds. Counihan, C. and P. Van Esterik. London: Routledge, 2013. 394-409.

Levkoe, Carol Z. "Towards a transformative food politics." *Local Environment* 16 7 (2011): 687-705.

Lewellen, Ted C. *Political Anthropology: An Introduction (Third Edition)*. London: Praeger, 2003.

Marcus, E. George, ed. *Critical Anthropology Now. Unexpected Contexts, Shifting Constituenceies, Changing Agendas*. Santa Fe: School of American Research Advanced Seminars Series, 1999.

Martino, Gaetano. "Pratiche contrattuali e ruolo delle consuetudini. Le transazioni di olio di oliva in un'indagine sul campo nel territorio umbro." *PhD Thesis, Dottorato di Ricerca in "Culture e Linguaggi"* Ciclo XXVII, 14 febbraio 2015, Università degli Studi di Perugia (2015).

Mintz, Sideney W. "Afterword (special issue on Trash Foods)." *Ethnology* 47 2 (2008): 129-35.

—. *Sweetness and power: the place of sugar in modern history*. NewYork: Penguin Books, 1985.

Müller, Birgit. "The Elephant in the Room. Multi-stakeholder Dialogue on Agricultural Biotechnology in the FAO." *Policy Worlds: Anthropology and the Anatomy of Contemporary Power*. Eds. Però, Davide, Cris Shore and Sue Wright. Oxford: Berghahn 2011. 282-99.

Munn, Nancy D. *The Fame of Gawa: A Symbolic Study of Value Transformation in a Massim (Papua New Guinea) Society*. Durham: Duke University Press, 1992.

Nonini, Donald M. "The local-food movement and the anthropology of global systems." *American Ethnologist* 40 2 (2013): 267-75.

Ohnuki-Tierney, E. *Rice as Self: Japanese Identities through Time*. Princeton: Princeton University Press, 1994.

Paley, Julia. "Toward an Anthropology of Democracy." *Annual Review of Anthropology* 31 (2002): 469-96.

Papa, Cristina. "Il prodotto tipico come ossimero. Il caso dell'olio extravergine d'oliva umbro." *Frammenti di economie*. Ed. Siniscalchi, Valeria. Cosenza: Pellegrini, 2002. 159-93. Print.

—. "What Does It Mean to Conserve Nature?" *Nature Knowledge. Ethnoscience, Cognition, and Utility*. Eds. Ortelli, G. and G. Sanga. London: Berghahn, 2004. 339-59. Print.

Parkins, Wendy, and Geoffrey Craig. *Slow living*. London: Berg, 2006. Print.

Pilcher, Jeffrey M. *The Oxford Handbook of Food History*. Oxford: Oxford University Press, 2012.

Pink, Sarah. "Re-thinking contemporary activism. From community to emplaced activism." *Ethnos* 73 2 (2008): 163-88.

Rabinow, Paul. *Marking time. On the anthropology of the contemporary*. Princeton: Princeton University Press, 2008.

Rosa, Hartmut. *Alienation and Acceleration: Towards a Critical Theory of Late-modern Temporality.* New York: NSU Press, 2010.

—. *Weltbeziehungen im Zeitalter der Beschleunigung: Umrisse einer neuen Gesellschaftskritik.* Frankfurt a. M.: Suhrkamp, 2012.

Scalacci, Roberto. "I prodotti tradizionali e l'igiene degli alimenti." *Prodotti agroalimentari tradizionali: un'opportunità da valorizzare.* Eds. Scalacci, Roberto, Daniele Vergari and Fabio Panchetti. Firenze: Associazione Giovani Imprenditori Agricoli Toscana, 2007.

—. "L'analisi del rischio come strumento di valutazione igienico sanitaria e l'indagine dell'Istituto Zooprofilattico Sperimentale per il Pecorino "Marzolino di Lucardo"." *Il Marzolino di Lucardo. Un formaggio ritrovato.* Eds. Scalacci, Roberto and Daniele Vergari. Firenze: Confederazione Italiana di Agricoltura, Toscana, 2009. 47-50.

Scott, James C. *Weapons of the Weak: Everyday Forms of Peasant Resistance.* New Haven: Yale University Press, 1987.

Shore, Chris. "Audit culture and Illiberal governance: Universities and the politics of accountability." *Anthropological Theory* 8 3 (2008): 278-98.

Shore, Chris, and Susan Wright. *Anthropology of Policy: Critical Perspectives on Governance and Power.* London: Taylor & Francis, 1997.

Strathern, Marilyn *Audit Cultures: Anthropological Studies in Accountability, Ethics and the Academy.* London: Taylor & Francis, 2000.

Taylor, Charles. *Multiculturalism: Examining The Politics of Recognition.* Princeton: Princeton University Press, 1994.

Wedel, Janine R., et al. "Toward an Anthropology of Public Policy." *The ANNALS of the American Academy of Political and Social Science* 600 1 (2005): 30-51.

Willis, Paul, and Mats Trondman. "Manifesto for Ethnography." *Cultural Studies & Critical Methodologies* 2 3 (2002): 394-402.

Wolf, Eric. *Pathways of Power. Building an Anthropology of the Modern World.* Berkeley, Los Angeles, London: University of California Press, 2001.

Wu, David Y.H., and Sidney Cheung, eds. *The globalization of Chinese food.* Richmond: Curzon, 2002.

Zinn, Dorothy. "The Case of Scanzano: Raison d'Etat and the Reasons for Rebellion." *Policy Worlds: Anthropology and the Analysis of Contemporary Power.* Eds. Shore, C., S Wright and D. Pero. London: Berghahn, 2011.

Notes

[1] I wish to acknowledge the suggestions, help and advice provided by Sergio Cabras, Massimiliano Benelli, Roberto Scalacci, Katrina Campbell, Moira Dean, Tullio Seppilli, Cristina Papa and the various people that I have met during my fieldwork. Time allocation for central parts of this work has been supported by the Economic and Social Sciences Research Council, UK [grant number ES/M003094/1].

[2] The main points of criticism refer here to the implementation of practices to certify organic agriculture with the implementation of the EU-Eco-regulation 1992. In Italy, supervision of certification bodies is handled on the national level through private third bodies and is associated with considerable bureaucratic efforts and high costs. Another point of criticism relates to the introduction for all those who process primary agricultural products of the procedures- Hazard Analysis and Critical Control Points (HAACCP) for processed food introduced in Europe through 43/93/CEE. The way these procedures are implemented at local level is often perceived as discriminatory for independent small-scale farmers, with some exceptions (cfr. Scalacci 2007, 2009).

[3] Precursors of food activism studies are analyses of how industrialization and globalization affect eating (Mintz 1985, 2008). As studies of the reactions to industrialized food and its alienation, anthropologists have been at the forefront of those who investigate ethical consumerism.

[4] In Italy, the work of Cristina Papa (2002, 2004) provides ethnographic evidence of long-standing practices of farmers to circumvent or silently subvert official standards of certification, by keeping alive a range of informal sets of practices. For similar arguments, related to informal practices that produce trust, see Martino (2015).

[5] These studies have shown the importance of understanding local ideas of change in broader policy implementations (Herzfeld 1992; Scott 1987). Landmark studies that uncover the multiplicity of everyday life behind the objectifying processes of standardizing policies are those considering the implications of the 'audit culture' of 'accountability' (Strathern 2000; Shore 2008).

[6] Media coverage has made the case widely public. See for example, 'How the horsemeat scandal unfolded – timeline'. The Guardian, 15 February 2013; 'Slaughterhouse boss admits charges over UK horsemeat scandal', The Guardian, 28 January 2015.

[7] 'Goodman firm says horse meat crisis has changed it for the better', The Irish Times, 13th January 2014.

[8] See, Christopher Elliot et al., 'Elliott review into the integrity and assurance of food supply networks: interim report' Department for Environment, Food & Rural Affairs, 12 December 2013.

[9] All names of people and places are changed.

[10] In particular, for Rosa, the origins of the proliferation of de-personalised relations derives from the politics of 'social acceleration' as a key feature of modernity, constituting acceleration as an intrinsic value functional of contemporary capitalism (cfr. Rosa 2010).

PART II:

SUSTAINABILITY IN PRACTICE

CHAPTER FOUR

TRANSFORMING SUSTAINABILITY INTO ACTION: CHALLENGES OF A TRANSDISCIPLINARY PROJECT WITH MULTI-ETHNIC ACTORS IN THE SOUTH CAUCASUS/GEORGIA

ANJA SALZER, MARINUS GEBHARDT, SUZANNE ELSEN AND STEFAN ZWERBE

Introduction

The political transformation in the former Soviet republics of Central Asia and the Caucasus was accompanied by a fundamental socio-economic re-organisation. Within this process, ecological and economic claims often stand in contradiction to each other. As the access to natural resources as well as strategies of securing livelihoods have changed, and receive new significance and awareness, new challenges for the local ecosystems and their biodiversity have arisen. In particular, in the high-mountain areas of the crisis-ridden Caucasus region, the degradation and transformation of sensitive alpine steppe ecosystems is proceeding rapidly, mainly due to unregulated pasturing (Williams et al. 2006) and climate change.[1] Thus, the challenge of the following decades will be to elaborate ways for sustainable regional futures, especially land-uses that are flexible enough to adapt to the new socio-economic situation and the changing environmental conditions in the region. In transforming this challenge into sustainable action, the common understanding of "sustainability" among all stakeholders is seen as a key.

In order to face the complex problems of global change, the knowledge of a single discipline is certainly not far-reaching enough. Therefore, an integrative, interdisciplinary approach is essential. However, proposals on sustainable future processes such as land-use management are only applicable when considering local knowledge and needs, as well as local identities. There is an urgent need to discuss applicable concepts of sustainability within the conflicting priorities of cultural/social and natural scientific approaches.

The aim of the following chapter is to address the theoretical and practical challenges researchers face with transformative types of research within the thematic area of sustainability. Based on a case study in the form of a specific project, this chapter discusses a potential methodology with which to better understand sustainability – implying a participatory reflection and the development of a vision of sustainable futures. Therefore, the following chapter seeks to provide answers to the question of the role of anthropology within research and practice for sustainability and sheds some light on the learning processes, as well as the potential positioning and responsibilities of applied anthropology within an interdisciplinary project focused on fostering the co-construction of knowledge by transforming it into action. This chapter intends on deepening the understanding of the concept of sustainability and its potential implementation from a social scientific perspective. In addition, theoretical approaches towards processes of socio-ecological alteration (in general) will be discussed.

1. Case study – sustainable futures in a village community in the Javakheti Highlands of Georgia

Javakheti is a region that combines the life and survival strategies of all the major ethnic groups of the Caucasus. The highlands, a volcanic plateau with a base altitude of 1900m a.s.l. (above sea level), and mountains reaching up to 3000m a.s.l., are situated in the border triangle of Georgia, Armenia and Turkey. The landscape is primarily characterised by grasslands and sub-alpine and alpine meadows – testimony to thousands of years of land-use, such as transhumance[2]. At lower altitudes, deep, fertile black soils are found – a result of climatic processes – which, since the collapse of the Soviet Union, are mainly used privately for the cultivation of potatoes. Due to the uniqueness of the Javakheti Highlands, parts of the region were designated a protected area encompassing a national park and several managed wetland reserves. With its high diversity of ethnic groups and farming practices, but also of nature – as part of the Caucasian biodiversity hotspot, with a high rate of endemic species (Williams et al. 2006) – the highland can be seen as a prism for many developments and events of the past, the present and the future in the region.

The project on biodiversity and sustainable management of mountain grasslands focuses on the recently legislated Javakheti protected areas and its surroundings. The protected areas system is funded by an international development bank and implemented by the national agency for protected areas- with the support of an international NGO (Non-Governmental Organisation). The main reason for the establishment of the national park was its identification as a priority conservation area by the government and the international community due to the uniqueness of the landscape in the Caucasus region, its function as a biodiversity corridor (Williams et al. 2006) and its function in trans-boundary peacekeeping (Caucasus Initiative of the BMZ, 2001). In addition, the region is of international interest due to the Baku-Tbilisi-Ceyhan pipeline and the Baku-Tbilisi-Kars railway crossing the highlands. In the course of the establishment of the Javakheti protected areas, their surroundings, the so-called support zone, received special attention in terms of development measures for local residents in order to enhance rural economy.

Although, the whole region bears a high diversity in terms of ethnic groups, including Georgians, Armenians and Azeri, the case study concentrates on a mountain village inhabited by ethnic Armenians. Armenian groups settled the highlands around 200 years ago during the war between the Russian and the Ottoman Empires, when Javakheti came under the control of Russia's Imperial Army (Guretski 1998; Wheatley 2004; Øverland 2009). With its 130 households and 690 inhabitants (Tarknishvili et al. 2001), the village is still dominated by three main lineages. Most of the extended families live in multi-generational households of at least three generations. For the greater part of the households, at least one (male) family member is periodically abroad for labour migration to Russia or Armenia. Social networks, for the most part, are face-to-face and multiplex, promoting social compliance as a result of high social cohesion. This highly bonding social capital[3] is a result of identity constructions based on a minority status within Georgia and the specific history of the region, as from 1910 to 2007 the Russian Army maintained a military base in the Javakheti region, which retained the status of a border zone between the Soviet Union and Turkey, a NATO country (Wheatley 2004; Lohm 2007; Øverland 2009)[4]. This made Javakheti strongly separate not only in terms of infrastructure, but also politically, socio-culturally and economically (Tarknishvili et al. 2001; Lohm 2007; Øverland 2009). Since the breakdown of the Soviet Union, and the closure of the military base, almost the complete industrial sector, as well as the local Kolkhoz agriculture, has disappeared. Nowadays, the main economic activity of the villagers is primarily subsistence farming.

The farming practices tend to consist of two main activities, i.e. diary, in particular cattle, farming on mountain pastures and potato production on the fertile black soils at lower areas in the region. The access to markets is compounded by the poor state of the village road. By virtue of post-Soviet land reforms, cattle are herded on joint community pastures, whereas hay meadows and arable lands are privatised.

The transdisciplinary project aims to integrate landscape ecology, soil-science, socio-anthropological and sociological approaches in order to face these challenges on a local level. The project is conducted by researchers from different academic and ethnic backgrounds: one geographer, one social anthropologist both trained in Germany, a third – an environmental scientist – trained in Kyrgyzstan and the project leadership is run by a biologist and a sociologist. Consequently, the interdisciplinary cooperation itself represents a challenging grade of diversity.

The starting points of the research group were, on the one hand, the presumption of a loss of biodiversity and the risk of erosion by overgrazing- stated by an international environmental NGO, and on the other hand, the establishment of a trans-boundary protected areas system as a point of departure for processes of change in the region. Preliminary research has shown the need for a holistic view of the area (natural conditions and living world of the local actors). Active transdisciplinary cooperation and the joint formulation of hypotheses and definitions has led us to reconsider various assumptions, categories and perspectives.

With the integration of applied social sciences in particular, the fact was stressed that the entire process of knowledge production, as well as the results based on natural science only become relevant when they are communicated, accepted, and transferred into action by the respective land-users and stakeholders. As the project aims at the development of vision and practice for sustainability in mountain regions in the Caucasus (which also could be applied in other post-Soviet mountainous regions), the accordance with local land-use practices and the socio-cultural background of the local population is considered as key. Such a setting implies not only classical anthropological or sociological methods, but participatory and activist approaches. This involves a new effort to (jointly) build a community programme that addresses local natural resources and life-world problems as consequences of global change. Although global change affects everyone, it disproportionately threatens low-income communities that have less access to knowledge, greater existing economic problems, and fewer resources to protect against extreme weather events and other adverse consequences of global change (Singer 2011: 7). In this respect, projects dealing with sustainability in a certain region must also envision the vulnerability, resilience and capabilities of the local population. The social sciences part of the project, in particular, is based on the elaboration of different forms of local knowledge through participatory work with community members to jointly produce a vision for and practice in regional sustainability.

A local notion of life-worlds, strategies and prospective options for action implies a joint perception of "sustainability" and indicates the reason for working on this issue as one of the first research steps. To summarise, the described research setting leads to sustainability being our central concern and key component of the project. Furthermore, a joint notion of sustainability is seen as common ground, and thus a prerequisite for successful cooperation with all actors involved, internally and externally.

2. Sustainability – an approximation

Sustainability is a concept with a diverse array of meanings and definitions. Nowadays, however, it is a glamorous, ambiguous, ambivalent and vague concept widely used by different stakeholder groups in various ways. Presumably, to avoid debating terminology, or to avoid confrontation with a definition, the concept of sustainability is most widely broken down as a planning process (Döring and Muraca 2010). That is why, most commonly, sustainability is understood as sustainable development.[5]

Sustainable development, adopted after the Brundtland Report of 1987, is a planned, goal-driven and process-oriented procedure that meets the needs of today's generations without endangering the needs of future generations and world regions (Ott & Döring 2004, 2006).[6] The principle of sustainability describes the efforts of the international community, all countries and people to create equal opportunities for development by explicitly taking into account the interests of future generations. Most frequently, the concepts of sustainability are based on a triple bottom line represented by three pillars: ecology, economy and social security (e.g. by the Enquete Commission, 1998; Cirella and Zerbe 2014). Apart from the general weaknesses of the column model, that is the interchangeability of dimensions and the ignorance of (social) relatedness (Ott and Döring, 2004),[7] the definition of sustainability (the model is illustrating), is seen as a bad compromise between the needs for conservation of natural resources and the aspirations for economic growth by some scholars (Döring and Muraca 2010). Irrespective of these problems, the model sometimes competes with other pillars such as "knowledge", "institution", "governance", "arts" or the like (Ott and Döring 2004). Yencken and Wilkinson (2000), in turn, propose the idea of "culture" as a fourth pillar of sustainability in their paper "Resetting the Compass". What they therewith address is the value of a specific cultural perspective.

However, an intrinsic character of the concept of sustainability itself – apart from being normative, ambiguous and subjective (Loorbach and Rotmans 2006) – lies in its requirement to be lived and thus transformed into action (Elsen 2013). Some scholars argue that the socio-cultural aspects of sustainability are not a by-product of the environmental and economic dimensions of sustainability but play a key role in the evolution of sustainability (Elsen 2013).[8] Thereby, the concept posits change as an explicit and necessary aim of social science knowledge production. Since the concept is virtually constructed and interpreted by humans, sustainability entails multiple ways of knowing the same information. Thus, sustainability and sustainable action strongly depend on the actors' knowledge, attitudes, competencies, options and restrictions within their respective context of action (Guyot 2010). Hence, a practical implementation, "(...) has to incorporate the inherent conflicts between the values, ambitions and goals of a multitude of stakeholders" (Loorbach and Rotmans 2006: 188). Therewith, an approximation towards sustainability becomes a complex endeavour. Bearing in mind its contextual character, we propose culture should not be seen as another pillar, but as a basis of perception and evaluation of sustainability and its transformation into practice. For if we believe culture is seen as a whole complex of ideas, ways of thinking, feeling, values and meanings and the ways they are expressed, then they are the constitutive elements of culture, and thus the basis of society/groups upon which all else is built. Such a perspective helps us understand processes of global change as social processes embedded in specific social systems (and historical contexts), thus in line with one of the most central concepts of anthropology. Nevertheless, a scientific confrontation with the concept of sustainability, its application and transformation into practice is challenging and requires reflection on different levels and dimensions[9].

2.1 Exemplified through the example of a transdisciplinary research project on sustainable regional futures in Georgia, the following discourse will illustrate challenges and approaches to counter the problem. Insights into the "field": translating sustainability into research practice

Within the integrative project in Georgia, we understood the need to form different perceptions of sustainability and different disciplinary findings into a joint research question. This, in turn, required a common perception of the central approaches and concepts of the project. The starting point of the negotiation process was the adoption of the concept of *strong sustainability*. Strong sustainability refers to an approach in which natural capital (i.e. natural resources) is regarded as non-substitutable. Since natural resources are limited, they form the basic prerequisite for them (Döring 2004). However, the question remains: how to deal with the other dimensions of sustainability and where to locate culture? Through mutual exchange of research ideas and approaches, a model of how a sustainable project cooperation should look like was formulated. Although, different approaches such as landscape ecology, hydrology, anthropology and sociology meet within the project, the different disciplines and research areas overlap at the joint aim of understanding sustainable pasture use (Figure 1). However, culture, in particular local and academic identities, needs and knowledge frame and influence all components of the joint project.

Further, the context of the research (that goes beyond classical anthropological work) requires a different approach, i.e. a reflection on locally applicable solutions that can be linked to global change and a joint local definition as a core component. "Integral Sustainability" emphasises the mutual lineage and dependency of the individual dimensions (Kopfmüller 2007) and is suitable as a framework for the elaboration of a joint idea of sustainability. The concept enables individual dimensions with specific local focus to be defined without losing the perspective of the global concept of sustainability.

Figure 4.1: Sustainability within the project with regard to landscape ecology, hydrology, and anthropology.

3. Transdisciplinarity and its implications for research and practice for sustainability

(...) if the fundamental causes and consequences of global change are social, then so must the solutions be. (Hackmann and St.Clair 2012: 9)

The challenges of global change and ensuant life-world problems at the local level are often highly complex and located at many different levels. In such comprehensive fields, disciplinary analyses quickly reach their limits (Jahn 2001; Dubielzig and Schaltegger 2004; Hanschitz et al. 2009; Elsen 2011; Schneidewind and Singer-Brodowski 2013). Research for sustainability requires different approaches. The complexity of research questions that arise from attempting to grasp "sustainability" in all its dimensions, especially in terms of a future orientation, requires comprehensive and integrated approaches.

In this broad spectrum, the concept of sustainability already implies certain "access requirements". These refer, on the one hand, to the multidimensional nature of sustainability, and involve, on the other hand, the normative claim to intergenerational justice- which is often associated with an immediacy of response. Knowledge as a desirable state and a vision of "futures," in turn, is the explicit property of transdisciplinary and transformative types[10] of research (Dubielzig and Schaltegger 2004: 6). Transdisciplinarity[11] is defined as science and research released from their professional and disciplinary boundaries. By facing non-scientific social problems, research questions are defined and specifically targeted, and subsequently, transformation paths developed, so as to solve these problems independently of discipline and profession (Jahn 2001; Schneidewind and Singer-Brodowski 2013). Hence, the integration of different claims and types of knowledge, as well as the action-oriented pooling of resources and skills for designing transformation becomes a specific feature of transdisciplinary and transformative types of research.

In anthropology, there has been an increasing awareness of the need for a more engaged role in both academia and the public arena over the past number of decades (Rylko-Bauer et al. 2006). Also, the relevance of addressing social problems and the structures that produce and maintain them has been discerned. But up to now, much of this discussion has taken place within the academic milieu, and has focused on new approaches (such as public anthropology), and other ways in which anthropologists can expand the impact of their ideas and connect with broader audiences (Forman 1995; Basch et al. 1999; Borofsky 2000)" (Rylko-Bauer et al. 2006: 178).[12]

An engagement with sustainability requires integration as a main principle of research.[13] Life-worlds and the structures of relevance of the stakeholders or actors serve as central points of reference. In so doing, social actors are involved in the "co-design" and "co-production" of knowledge (Schneidewind and Singer-Brodowski 2013). This kind of access implies the simultaneity of two paths. One is the path of practice-that is exploring new options for action in resolving social problems (utility) by the involvement of actors. The other one is the path of science, which is a methodological innovation in any research as approaches are developed in conjunction with practice (c.f. Schneidewind and Singer-Brodowski 2013). In other words, transdisciplinarity contains a dual commitment, i.e. firstly to study a "system", and secondly, to collaborate with members of the system "(...) in changing it in what is together regarded as a desirable direction" (O'Brien 2001: 3).

Action anthropology,[14] whose roots trace back to 1951 according to Sol Tax (1975: 515), has two comparable goals that are coordinated and "to neither none of which (...) will [be] delegated to an inferior position." On the one hand, action anthropology's goal is to help a group of people to solve a problem; on the other hand, it aims to learn something in the process: he [the anthropologist] refuses to think or to say that the people involved are a means of advancing his knowledge; and he refuses to think or say that he is simply applying science to the solution of those peoples' problems (Tax 1975: 515).

Conducting action anthropology, Tax furthermore states, would not be possible if there were not such great tolerance for ambiguity.[15] Transdisciplinarity is a scholarly driven process which functions successfully in facing this ambiguity; it is an integrated access, a form of academic research and a principle, which raises a claim through its democratic approach that goes beyond the concept of representative democracy. Rather, it is grassroots participation. Thereby, the idea of participation becomes a defining feature of transdisciplinary research (Hanschitz et al. 2009). With the usage of the term "participation", numerous problems arise. One of the main problems is that the term recently has been misused, in particular, with regard to development cooperation or environmental policy decision-making, where citizens are often allowed to participate. However, in spite of requirements that mandate public participation or institutional practices, citizens are often excluded from anything other than a superficial role, whereas the way participation is engaged in transdisciplinary or transformative types of research usually implies the involvement of social actors in the whole process of knowledge generation. Therewith the basic premise of such types of research is, at its best, the co-design and co-production of knowledge within the whole research process, focusing on locally defined priorities and local perspectives (Cornwall and Jewkes 1995). Therefore, the integration and coordination of diverse knowledge becomes one of the main objectives of this type of research, which in turn leads to one of the major challenges of transdisciplinary, transformative research, i.e. the achievement of a culture of collaborative knowledge production among different actors.

Methodologically, action research is primarily defined by its design consisting of three recurring stages i.e. inquiry, action and reflection (Lewin 1947; Kemmis and McTaggart 1988; 2005). Through multiple cycles of these stages, improvements in the knowledge and understanding of those involved in the inquiry leads to social action. Reflections on actions lead to new understandings and open up new areas of inquiry (Greenwood and Levin 2003; Mackenzie et al. 2012).[16] Constituting a methodological framework for transition management in transformational sciences, the transition cycle consists of comparable steps (Schneidewind and Singer-Brodowski 2013). The cycle is based on four consecutive steps of inquiry: 1) problem assessment, 2) vision development, 3) experiments, and 4) learning and up-scaling (Loorbach and Rotmans 2006). Thereby, it is aimed at three different forms of knowledge, i.e. system, future, and transformation knowledge. Research for sustainability implies the alteration of at least two of these forms (system and future knowledge) that methodologically have to be considered and reflected on, whereas practice for sustainability, in particular, has to be confronted with transformational knowledge.

3.1. Cognitive mapping of local sustainability – combining system and future knowledge

The means used to mediate and work out relevant knowledge on the concept of sustainability in Javakheti was an integrative discussion, structured using the cognitive mapping method. A cognitive map can be described as a qualitative model of how a given system operates. The map is based on defined variables and the causal relationships between these variables (Özesmi and Özesmi 2004). These variables can be physical quantities, such as the amount of precipitation or percentage vegetation cover, or complex aggregates and abstract ideas, such as political forces or aesthetics. The important variables that affect a system are decided by the actors developing the cognitive map. In a second step, causal relationships among these variables are drawn. Within the research project, the participatory cognitive mapping process is targeted on a "common" perspective of sustainability. Hence, the concept was heuristically divided into its main dimensions, i.e. social, economic and ecological. The stakeholders were invited to contribute to a joint discourse on the local context of the single dimensions of sustainability, and in further steps, to denominate connections between the dimension and possible effects and problems of changes within this "system". The approach allows different stakeholders in a participatory process to arrive at a representation of local perceptions, evaluation and interpretation of sustainability. By this, it is likely to generate system knowledge (according to a predefined order) and a holistic identification of real-life problems. The latter delineates the point of departure in defining objectives of research in transformational sciences, and thus, is an important distinguishing feature. The other important part of the mapping process is the joint development of a vision of desired local futures, which corresponds to the generation of future knowledge in transformational sciences.

   The outcome of this research process is seen as a first step towards prioritising key issues and tasks for the research agenda, resulting in a clearer picture of what needs to be addressed, and what is required for implementation. The mapping process- with mostly young people (18-32 years)-from the village- revealed some key concepts with regards to sustainability- that appeared to be of special importance. The mappings with stakeholders in Javakheti show a clear correspondence in terms of content and assumptions concerning the individual dimensions of sustainability:

- From the perspective of the stakeholders, the local economy is (almost exclusively) determined by animal husbandry and potato farming- being primarily the only sources of income. At the same time, the necessity of alternative income opportunities is emphasised, which would prevent the tendency to migrate, in particular, for the younger population.

- Concerning the social or cultural dimension of sustainability, the emphasis on specific local traditions is paramount. With it, special reference is made to a local holiday[17]. At the same time, a high priority is given to Soviet-imprinted elements of advanced civilisation. The latter is related to the fact that cultural institutions such as the local clubhouse were closed down after the dissolution of the Soviet Union. Future visions for the socio-cultural aspects of a sustainable local community, formulated by community members, are closely linked to the reactivation of cultural events such as cinema and concerts- but also internet-related education and leisure activities.

- With regards to the importance of the environment, the actors are mainly aware of the risk of the drying out of the local lake, whereas land-use related issues (e.g. erosion of grazing land) are rarely perceived as a problem. However, it should be pointed out that the biggest variety of answers appeared in relation to the perception of the environment. For some of the stakeholders of the inquiry, nature is seen as an important resource- (being in a good state, especially for cattle breeding and potato farming)- providing good soil and plants with a high fodder value. For others, the environment is in a bad state, in particular due to the destruction of nature by uncontrolled garbage disposal (as a result of the absence of state-regulated waste disposal). Special attention is not only paid to the weak condition of the local lake but also to the necessity of planting trees as a vision for a local sustainable future. In this respect, it has to be considered that a reason for these focal points could lie within the ecological campaign by an international NGO in the course of its awareness-raising concerning the Javakheti protected areas.

- However, altogether, the recognition of connections and dependencies (a core element of integrated sustainability) between the different dimensions of sustainability and their local interpretation tends to be weak.

To summarise, the ongoing research process on the participants' side reflects upon their assumptions, as well as their views on a living-environment and future. For us as scientists, the approach revealed first insights for further research on local perceptions, needs, contradictions, constraints and limits, and thus serves as a sound base for future research and action. The understanding of the concept of sustainability and its potential implementation could be deepened, enriched and rooted in the local life-worlds, perspectives and views. The significant similarities between the stocks of knowledge and the structures of perception of individual stakeholders point to the importance of the socio-cultural context in terms of learning and perception. Some of the specifics can be found in other post-Soviet transition countries as well. Knowledge, for example, was highly specialised and centralised by the state during the Soviet period, promoted and controlled by local institutions (Ul-Hassan et al. 2011). Whereupon the collapse of the Soviet Union in 1991 led to a loss of institutionalised knowledge, resulting in knowledge gaps in the academic field, and a mismatch of local knowledge with today's institutional structures (Wall 2008).

Cognitive mapping processes not only contribute to a holistic identification of practice problems, but also promote capacity-building. One of the perceived great strengths of the explicit mapping of sustainability is to generate knowledge in the sense of a local notion of sustainable options for the future. In this regard, the equal relevance of all dimensions of sustainability could be elaborated together with the local stakeholders. Specific regional problems, in particular the need for economic diversification as a condition to prevent young people from migration, could be focused upon in detail. Furthermore, initial steps towards and visions of local, sustainable futures (in part) were developed. The implementation, i.e. the transformation of proposals for sustainable future processes into action by scientific and local stakeholders, is the next research phase. As such, the developments of competencies in order to actively mould future processes are at the centre of this project.

The evidence presented can thus be seen as the first step towards the transformation of a (theoretical) concept into practice. Cognitive mapping processes therein are just one potential tool to arrive at a joint definition of sustainability, which has to be addressed and discussed in consecutive steps in more detail. As future knowledge is highly informed by the experiences, perceptions and language of those whose futures are at stake (Singer-Brodowski 2013), the presented effort to resolve the issue of defining sustainability on a local level must be seen as one particular approach that is neither useful in some kinds of research nor necessarily meaningful for a whole community. Hence, generally speaking the choice of method to arrive at a joint aim must be reflected on with regard to the participating community, but it also must be appropriate for the object of research (Von Unger 2014). Thus, the joint definition of sustainability by means of cognitive mapping must be seen as a locally specific attempt within a range of flexible and process-oriented methods that can only be developed "on site".

The approach has proven effective in overcoming community hesitancy to engage in collaboration with university personnel (Singer 2011). Preconditions of such a process are communication and the initiation of reflection processes; thus rooting sustainability locally as part of the life-world. The core issue will be the promotion of competencies to modify and to mould the future in an active and accountable way involving as many people as possible. Therefore, it is necessary to meet and join them where they are. To make sustainability initiatives relevant for the target audiences, it is necessary to adapt the culture and language of science to community cultures and languages of diverse groups (Singer 2011). Additionally, according to Singer (2011), useful capacities must be transferred to the locals through awareness-raising and educational processes. Participatory research itself can be regarded as a joint (social) learning process in which capacity building takes place. Assuming that the aim of the learning process is arriving at transformative literacies with regard to sustainable futures,[18] the enhancement of analytic abilities for assessing and responding to future scenarios and interconnectedness between different dimensions of sustainability is a main target. As a result, it is hoped that global change and sustainability issues will not be perceived as one more burden, but rather as a significant encounter that can be addressed with practical, science-based skills and perspectives.

1.1. *Transforming sustainability into action – an ongoing process*
Not only is the data generation process itself an important stage of research, but also the spreading and use of the findings- as well as a joint critical and reflective evaluation of methods and results are of importance. Based on the current analysis of results and the problems identified during our research, action-oriented strategies that address some of the main problems of sustainable regional development/perspectives are on their way to being developed. In particular, the diversification of options for young people – whether these are alternative income options or educational or leisure activities – to prevent migration- are targets of action. Other focuses for research and practice on local transformations are grazing management strategies, as well as the different cultures of

knowledge, in combination with a high staff turnover, that are a result of post-Soviet transformation processes.

The activation of community members by means of cognitive mapping has led the initiative to deploy a working group. Thus joint work on defining local sustainability created a vision connected with the idea of establishing local structures that are capable to act as a gateway and platform for local community members and external stakeholders such as, NGOs, sponsors and visitors of the protected areas in order to enable different user groups to engage fairly and respectfully with one another, and further, obtain goods and services needed. The concept of a sustainable community platform can be seen as a framework to guide future action as it addresses some major local issues in response to the following problems (formulated by community members):

The lack of continuous income sources compatible with the agricultural and herding lifecycle of the community;

- The necessity of employment and leisure opportunities that fit the needs of the globally and socially connected lifestyles of young villagers on a local level in order to prevent the tendency of migration (a high priority given to cultural and community institutions and offers such as a clubhouse, cinema, theater, concerts and sports activities, but also the provision of internet and a meeting place).
- The increasing trend of tourism that impacts the community and its environment, but up to now brings little or no benefit to the community.
- The awareness of problems connected to the environment, such as uncontrolled garbage disposal due to lacking infrastructure, the risk of the drying out of the local lake, etc.
- The wider problems of marginalization through infrastructural (state of the road) and marketing conditions for local products.

Nevertheless, the formulation of targets for action based on compiled definitions and reflective learning must be seen as a gradual, long-term process with changing directions of impact. This is due to changing local economic and political conditions and options- as well as individual and collective time requirements with regard to knowledge production, etc. Thus, the aims and ideas (see above) for a local sustainability vision must be seen as a snapshot that is dependent on the commitment and engagement of community members, researchers and other stakeholders involved. In the case of the cognitive mapping process, only a small group of young and active community members could be reached. Thus, their respective life situations and perspectives are as important to the further course, as the perceptions, understanding and commitment of a larger group of community members.

Altogether, the real transformation of the formulated visions and needs into action depends on several interdependent factors and aspects. Firstly, the responsibilities and commitment of stakeholders in pursuing a long-term vision and action. Secondly, financial means and funding structures for research and practice also play a major role. Additionally, the formulation of practice targets should be acceptable to all stakeholders, realistic and terminated. Von Unger (2014) furthermore recommends a helpful division between far-reaching visions, on the one hand, and concrete targets that can be reached within a certain time frame, on the other hand.

However, the main difficulty with regards to the planning of exploratory and activation processes is that at the beginning of such a process it is not possible to exactly determine how the research process will run and to what results it will lead.

Conclusion

Facing scenarios of planned eco-social change targeted on sustainability as subject and subjective guiding principle of such transformations represents a genuine challenge to academic research cultures, as it implies a reflection of the researcher's position with regards to the modalities of knowledge production. The highly complex and dynamic fields and discourses of eco-social change, notably involve critical reflections and negotiations of disciplinary assumptions, and an extended understanding of the researchers (professional) positioning. This, in particular, involves the establishment of dialogues on locating anthropology related to different types of applied or activating social sciences and their recent developments. Thus, asking for the role of anthropology in developing a common understanding of sustainability implies an extended understanding, in terms of a confrontation with the strengths and weaknesses, of one's own discipline by acknowledging various approaches and engaging in constructive dialogues, since the topic is about no less than ensuring future abilities. In this sense, the ISSC (International Social Science Council 2012) takes a specific point of view to the question of sustainability by generally asking about the role of social sciences to be more prominent in responding to issues of global change. The council has developed cornerstones that articulate a framework for understanding processes of global change as social processes embedded in specific social systems, past and present. Together, the 6 cornerstones[19] "(...) provide tools for critically questioning and rethinking the shape and course of these processes and systems in the future. The cornerstones are called transformative because they work together to inform action for deliberate transformation that is both ethical and sustainable" (Hackmann and St. Clair 2012: 15). The ISSC (2012) is supporting the above mentioned understanding of sustainability by understanding climate change and global environmental change as social processes embedded in specific social and historical systems, and thus as a cultural issue. One of the 6 cornerstones of the ISSC is responsibility. In general, the transformation of sustainability into both research practice and action can be understood as a commitment to accept responsibility as a researcher. But what is the specific responsibility of applied social sciences within a transdisciplinary project aimed at transforming knowledge into action?

In a transdisciplinary setting, the role of social scientists is eclectic in developing a common understanding of sustainability and, in particular, visions of sustainable futures. One of the major contributions is the holistic perspective[20] on culture- with special attention to the interaction of local and extra-local perspectives. This recognition of complexity is well suited to capture sustainability in all of its dimensions and interrelatedness, "While anthropological assessments of societal and environmental interaction are considerable, anthropology has not defined itself or been viewed by others as a sustainability science" (Singer 2011: 5). There is no reason for restraint. As anthropology emphasises the local level, with its emic[21] informed approaches, it not only complements but enriches other scientific approaches in particular natural sciences. Indispensable qualifications for participatory transdisciplinary approaches are the ability to obtain local knowledge and the appreciation of alternative views, which again, are central competencies of anthropologists. In the example of dealing with the concept of sustainability, anthropology is able to reveal potential barriers and Euro-centric perspectives towards the concept. Applied anthropology, understood as a form of commitment to "rolling up the sleeves" and getting involved, and thus an activating social science is capable of making a difference by putting the person in the centre (c.f. Guyot 2011). In doing so, social sciences become key sciences in the development of strategies for knowledge production and the transformation of sustainability into action.

Working with scientists of other disciplines on a transformation towards sustainability offers huge opportunities. The co-construction of knowledge opens perspectives that inform and transform one's own perspective and vice versa. At the same time, transdisciplinary work *creates*. In this context, an important issue has to be taken into account that arises with regard to the sustainability of transdisciplinary research processes in a specific way, i.e. the complexity and long-term processes of social change, but also the persistence of problems stands in contradiction to the generally relative short-term nature of academic research projects and funding structures. Therefore, a central objective is the development of self-supporting structures and the self-empowerment of the actors as well as the establishment of action and design competence. Sustainability means to enable practitioners by and through the experience of the transdisciplinary exchange process to autonomously control further processes (Hanschitz et al. 2009). This implies that one of the main goals of transdisciplinary research and education processes within a sustainability project must be the development of structures that are adapted to the continuously varying local contexts. For this purpose, it is necessary to create the appropriate contextual framework. One of the major challenges in our opinion is time. Time is necessary for the co-construction of knowledge, updating the individual findings, joint formulation of hypotheses and concepts, and the agreement on communication strategies, as well as finding ways to understand one another. Crucial points are, in this case, responsibility and real cooperation within inter- and transdisciplinary teams, amongst all potential non-scientific actors and local stakeholders, as well as within the wider community of scientists. However, to put it in the words of Redman (2011), "We cannot answer the challenges facing us today with the traditional kinds of knowledge and approaches we've used in the past" (c.f. Guyot 2011). Within this new field of knowledge production, the role of social scientists can be seen as communicators and mediators (how and why) between different perceptions, beliefs, values and life worlds. But not only should the role of a "cultural" translator be considered. Within transdisciplinary action-oriented research for sustainability, the researcher may also play the role of a catalyst (Tax 1975). And even though the role of a "facilitator" for the co-construction of knowledge might be seen as problematic within the anthropological community, the approach of facilitating, joint learning and empowerment for change is of utmost importance. Anthropology plays a key role in providing and transforming indispensable knowledge of "(…) more effective, equitable and durable solutions to today´s sustainability challenges" (ISSC/ UNESCO-Summary 2013: 4), by providing the theoretical and empirical basis and applied knowledge to bear on the urgent challenges of today's global world and providing knowledge about (historical) conditions but also (local) visions for change.

Even if a further confrontation with the challenging and critical relationship (arising from the historical development) of anthropology with application-oriented approaches such as transformative research might be necessary, we agree with the optimism of Charles Redman (2011) about the potential role for anthropology in sustainability sciences. We believe that engaging with the concept of sustainability is tremendously important in enhancing the role and impact of anthropologists in a world of rapid global change. Thus, a vision for a sustainable future of anthropology would be anthropologists being engaged in different fields and levels, actively framing the perception of global change and sustainability, mobilising a wider social science community to engage more effectively, and taking action in developing a more integrated and transformative science of global change and sustainability.

Acknowledgement

The project "Biodiversity and sustainable management of mountain grassland in the Javakheti Highland, South Caucasus, Georgia (BIOMAN)" is funded by the Bauer Foundation within the *Stifterverband für die Deutsche Wissenschaft* and the Foundation of the Free University of Bozen-Bolzano.

References

Balsiger, Philipp.W. "Supradisciplinary research practices: history, objectives and rationale." *Futures* 36 (2004), 407–421.
Bell, Simon, Stephen Morse and Rupesh, A. Shah. "Understanding stakeholder participation in research as part of sustainable development." *Journal of Environmental Management*, 101 (2012): 13–22.
Bergmann, Matthias, Thomas Jahn, Tobias Knobloch, Wolfgang Krohn, Christian Pohl, Engelbert Schramm. *Methoden transdisziplinärer Forschung*. Franfurt/New York: Campus Verlag, 2010.
Bourdieu, Pierre. Ökonomisches Kapital, kulturelles Kapital, soziales Kapital. In *Soziale Ungleichheiten* edited by Kreckel, Reinhard. Soziale Welt/Sonderband 2. Göttingen: Schwartz, 183–198, 1983.
Browne, Stephen. *Aid and Influence: Do Donors Help or Hinder?* London: Earthscan, 2006.
Brundtland, Bericht. "Our Common Future" *UN Komission für Umwelt und Entwicklung*, 1987.

Caister, Karen, Maryanna, Green and Steven Worth. "Learning how to be participatory: An emergent research agenda." *Action Research 10* (2012): 22–39, first published on August 4, 2011.

Cirella, Guiseppe Tommaso and Stefan Zerbe. Quizzical societies: A closer look at sustainability and principles of unlocking its measurability. *The International Journal of Science in Society* 5/3 (2014): 29-45.

Cornwall, Andrea and Rachel Jewkes. "What is participatory research?" *Social science & medicine*, 41/12 (1995): 1667–1676.

Dubielzig, Frank and Stefan Schaltegger. *Methoden Transdisziplinärer Forschung*. Lüneburg: Center for Sustainability Management, 2004. Accessed February 02, 2010. http://www2.leuphana.de/umanagement/csm/content/nama/downloads/download_publikation

Döring, Ralf, „Wie stark ist schwache, wie schwach starke Nachhaltigkeit?" Wirtschaftswissenschaftliche Diskussionspapiere. Ernst-Moritz-Arndt-Universität Greifswald: Rechts- und Staatswissenschaftliche Fakultät, No. 08, 2004.

Döring, Ralf and Barbara Muraca. *Sustainability Science – The Greifswalder Theory of Strong Sustainability and its relevance for policy advice in Germany and the EU*. Oldenburg/Bremen: Yearly Conference of ISEE (International Society of Ecological Economics), 2010.

Easterly, William. *The White Man's Burden*. Oxford: Oxford University Press, 2007.

Elsen, Susanne (Hg.). *Ökosoziale Transformation. Solidarische Ökonomie und die Gestaltung des Gemeinwesens. Perspektiven und Ansätze von Unten*. Neu Ulm: AG SPAK Bücher, 2011.

Elsen, Susanne. Nachhaltigkeit. In *Handbuch Soziale Arbeit* edited by Otto, Hans-Uwe and Hans Thiersch. München: Ernst Reinhardt Verlag, 2013.

Gebhardt Marinus. *Landschaftsökologische Bestandsaufnahme im Rahmen des WWF Weidemanagements im Lake Arpi & Javakheti National Park*. (Unpublished Diploma thesis), 2004.

Görgen, Maraile and Soete Klien. "Die Akteursanalyse." *Organisations Entwicklung*. Heft 2 (2009): 87–91.

Greenwood, Davydd J. and Morten Levin. Reconstructing the relationships between universities and society through action research. In *The Landscape of Qualitative Research: Theories and Issues,* edited by Denzin, Norman K. and Yvonna Lincoln. London: Sage Publications, 131–136, 2003.

Guretski, Voitsekh. "The Question of Javakheti."*Caucasian Regional Studies*, 3 (1998): 1–18.

Guyot, Jodi. *Anthropology as Key to Sustainability Science.* An Interview with Charles Redman by Jodi Guyot. Arizona State University. Anthropology News, April 2011. Accessed February 20, 2014. http://shesc.asu.edu

Häberli, Rudolf, Alain Bill, Walter Grossenbacher-Mansuy, Julie T. Klein Roland W. And MarthaWelti. Synthesis. In *Transdisciplinarity:Joint Problem Solving among Science, Technology, and Society* edited by Thompson Klein, Julie. Basel: Birkhauser, 6–22, 2001.

Häberli, Rudolf and Scholz, Roland W. *Transdisciplinarity: Joint Problem-Solving among Science, Technology and Society.* Workbook I: Dialogue Sessions and Idea Market.Zürich: Swiss Federal Institut of Technology, 2000.

Hackmann, Heide and Asunción Lera St. Clair. *Transformative Cornerstones of Social Science Research for Global Change.* Report of the International Social Science Council. Paris, 2012.

Haller, Dieter (Ed.). *Dtv-Atlas Ethnologie.* München: Deutscher Taschenbuch Verlag, 2005.

Hanschitz, Rudolf-Christian, Schmidt, Esther and Guido Schwarz. *Transdisiziplinarität in Forschung und Praxis-Chancen und Risiken partizipativer Prozesse.* Wiesbaden: VS Verlag für Sozialwissenschaften, 2009.

ISSC/UNESCO. *World Social Science Report: Changing Global Environments - Summary.* Paris: OECD Publishing/UNESCO Publishing, 2013.

Jahn, Thomas. *Transdiziplinäre Nachhaltigkeitsforschung – Konturen eines neuen disziplinenübergreifenden Forschungstyps.* Frankfurt am Main, 2001. Accessed February 20, 2014. http://www.isoe.de/ftp/Jahn-ISOE.pdf

Jantsch, Erich. Towards interdisciplinarity and transdisciplinarity in education and innovation. In *Interdisciplinarity. Problems of Teaching and Research in Universities* edited by Centre for Educational Research and Innovation (CERI). OECD,97–121, 1972.

Kemmis, Stephen and Robin McTaggart (eds.). *The Action Research Planner.* Victoria: Deakin University, 1988.

Kemmis, Stephen and Robin McTaggart. Participatory Action Research: Communicative Action and the Public Aphere. In *The SAGE Handbook of Qualitative Research,* edited by Denzin, Norman K. and Yvona S. Lincoln, 3rd Edition. Thousand Oaks: Sage, 559–604, 2005.

Kopfmüller, Jürgen. „Auf dem Weg zu einem integrativen Nachhaltigkeitskonzept." *Ökologisches Wirtschaften* 1 (2007): 16–18.

Lewin, Kurt. "Frontiers in group dynamics: social planning and action research." *Human Relations* 1 (1947): 143–153.

Lewin, Kurt (ed.). *Feldtheorie in den Sozialwissenschaften.* Stuttgart, 1963.

Lohm, Hedvig. "Javakheti after the Rose Revolution. Progress and Regress in the Pursuit of National Unity in Georgia." *ECMI (European Centre of Minority Issues) Working Paper*, 38, 2007. Accessed January 30, 2014. www.ecmi.de

Loorbach, Derk and Jan Rotmans. Managing Transitions for Sustainable Development. In *Understanding Industrial Transformation. Views from Different Disciplines* edited by Olsthoorn, Xander and Anna J.Wieczorek. Dordrecht: Springer, 187–206, 2006.

McKay, Judy and Peter Marshall. "The dual imperatives of action research." *Information Technology & People*, 14 (2001): 46–59.

Mackenzie, John, Poh-Ling Tan, Suzanne Hoverman and Claudia Baldwin. "The value and limitations of Participatory Action Research methodology." *Journal of Hydrology* 474 (2012): 11–21.

Meppem, Tony and Roderic Gill. "Planning for sustainability a learning concept." *Ecological Economics* 26 (1998), 121–137.

Morris, Michael W., Leung Kwok, Daniel Ames and Brian Lickel. "Views from Inside and Outside: Integrating Emic and Etic Insights about Culture and Justice Judgement." *Academy of Management Review*, 24/4 (1999): 781–769. Accessed March 3, 2013. http://hunter.bschool.washington.edu/main/DissertationProposalGrant/ Morri%20emic-etic%20AMR%201999.pdf

Myers, Norman, Russell A., Mittermeier, Cristina G. Mittermeier, Gustavo A.B. da Fonseca, and Jennifer Kent. "Biodiversity hotspots for conservation priorities." *Nature* 403 (2000): 853–858.

Ott, Konrad and Ralf Döring. *Theorie und Praxis starker Nachhaltigkeit.* Marburg: Metropolis, 2004.

Ott, Konrad. *Umweltethik – zur Einführung.* Hamburg, Dresden: Junius, 2010.

O'Brien, R. Umexame da abordagem metodlógica da pesquisa ação [An Overview of the Methodological Approach of Action Research] In Ricardson, R. (Ed.), *Theoria e Práctica da Pesquisa Ação* [Theory and Practice of Action Research] João Pessoa, Brazil, Universitad Federal da Paraiba. 2001. Accessed February 20, 2014. http://www.web.ca/~ribrien/papers/arfinal.html

Øverland, Indra. "The Closure of the Russian Military Base at Akhalkalaki: Challenges for Local Energy Elite, the Informal Economy and Stability." *The Journal of Power Institutions in Post-Soviet Societies* [en ligne], 10, 2009. Accessed January 30, 2014. http://pipss.revues.org/3717?lang=fr

Özesmi, Uygar and Stacy LÖzesmi. "Ecological models based on people's knowledge: a multi-step fuzzy cognitive mapping approach." *Ecological Modelling,* 176 (2004): 43–64.

Piaget, Janet. 1972. The epistemology of interdisciplinary relationships. In *Interdisciplinarity. Problems of Teaching and Research in Universities* edited by Centre for Educational Research and Innovation (CERI). OECD, 127–139, 1972.

Rockström, Johan, Will Steffen, Kevin Noone, Åsa Persson, Stuart F. Chapin, Eric Lambin,Timothy M. Lenton, Scheffer, Marten, Carl Folke, Hans Joachim Schellnhuber, Björn Nykvist, Cynthia A. de Wit, Terry Hughes, Sander van der Leeuw, Henning Rodhe, Sverker Sörlin, Peter K. Snyder, Robert Costanza, Una Svedin, Malin Falkenmark, Luise Karlberg, Robert W. Corell, Victoria J. Fabry, James Hansen, Brian Walker, Diana Liverman, Katherine Richardson, Paul Crutzen and Jonathan Foley. "Planetary boundaries: Exploring the safe operating space for humanity." *Ecology and Society* 14, 2009.

Rylko-Bauer, Barbara, Merrill Singer and John Van Willigen. "Reclaiming Applied Anthropology: Its Past, Present, and Future." *American Anthropologist* 108 (2006): 178–190.

Schneidewind, Uwe."Transformative Literacy. Gesellschaftliche Veränderungsprozesse verstehen und gestalten." (Transformative Literacy. Understanding and Shaping Societal Transformations). *GAIA* 22/2 (2013): 82–86.

Schneidewind, Uwe and Mandy Singer-Brodowski. *Transformative Wissenschaft. Klimawandel im deutschen Wissenschafts- und Hochschulsystem.* Marburg: Metropolis-Verlag, 2013.

Singer, Merill. "Anthropology as a Sustainability Science." *Anthropology News*, 52/4 (2011): 5–10.

Smyth, Luke. "Anthropological Critiques of Sustainable Development". *Cross-sections, The Bruce Hall Academic Journal*VII, (2011): 77–85.

Tarknishvili, David, A. Gavashelishvili, O. Ginosyan, , N. Ginosyan, , G. Darchiashvili, , N. Janashia, Z. Javakhisvili, A. Kandaurov, A. Makaryan, and M. Matcharashvili. *Land Use and Landscape Conservation in Southern Georgia.* Tbilisi: Georgian Centre for Conservation of Wildlife, 2001.

Tax, Sol. "Action Anthropology." *Current Anthropology*, 16/4 (1975): 514–517.

Thompson-Klein, Julie. „Prospects for transdisciplinarity." *Futures*, 36/4 (2004): 515–526.

TJS, *Protected Areas and Rangeland Management Planning in the South Caucasus: A Review of Current Approaches*. Baku and Tbilisi: BMZ/KfW Ecoregional Programme for the Southern Caucasus, 2008.

Tress, Bärbel, Gunther Tress and Gary Fry. "Integrative Research on Environmental and Landscape Change: PhD Students Motivations and Challenges." *Journal of environmental management*, 90/9 (2009): 2921–2929.

Ul-Hassan, Mehmood, Anna-Katharina Hornidge, Laurens van Veldhuizen, Akmal Akhramkhanov, Inna Rudenko and Nodir Djanbekov. *Follow the Innovation: Participatory Testing and Adoption of Agricultural Innovations in Uzbekistan*. Bonn: Zentrum für Entwicklungsforschung, 2011.

Von Unger, Hella. *Partizipative Forschung. Einführung in die Forschungspraxis*. Wiesbaden: Springer VS, 2014.

Wall, Caleb. *Buried Treasure: Discovering and Implementing the Value of Corporate Social Responsibility*. Sheffield: Greenleaf, 2008.

Wallimann, Isidor. Environmental Policy is Social Policy – Social Policy is Environmental Policy. New York: Springer, 2013.

Watson-Gegeo, Karen Ann. "Ethnography in ESL: Defining the Essentials." *Tesol Quarterly*, 22 (1988): 575-592.

Williams, Laura, Zazanashvili, Nugzar, Sanadiradze, and Giorgi Sanadiradze (Eds.). *An Eco-regional Conservation Plan for the Caucasus*. Second Edition. Tbilisi: Contour Ltd., 2006.

Wheatley, Jonathan. *Obstacles Impending the Regional Integration of the Javakheti Region of Georgia*. ECMI (European Centre of Minority Issues) Working Paper, 22, 2004. Accessed January 30, 2014. www.ecmi.de

Wright, Michael T., von Unger Hella, and M. Block. Lokales Wissen, lokale Theorie und lokale Evidenz für die Gesundheitsförderung und Prävention. In *Partizipative Qualitätsentwicklung in der Gesundheitsförderung und Prävention* edited by Michael T. Wright. Bern: Huber, 53–74, 2010.

Yencken, David and Debra Wilkinson. *Resetting the Compass – Australia's Journey Towards Sustainability*. Collingwood: Csiro Publishing, 2000.

Notes

[1] Conservation International (2007) assumes that overgrazing has eroded the natural vegetation in more than 30% of the sub-alpine and alpine summer ranges in the Caucasus. According to Myers (2000), obout10 % of 500,000 km² original extent of primary vegetation remains in this Caucasus biodiversity hotspot. A system of protected areas is being established in order to maintain biodiversity in several parts of the Caucasus Eco-region (Williams et al. 2006).

[2] Transhumance is a semi-nomadic form of pastoralism. The term describes the action or practice of seasonal livestock migration from one grazing ground to another (typically to lowland pastures in winter and highlands in summer). According to some definitions another part of the group settles in villages and practices agriculture (c.f. Haller 2005: 166f.).

[3] According to the understanding of Pierre Bourdieu (1983) and his article "economic capital, cultural capital, social capital" published in 1983, social capital, is the capital of social relationships, which again is subject to certain conditions, mechanisms and obligations. Social capital is institutionalized for example through the adoption of a common family name.

[4] For the Russian Empire it was a remote outpost against the Turks. For the Armenian, the Russian presence provided security guarantee against their Turkish neighbours." (Øverland 2009: 1). The base further fulfilled many of the traditional state functions such as providing education and (social) security to the local population (Wheatley 2004).

[5] "A distinctive characteristic of the anthropological critique of sustainable development is the argument that sustainable development projects often fail to primarily serve the interests of target communities, and instead conform largely to the desires and expectations of the involved external stakeholders, such as foreign donors, non-governmental organisations, and the state. This can be explained through sustainable development's particular attention to environmental concerns; this results in the dominant discourse of sustainable development privileging ethical perspectives in such projects, and discounting local knowledge." (Smyth 2011: 78)

[6] Pearce et al. (1989) have listed more than 20 possible meanings of sustainable development, many of them have proposed that Sustainable Development in fact as an oxymoron (Meppem and Gill 1998: 122).

[7] According to Ott and Döring (2004), the model is representing a concept of weak sustainability and refers to the idea that environmental, economic and social resources can be outweighed against each other.

[8] Whereas in the early 2000s the main focus was on the economic and ecological dimension of sustainability, since the late 2000s social sustainability, as democratic, distributive and integrative policy issues, moved into the centre (Wallimann 2013). It's about the preservation of society through equitable participation, democracy and participation (Elsen 2013).

[9] Culture is one of the most complex and contested words and concepts that bears a long tradition of discussion and theoretical definition processes in scholarly

literature but also has an everyday use all over the world. Overall, the diversity of cultural terms underlines the understanding of culture as a discursive construct that can be understood, defined and explored in different ways.

[10] Especially, in German speaking countries, transformational sciences are an advancement of sustainability sciences (Schneidewind and Singer-Brodowski 2013).

[11] A definitional approximation to research in the relatively young field of academic research in the German-speaking countries that is explicitly designated as transdisciplinary shows a range of definitions with widely differing focal points. According to Jahn (2001), transdisciplinarity is science or research released from their professional disciplinary boundaries. Problems are defined with a view to non-scientific social developments and are then solved independent of disciplinary boundaries (Jahn 2001). Häberli et al. (2001), Thomson-Klein (2001) and Balsinger (2004) support this understanding of transdisciplinarity, whereas Jantsch and Piaget (1972) regard transdisciplinarity as final integration or unification of knowledge among disciplines, and thus describe the development of inter- to transdisciplinarity (see Tress et al. 2009; Dubielzig and Schaltegger 2004). What is common to these definitions is the fact that transdisciplinarity is seen as an integrated access, i.e. a science and research principle. Considered the case, disciplinary boundaries are broken down and a collaboration between natural sciences and technology with social and cultural studies induced. Disciplinary knowledge in this context is (only) relevant insofar as it is used for joint problem-oriented question solving (Tress et al. 2009).

[12] In many other parts of the world, "(…) anthropological work by resident scholars is often driven by critical socio-economic and structural issues, thus merging theory and engaged praxis (Baba and Hill 1997; González 2004; Guerrón-Montero 2002)" (Rylko-Bauer et al. 2006: 178).

[13] In the work of the ISSC (2012), the notion of integration is understood as referring to the co-design and co-production of knowledge across scientific borders, across national boundaries and with the involvement of so-called research users. In other words, it refers to research, i.e. "a) inter-disciplinary, including and working across all disciplines and fields of science, b) trans-disciplinary, collaborating with multiple societal actors, including decision makers, practitioners and civil society organisations, and c) truly global in nature, working with multiple socio-geographic perspectives and approaches, incorporating communities of practice and epistemic frameworks from all parts of the world." (Hackmann and St.Clair 2012: 9).

[14]"Whether action anthropology is a variety of applied anthropology, or something quite different depends on one´s conception of applied anthropology, which is itself changing rapidly" (Tax 1975: 515).

[15]Thus, one of the major characterisations of action anthropology is that a community not only is subject of study, but also its object (Tax 1975).

[16] Action research becomes participatory action research depending on who is involved in each of those stages and to what extent. At its most participatory stage, researchers engage with participants as collaborators who can inform project

design, propose methods, facilitate some of the project activities and, importantly, review and evaluate the process as a whole. (Bell et al. 2012.). Therefore, one of the biggest challenges is to connect the complexity and hybrid character of life-world problems with accountable scientific approaches. According to Caister et al. (2012: 33- 36), it is "the attitude, the environment and the issues, not the particular tools that achieve participation. [...] The participatory nature of research is determined by how relationships are developed and managed". This building up of networks of trust is seen as a first important step of research but is also a necessary implication throughout the whole research process. Therefore, reliability and reflexivity are necessary preconditions. The first research phase was, among other things, scheduled to establish networks and confidence through participatory observation. Without this the second research phase, which is aligned with the approach of "cognitive mapping", would not have been possible.

[17] In particular, the "festival of flowers" seems to be of great importance. The festival only exists in this specific village and is connected to a flower (*Anemone fasciculata L.)* that can be found on the slopes nearby.

[18] According to Schneidewind (2013: 83) this is: "The ability to read and utilize information about societal transformation processes, to accordingly interpret and get actively involved in the processes".

[19] 1) Historical and contextual complexities, 2) consequences, 3) conditions and visions for change (future knowledge), 4) interpretation and subjective sense making, 5) responsibilities, 6) governance and decision making (ISSC 2012: 15)

[20] A strict holistic perspective in ethnography would be the description and explanation of all aspects of a culture in relation to the whole system of which it is a part (Firth 1961; Diesing 1971; cited in Watson-Gegeo 1988).

[21] The emic, or inside perspective, describes thought and actions primarily in terms of the actor's self-understanding. Historically, the conception is based in cultural anthropology striving to understand culture from a "native's point of view" (Malinowski 1922; cited in Morris et al. 1999).

CHAPTER FIVE

SENSORY HOUSES: CROSS-SENSORIAL LEARNING IN THE ANTHROPOLOGY OF DEVELOPMENT FOR ALL AGES

NADEZHDA SAVOVA-GRIGOROVA

Introduction: Make bread, not war!

Fig.5-1. People gathered for a collective bread-making event at the first Bread House community center in Gabrovo, Bulgaria.

I was surprised at not being surprised when during the protests in 2013 against the government corruption in Bulgaria-various people, organizations, and journalists suggested to me to set a table in front of the Parliament and invite politicians, protesters and policemen to make and break bread together. In Bulgaria, these protests were the culmination of over two decades of what people in the country called with irony "the transition" from Communism/Socialism to democracy. The period was marked with large popular disillusionment and resentment towards the falsehood, hypocrisy and corruption of both systems, which claimed to be one thing, both supposedly very different, and ended up being the same destructive type of structure offering, as such, to the common person- no real improvement in quality of life. In 2013, a lot of young people, ignited by large protests in the main universities in the capital Sofia, rose to protest in front of the Parliament building, joined by thousands of others. People wanted real "transition", real change, and real life in the vacuum of so many false promises.

I was admittedly not surprised by the suggestion to set a kneading table and bake with the feuding sides in front of the Parliament, since for the past three years my *action research* and applied development work in Bulgaria had been experimenting and proving successful new methods for community engagement, dialogue, and cooperation – all focusing on forms of collective bread-making. These community activities are "not by bread alone", for they always include "kneading with metaphors", or a way of engaging all participants to share about their lives, fears, and hopes, and discuss their community, society and the future – again, all by thinking through the bread ingredients (flour, yeast, salt, water, etc.) and the bread-making processes (sifting, mixing, rising, shaping, proofing, baking, breaking and sharing).

The baking events quickly grew from one city, Gabrovo, to more than a dozen other cities in Bulgaria. They became catalysts for local creativity, as locals started shaking off their embarrassment and undertaking the initiative to present their art and engage others in co-creation (music, painting, pottery, theatre, etc.). What was surprising to me and is striking in general for the context of Bulgarian society, which has been highly divided and divisive since the fall of socialism (and as many would argue has been so for centuries as a national cultural trait), is that people of all walks of life tend to come and mix freely at these events. People come because they have heard by word of mouth or through the media, others, indeed those who are vulnerable or isolated from mainstream society, often come as a collective, organized by the social institution that takes care of them (orphanage, rehab center, hospice, etc.). The important thing, however, is that bread-making is not the main goal or focus for people, but it becomes a vehicle for communication and friendships: very diverse groups come together and engage in the same simple act of baking and sharing, which makes hardly any distinction among the diverse abilities, skills, or educational backgrounds of the participants.

From one town to another, around 20 cities in Bulgaria currently have initiated their own community baking activities, asking me to train them at the beginning and then continuing on their own. Beyond Bulgaria, the network of people and organizations who have embraced the vision and have used the baking-with-metaphors and bread therapy methods includes (chronologically) Italy, Peru, South Africa, Israel and Palestine, Russia, Brazil, Hungary, UK, Scotland, USA, Spain, Mexico, Switzerland, Serbia, Tadjikistan, Thailand, Portugal, New Zealand, and it keeps growing (for more information see www.breadhousesnetwork.org). Across these diverse countries, the groups that have been engaging in collective bread-making are even more diverse and often hard to imagine making and breaking bread together: former prisoners and local families, gang members in low-income ghettoes, women war veterans and university students, orphaned children and elderly people from hospices, foster families helping to inspire girls escaped from trafficking to keep their unwanted children, women victims of domestic violence and their children, young men suffering drug and alcohol addictions, sight-impaired and deaf people, people with various physical and mental special needs (Down Syndrome, autism, cerebral palsy) and with mental illness (depression and mild schizophrenia), businessmen and women and low-income immigrants, refugees, university students, professors and the university janitors (just to mention a few), but it is, indeed, sometimes hard for the participants to believe their eyes that some of these people are at all making bread, let alone making it shoulder to shoulder with those whom they may otherwise never encounter.

If we are to summarize why the activities and methods spread so quickly, then what I would point to are some of my research and project participant's opinions and claims that the most appealing aspect to all is the simplicity and yet inspiring creativity of baking with metaphors – anyone can make bread and break it, and at the same time it nurtures not only the belly but even more so the mind and the heart. Bread-making triggers intriguing, unexpected and rich meaning-making processes from memories, associations, and stories that the multi-sensorial experience catalyses.

When I set off in 2007 to study the effects of national and transnational (UNESCO) cultural policies in Bulgaria, Cuba, and Brazil, I never expected that I would end up making bread or studying bread and bread-making as a locally-meaningful cultural practice and symbol. Yet, indeed, bread proved to be a particularly relevant analytical tool, both phenomenologically and semiotically, to help me observe and understand otherwise largely invisible or unspoken cultural schemata and process in community building and development. In fact, bread proved to be as important a symbol of cultural, social, economic, political, and ecological issues and transitions as was salt in India-particularly in relation to the British salt monopoly that Gandhi first rose up against.

The Salt March, also known as the *Salt Satyagraha*, was an important part of the Indian independence movement in 1940. It was a nonviolent protest and direct tax resistance against the British salt monopoly in colonial India, and triggered the wider *Civil Disobedience Movement*. The Salt March began on 12 March 1930, lasted almost a month until Gandhi reached the town of Dandi, and after making salt in Dandi, Gandhi continued southward along the coast, engaging in making salt, and simultaneously, political discussion and community meetings along the way.

The symbolic act of making salt with the people and sharing it freely was as powerfully symbolic as is baking and breaking bread with someone in the Bulgarian cultural context, or, for that matter, in many of the other wheat-based European, North American, and Middle-Eastern cultures. As a sign of sharing and friendship, on the one hand, bread has also been, on the other, a highly politically charged symbol of protest, struggle for change and hope for peace. "Bread and Roses" was the slogan that acquired an idiomatic and iconic value after the workers' protests in 1912 in the USA, when people called for dignity, not only in terms of working conditions and wages (the "bread"), but also in their striving to secure leisure time and access to the arts (the "roses").

In the case of Bulgaria, bread is used in many popular expressions and idioms, for it is also the main element present in key religious rituals marking the central rites of passage in one's life. This is so in the general practice of Eastern Orthodox Christianity, but in Bulgaria there is also a long per-Christian bread tradition that makes bread such a recognizable cultural sign. Thus, the wide affection of people towards bread as a key religious and social symbol in Bulgaria was one of the reasons why I became interested in it as a topic of research and, later on, it evolved as a tool for community engagement and discussion.

As a researcher and community activist, I envisioned collective bread-making at its inception as an auto-ethnographic project, in which the shared space, time, and action could serve as a forum for discussions and dialogue, a form of improvised focus groups to discuss the social and cultural transformations in Bulgaria during the so-called "transition" period. In the process over months and years, however, these gatherings became so popular that they evolved as a form of civic fora geared towards local development.

These baking sessions were often used as platforms for civil society to voice its plea to the authorities, as sometimes members of the local authorities, mayors, school masters, even once the President of Bulgaria, took part in the baking events, and got involved not only in "dialogue," but also in collective "doing". Instead of purely discursive "roundtable" discussions these became engaged experiences around a tangible round table where the hierarchical structures of power and communication re-aligned temporarily through the breaking of bread. Though to some extent this might appear utopic, it has turned out to be quite simple, applicable, and successful in bringing people together to talk to each other – quite often even people who otherwise traditionally feud with each other, such as different ethnic groups or socio-economic classes.

Again, similar to the way Gandhi used salt, both as a concrete contested issue, and as an important symbol and trigger for civic activism, the enthusiasm and civic initiatives inspired by collective bread-making in Bulgaria reflect the hunger for unity and change for the very many diverse groups of people and communities, divided by the harsh economic and social inequalities of "the Transition" period. What is so important in the cases of bread in Bulgaria and salt in India as tools in social activation is that popular symbols turned out to be very powerful in organizing and uniting people, but also in having a lasting emotional effect on people, sustaining the momentum towards longer-term engagement with transformation at the community-level rather than short-term protests. In this sense, I argue that when discussing issues of sustainability in social change, it is crucial to understand the signs, symbols, idioms, and thus the subtle ranges of sensitivity of a culture or a group of people in order to comprehend what is meaningful for them in "development" or "sustainability", and what symbols or ideas inspire them to imagine new paths in those directions.

In this auto-ethnography, I analyse and frame what I call *cross-sensorial learning* processes in informal "communities of practice" and the role of co-creation activities, with the main case study of collective bread-making, as catalysts for social transformation and community development. These observations reveal the importance of such co-creative activities in generating, what in previous works, I have defined as *community creative capital* (Savova 2007). *Community creative capital* defines a wide range of community-arts-driven social relations, networks, and forms of cooperation that are at the crossroads of various types of "social capital" and "cultural capital". The intriguing effects of the arts and creativity on people and communities examined in the generation of *community creative capital* give these two widely accepted concepts of social relations new perspectives and important understanding of the dynamics of human behaviour and social psychology.

Herein, I analyse the role and effect of the senses and various sensory experiences on the ways people engage with each other and build a sense of belonging and community, of meaning and purpose. The study examines how people involved in sensorially-stimulating, experiential informal learning dynamics develop various channels of transmission of knowledge, skills, ideas, values, and cooperation. The main question it poses is: "Does the sensorial engagement in co-creation affect and change the structures of power, communication, and cooperation across socio-economic, ethnic, or cultural boundaries?" The role of the senses in community engagement and development dynamics is understood through the processes of production and circulation of social capital, cultural capital, and *community creative capital* -in the particular case of collective bread-making.

The overall theoretical frameworks were developed in my dissertation defended at Princeton University's Anthropology Department and titled *Bread and Home: Global Cultural Politics in the Tangible Places of Intangible Heritage* (2013). This research examined the meanings of production of cultural capital and cultural policies fostering arts centres as spaces for integrated social development. While the main research method at the outset of my dissertation research was the classical anthropological "participant observation", as the study evolved I started being actively engaged in creating occasions and activities with the communities- leading to the birth of a non-governmental organization, the International Council for Cultural Centres- that I later analysed through "action research" methods (Torbert 2001).

This paper analyses the Bread House project which I developed in Bulgaria as an auto-ethnographic project. In many ways, such endeavors are much more complex than a standard ethnography because in action research the researcher faces various issues of self-reflexivity and subjectivity. In either case, however, anthropologists have widely agreed that the ethnographic field is always affected- and in varied degrees- constructed by the fieldwork, thus leaving aside as unrealistic and unnecessary any claims to pure "objectivity" and "non-interference".

Nowadays, more and more anthropologists see the benefits of action research, as well as that of multi-sited and multi-locale ethnographies (Amit 2000, Marcus 1995). The field of engaged, applied anthropology is also growing for its potentially concrete contributions to society. I certainly support this group of engaged scholarship as it is a field in anthropology that can bring very interesting and useful observations, new perspectives on common issues, and most importantly, it can contribute new ways of addressing social problems, in particular, when related to the wider sphere of research on sustainability that this book examines.

Liminality in Community Transformations: Sustainable Development from the Hearth

My hands-on community development work and action research led me to found in 2008- the organization called the International Council for Cultural Centers (I3C)[1]. I3C started off as a slow process of connecting community cultural centres- starting with the centres I was visiting and studying for my PhD dissertation in Latin America and Europe, and then connecting people to people from directors of regional NGOs to representatives of Ministries of Culture from around the world (many of whom I got to meet during my work as a consultant for UNESCO's Culture Sector in Paris in 2008). People representing national networks and the actual networks started getting associated with I3C, country after country, and the International Council is now connecting in an informal manner more than 50 countries with their national networks of community cultural centres offering arts-based life-long learning. I3C held the first World Summit of Community Cultural Centres and Networks in Bulgaria, when these people and networks from different continents met for the first time, and it is currently one of the largest platforms for community arts in the world.

While developing the I3C network, and researching community arts networks in Bulgaria, I started delving into the locally significant metaphors, symbols, and ritual practices around bread-making, since people often mentioned it when discussing cultural heritage and the meaning of creativity. Then I decided to start organizing collective baking sessions-this was indeed challenging having never made bread myself before. But the right moment came in a very unusual place with a very unusual kindred spirit.

In 2009, I found myself in the heart of the Peruvian Amazon jungle, in one of the most isolated by land cities in the world, Iquitos, at the "First Global Forum on Arts as a Bridge towards Wellbeing" organized by the World Health Organization. Side by side with Patch Adams, famous for his clown nose and doctor's garment, founder of the global movement to heal people with humor (humor therapy), Patch gave me the inspiration and the push to test my idea of using baking to unite and inspire people, which he perceived as a potential healing strategy –subsequently, I started thinking of it as a "bread therapy" similar to his "humour therapy".

On one of the Forum days dedicated to community workshops, I organized an event announced to the local community as an evening of making and sharing bread, nothing more than that. To everyone's amazement, especially mine, both men and teenagers came in addition to the women and children. Indeed, such male participation had not happened in any of the other workshops on different art forms that were being held and open to the community the whole week. The breaking of gender roles, stereotypes, and divisions that took place during this very first test workshop showed clearly how collective bread-making, mixed with spontaneous sharing and stories told, and the shaping of dough as a sculpting material was a form of collective, co-creative activity- not only appealing to all- but with the potential to help people rethink their social roles and behaviours. Already in those first experiences around bread, what was evolving was the *Theatre of Crumbs* method, which we currently use in Bulgaria, and in other countries, described further below.

One of the main reasons for the appeal of this type of collective event, expressed by many of the participants in these baking sessions, is that unlike other arts, bread does not require special skills and is not limited to certain levels of education or professions, neither gender nor age, and at the same time, it inspires creativity and sharing. With time I observed how the experience breaks socio-economic boundaries and naturally fosters integration and cooperation in a multi-cultural context- because it is both something very traditional and known- and at the same time- a very new kind of collective experience for mixed ages and backgrounds.

Many people who participate have shared that baking together with others is deeply healing and empowering for them, or, in the case of people with mental disabilities and psychological illness who cannot verbalize well, it is easy to notice significant improvement in their communication and self-confidence over time.

The touch of dough and, in particular, the aroma of hot bread unlocks hidden memories and soft emotional states in people with deep traumas. A young woman war-veteran suffering mental trauma after the fights in Afghanistan, and currently housed at a shelter for homeless veterans, looked with scepticism at the baking when professors and students from the University of Massachusetts-Amherst (USA) invited the women to bake. Then suddenly, the aroma of the other breads made her eyes water –

she remembered the aroma of her grandmother's biscuits when she was a child, which she stated was "one of the best times in my life." It was then possible for her to imagine a home and a new life after the horrors of war.

Similarly, another woman, victim of domestic violence who regularly attended Bread House gatherings in Bulgaria, in the town of Plovdiv, shared how they not only helped her cope with deep emotional traumas but even gave her the strength to become more independent. She writes:

> I was desperate and I had no direction. I did not have the courage to think of life improvements or turning a new page in my life. Baking therapy gave me more confidence and self-esteem to make responsible decisions.... Thanks to the talks and discussions during our meetings, I thought about the different stages of my life. It helped me a lot! Finally, I took the decision to buy my own home. All of my life I lived in rented space.

Fig 5-2. Bread puppets expressing the vision and hopes of the traumatized women in Plovdiv for a better future life, in a home where the aroma of hot bread is a marker of peace and love.

A foundational conceptual framework I found relevant in my analysis of these co-creative dynamics which often affect personal and communal transformations is the concept of the "liminal," or borderline, in general, and more particularly, the notion of "liminoid" space developed by Victor Turner in analysing play as a ritual practice (1979). While "liminal" denotes the state of transition and the ambiguity between categories of a person's position in society, "liminoid", from the Greek, means "resembling liminal." It defines ritual re-enactments that are framed as leisure and are open to choice and re-structuring. Turner argues that the key element that distinguishes leisure and play from traditional rituals is not the lack of seriousness (since we can "seriously" learn categories and norms through humor and game). Rather than seriousness, what distinguishes the "liminoid" from the "liminal" is the *freedom of choice* as to whether to participate in the activity, how to participate, and what to take out of it as applicable to one's daily life.

It is precisely this freedom of choice yet regularity of engagement in collective co-creation that I observed, negotiated, and enacted- first within the spatial and symbolic domains of the community cultural centres- and later, around the kneading tables of the Bread Houses. Within the community cultural centres the particular "framing" of traditional arts and modern arts as informal leisure activities allowed much space for bargains over meaning, substance, form, behavior, etc. Around the bread-making table, that open space for creativity was created by the lack of defining categories such as "art," but instead what existed was a simple, open, free collective bread-making. A particularly intriguing aspect of the relative freedom in these interactions is the opening of space and time for the sharing of intimate information among strangers, which in many cases is information kept away from close relatives and friends because of the many ties and webs of relationships that the information could affect and/or disturb.

The personal rethinking of one's role in society – thus a form of liminal role transition « in-between » already determined social categories – propelled wider communal transformations towards accepting and including, previously excluded, feared or scorned people and groups (ethnic minorities, mentally and physically disabled, orphans, the poor, the homeless, in short, the "Other").

One such story of the importance of the "liminoid" states and the shift of categories in the community happened to a young man with Down syndrome, Julian. He started coming regularly to the weekly community baking gatherings at the first Bread House community centre, and very soon the work with dough inspired him to work more and more with his hands, and Julian offered to give others massage. At first, the other participants were worried and a bit scared, because he usually rushed to strangers to hug them and people in town used to run away and tried to ignore him. But a few old ladies around the table finally agreed that he could give them a massage, and – what a surprise for all – Julian turned out to be very good at it (later on I discovered that one of the aspects of Down

Syndrome is that physically the hands can be extraordinarily strong). Overnight, Julian got to be liked and respected, and the old ladies would look forward to each weekly baking when they would also receive a free massage. The self-fulfillment visible on the young man's face could simply not be described. Indeed, overnight and through the regularity of community baking gatherings, he got to acquire a new status, a new category in the community, and the "liminoid", play-like context of the informal and entertaining collective baking further facilitated all these transitions.

Fig.5-3. Julian, a young man with Down syndrome, like many others found accepting environment and friends around the wood-fired oven and kneading table. People of all ages and all walks of life mixed without any unease, as if this is the most natural thing, and perhaps it is when the right conditions are at place.

To return back to the history of how the baking-with-metaphors method evolved and spread after my life-changing meeting with Patch Adams-after Peru, other conferences and projects took me around the world from New York to Japan, South Korea, South Africa, and Barcelona, and I took time beyond the conferences to organize bread-making evenings at local organizations I happened to come across. This is how more and more organizations and individuals started joining what was already growing as an informal social network and we could even call it an informal movement around bread as a widely accessible art form and a universal symbol of peace. At the COP15 ecological summit with a group of kindred spirits we called this simply the BREAD Movement, but filled the acronym with the meanings of what collective bread-making strives to achieve: *Bridging Resources for Ecological and Art-based Development.*

The first Bread House in this network, the first grain in the granary (a metaphor I further examine below), was an experiment and a collective volunteer undertaking that evolved when I donated for community use the old, uninhabited house of my great-grandmother to be turned into a local cultural centre where people could regularly come together for bread-making events. The idea of reviving the aroma of warm bread reminded many people of the old-time community bakeries, called *furni* in Bulgarian (similar to the words in Italy (*forno*), Spain (*horno*), and France (*four*), and similar traditions to the community baking spaces in those countries, and in Germany, Austria, and perhaps most European countries).

The memories of and nostalgia for the community bakeries that disappeared under socialism in Bulgaria, and the growing hunger for places for people to meet and interact without the requirement of financial transactions (which limits people from going to cinema, theater, restaurants, etc.) inspired many volunteers to help me fix the house, rebuild the old roof, donate old furniture and animate the whole space as a community center. In just a month, in December 2009, the Bread House was inaugurated, and since then more than 20 other communities across Bulgaria and more than 15 countries on 5 continents got inspired to try similar activities.

The second place that was quick to create a Bread House was the small town of Zlatariza, about an hour from Gabrovo. A teacher in Zlatariza, hearing about the community center in Gabrovo mixing all kinds of people around bread, imagined that bread-making might also help heal her community, which had been chronically suffering for centuries now from divisions and even conflicts among the five main ethnic groups (Roma, Turkish, Vlah/Romanian, Pomak/Bulgarian Muslims, and Bulgarian Christians as the majority). Thus, step by step, starting with children from the different groups, and then slowly inviting parents to informally join under the pre-text of helping their children in kneading the dough, adults who previously would not speak to each other started rubbing shoulders and kneading friendships around the kneading table.

Sensory Houses: Cross-sensorial Learning in Inter-generational/cultural *Doing*

Other cities and countries were inspired by the bread methods as a starting point – it further revitalized already existing community cultural centres or created new spaces with specially-built traditional wood-fired ovens, when people were particularly inspired to fully engage all senses. An intriguing case was one high-school in the Bulgarian town of Nova Zagora, whose Principal had the initiative to build a wood-fired oven in the school yard and, seeking locally people in need of socialization, she discovered a village with a refugee camp (full due to the Syrian refugee wave) and facilitated the meeting of the refugees with the students and other local people.

Fig.5-4. Students from the different classes at a high-school in Nova Zagora get united by their Director and vision to build a communal wood-fired oven, which becomes a focus of multiple inter-generational and inter-cultural gatherings – a perfect case of "cross-sensorial learning".

The inspiration that *cross-sensorial* experiences and the spaces meant to stimulate and host them provoked in people is the reason why I refer to these community spaces as *sensory houses*. Many people participating in the community-baking events have shared the fact that they love the aroma of the wood-fired oven and the hot bread, its taste, the tender dough touch, the sculptures made of it, the stories and often songs shared around the table – in sum, all 5 senses that the experience stimulates and engages.

While these deeply sensorial experiences are new to the conceptualization of culture and the arts, introducing touch and taste, a kitchen space or a kneading table and an oven, to the space of a cultural centre or a community centre helps shake the often stagnant, old-time programming of these spaces. And it is precisely the sensorial, as much as the semiotic analysis, of these communal spaces that is crucial to understanding their potential for fomenting sustainable community development, in particular because they manage to bring together diverse and often marginalized groups- that would hardly otherwise interact.

At different international conferences where I present my doctoral research or non-profit work with the International Council for Cultural Centres, during my presentations or in informal conversations with cultural workers, artists, and politicians from various countries, it was invariably the Bread House model that inspired them most to comment, share, envision, and even want to try such methods in their own cultural organizations and promote it through their cultural networks. As expressed by the President of the European Network of Cultural Centres, ENCC, the continental network of a dozen countries with networks similar to the *chitalishte*, "tastes and aroma lack widely in our cultural centres, and at the same time, they are crucial in attracting and connecting people, so we should really re-think the role of food alongside the arts.[2]"

I would define the Bread House as a type of community cultural centre engaging all senses as a *sensory house,* building on the formally accepted term "sensory room", which is a specially organized room used to stimulate the senses and help ameliorate learning processes for children with various types of disabilities. However, sensory rooms are usually fitted with mainly artificial materials to touch (plastic, rubber, and various artificial substances), lights, and sounds. Who has decided and why that these artificial sensory stimuli are better and more healing than natural elements is a pressing question? Why not touch wood and clay, plants and stones, flour and water (dough and bread), listen to birds singing and the wind whistling, or observe the natural play of the lights through tree leaves?

Most modern forms of therapy and therapy settings/spaces are created around various contemporary, artificially created materials (for example play-dough and sculpting clay, but not natural bread dough), and artificially designed processes (for example, sitting on a couch and trying to retell your life, or drawing or playing instruments as if to represent your inner world, rather than working the land and caring for plants and animals as a direct way to help you restructure and order your inner world). Having observed, as an anthropologist, traditional small-scale cultures and their traditional ecological and cultural knowledge, I am amazed that the increasingly "developed" world is coming up with new substitutes for things that have proven most useful and helpful to humankind for millennia.

The senses, which compose and affect most deeply our bodily and emotional states, are perhaps a main starting point for any healing process, whether officially called "therapy" or a process of community healing and building. Thus, the *sensory house* as a concept, though inspired by the concrete case study of the Bread Houses, could apply to any community centre or communal social space – a "third space" beyond home and work – where the activities stimulate a few or all human senses. Importantly, the sensorial stimulation should not be limited to reactionary experience (for example, watching a performance or listening to a concert), but through *active engagement* in creation. This engagement takes place through some form of co-creation rather than passive consumption of cultural, educational, or other products or services.

Out of the collective bread-making activities for mixed ages, professions, and ethnic groups, evolved a series of methods and processes of engagement, which I would define as *cross-sensorial learning* dynamics. These are based on the observations that when all senses are involved – different from the case of other artistic activities where taste especially is usually missing – people are additionally stimulated to open up and share intimate experiences, knowledge, emotions, and talents, and thus, learn together and from each other. To better understand these *mixed-group learning* (as an aspect of informal life-long learning) dynamics- but not in a didactic context- but an informal community setting, I analyse them through the theoretical framework of "experiential learning" and the formation of "communities of practice", developed by anthropologist Jean Lave (1982) and by Etienne Wenger (2002).

Many of the ways we have of talking about learning and education assume that learning "has a beginning and an end; that it is best separated from the rest of our activities; and that it is the result of teaching" (Wenger 1998:3), but in the late 1980s and early 1990s two researchers from different disciplines, anthropology and pedagogy, Jean Lave and Etienne Wenger developed a model of "situated learning[3]" that proposed how learning involves a process of engagement in a "community of practice" in various spheres of our daily lives and with various communities of people, but all these diverse kinds of knowledge are transmitted in direct personal contact and interactions, and best registered through hands-on engagement with things, people, and places.

An article on the various approaches to learning (Smith 1999) summarizes Wenger's (2007) three elements distinguishing a community of practice from other groups and communities:

> *The domain*: A community of practice is something more than a club of friends or a network of connections between people. It has an identity defined by a shared domain of interest. Membership therefore implies a commitment to the domain, and therefore a shared competence that distinguishes members from other people.

> *The community*: In pursuing their interest in their domain, members engage in joint activities and discussions, help each other, and share information. They build relationships that enable them to learn from each other.

> *The practice*: Members of a community of practice are practitioners. They develop a shared repertoire of resources: experiences, stories, tools, and ways of addressing recurring problems— in short, a shared practice. This takes time and sustained interaction.

The key here is that a community of practice involves much more than the technical skills and knowledge of a task, and what ultimately matters more, even most, to the members is their involvement in a set of relationships and common values and ways of coping with reality (Lave and Wenger 1991: 98).

I have been observing similar processes at the Bread Houses and through the Bread and Art methods in different communities and countries. People are coming together through the particular "domain" of knowledge of bread-making – traditions, recipes, stories, the *Theatre of Crumbs'* creative method, etc. Yet very soon it becomes clear in their comments, in the commitment in coming to the events where different recipes or skills are not necessarily introduced, but where instead personal stories and dreams start to be shared that collective bread-making gives them a sense of a collective identity and a constant source of informal learning much more than concrete bread-related knowledge.

The ultimate goal in these forming "communities of practice" is not bread-making itself, or bread as a food or product, but while the interest in bread has initially been the trigger to joining the community, in the long run what becomes more valuable to people is the shared "practice" of the mixture of bread-making and story-telling. I have previously referred to the relationships and networks triggered by community co-creative activities as the generation of *community creative capital* (Savova 2009). In fact, the generation of such *community creative capital* is interrelated with the formation of "communities of practice". They are a type of self-organizing system that has many characteristics of the associational life, as analysed mainly through the concept of "social capital" by Bourdieu, Robert Putnam, and others. However, the one main aspect that distinguishes *community creative capital* from other types of social or cultural capital is the regular *co-creativity*, a form of "liminoid" state that is both ritual and non-binding, and the unusual mixing of people from all walks of life inspired to engage in artistic creation out of love and searching for meaning and belonging. This is why such communal activities easily help transcend social barriers like class, economic limits, education, and different modes of behavior, thinking, and relating to others. Arts, and here I include bread-making as both an art and as a broader community creative practice, are liberating for they take people out of their standard categories, out of their comfort zone, and set them within a "liminoid" context where relationships and status categories are fairly flexible and prone to on-going restructuring.

Some art forms, in fact, emphasize specifically the need to interrupt people's comfort zones and let them enter zones that are often unknown and uncomfortable, such as the case of theatre and even more so psychodrama; in many cases, dancing as well. But other art forms, and this is particularly the case for bread-making as a form of sculpture, enable people to leave their own individual comfort zone and to collectively construct a new comfort zone that is comfortable and pleasant and stimulating to all. And this is also due to the way the smell, taste, and warmth of hot bread activate important archetypes (as Jung's psychological categories define them), or powerful associations with home and family and all of their derivatives – love, care, safety, sharing.

Communities of practice, in Lave and Wenger's analysis, also tend to create their own shared "repertoire of ideas", which include memories, vocabulary, symbols, tools, documents, and rituals that affirm the identity of the group and strengthen its shared practice (or a whole ritualized *praxis*). This is what happens also at the Bread Houses, where people have started developing their own language and gestures, related to bread-making ingredients, the stages of kneading, and baking and sharing – all evolving as metaphors and idiomatic expressions in daily life, pointing to processes and stages of relationships, of people's characteristics, and of issues in society and potential ways to cope with them. For example, a common phrase circulated among bread-making participants is that a personal or often political and social issue or situation needs to be allowed to "rise/proof", i.e. to evolve and get resolved with time.

Lave and Wenger further develop their concepts of the stages of learning, from "legitimate peripheral participation" to "full participation", through ethnographic observations of different apprenticeships (US Navy quartermasters, non-drinking alcoholics in Alcoholics Anonymous, meat-cutters, Yucatec midwives, Vai and Gola tailors). They found how initially people have to join the periphery of the communities of practice and gradually become more engaged with the main, core processes of the community. This is how they move from "legitimate peripheral participation" to "full participation" (Lave and Wenger 1991: 37), and in this sense, the key measurement indicator of the learning process is not the degrees or quality of knowledge acquisition but the degrees and quality of social engagement and participation. The main factor for participation is the situation, or the whole environment, of the learning process, and thus they define the "situational learning" process.

Similar to Lave and Wenger, over the years since 2009, I have been observing and analyzing how the Bread and Arts methods help form "communities of practice", inspired not only by the collective activity but, intriguingly, by the interesting to them diversity of the participants. At first, participants who are from minorities (such as the Roma in Bulgaria) or stigmatized communities (such as the low-income Afro-American neighborhoods) might remain at the periphery of the group, and yet even then, their participation is "legitimate peripheral participation" – they usually remain a bit to the side mainly because of their own self-awareness and insecurity rather than the others' negative behavior. However, usually only one subsequent bread-making gathering is enough to pull the previously peripheral participants to "full participation", because the informal, playful environment is conducive for people to quite easily let go of prejudices and fears, and in fact, often the diverse groups are themselves pleasantly surprised and excited that they can so easily feel free from previous stereotypes.

The role of the engagement of the senses in the stages and degrees of acquiring proximity, exchanging and thus learning and building social relations, from "legitimate peripheral participation" to "full participation", gives substance to my framework of *cross-sensorial learning.* The case of collective bread-making is a particular, in a way exemplary, case of *cross-sensorial learning*, for it engages not only all the physical senses - touch, taste, smell, sight, and hearing – but also triggers memories and associations, which could be referred to as a type of a "sixth sense" experience. As pointed out earlier, it is connected to most people's archetypal associations with home, family, and childhood memories. Intriguingly, sometimes people express what I analysed in my dissertation *Bread and Home: Global Cultural Politics in the Tangible Places of Intangible Heritage* (2013) as *non-memories*.

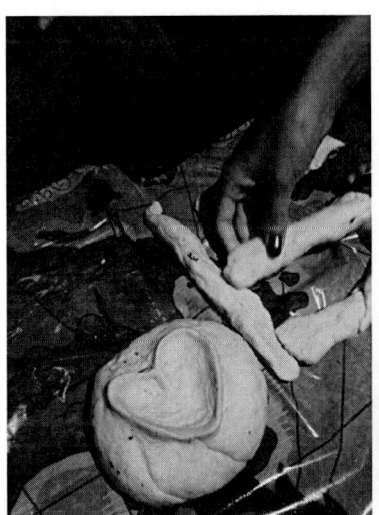

Fig. 5-5, 5-6. A young woman war-veteran in Massachusetts (USA), suffering mental trauma after the fights in Afghanistan, participates with enthusiasm in the baking after her initial skepticism – bread touches her because it reminds her of her grandmother. A young man from Harlem, NY, a hip-hop fan and possibly a gang member, also joins and becomes like a child around the dough, joking that it's better than the monetary "dough".

Non-memories refer to cases when people share that "bread reminds them of home," yet it turns out they had no actual such experience in their childhood or at present. Therefore, the *cross-sensorial learning* processes with other people seem to be producing and multiplying images and imagined scenarios for a happier past and more meaningful future.

Bread is clearly the one food that, when hot and fresh, does not leave people dispassionate, but, in the words of a middle-aged man in the USA engaged in the Princeton Bread House gatherings: "nothing can be more innocent but also more passionate than bread"! He used to describe the experiences of collective bread-making as "high-touch, rather than high-tech." In a society that is increasingly dependent on technology and often suffers distancing of real human relations due to disguised virtual proximity in online social networks, he pointed to bread-making gatherings as very much needed and useful in order to help people rediscover the meaning and joy in the basic things in life.

Observing the collective bread-making activities in particular in inter-cultural and inter-ethnic contexts (such as the USA, UK, South Africa, Peru, Spain, Austria, Tadjikistan, etc.), I realized that a key element of what makes these activities engage such diverse groups of people is the collective *doing* rather than "dialogue", and the possibility for *sharing* food, which is universally, a symbolic act and tangible experience of friendship. The activities foster both inter-generational and inter-cultural co-creation of both tangible objects and civic initiatives, projects, etc. Such processes can be defined as inter-cultural and inter-generational *doing*, rather than the concept of "inter-cultural dialogue", which is used as a common term – but often empty of substance and results – in policies and projects.

Building on the observations and lessons learned from the baking-with-metaphors activities, I started developing together with anthropology students a *cross-sensorial educational program* called « World Cultures: Cultural Anthropology for Children and Youth» to teach anthropology to the younger generations by taking them on a journey across countries in to the world where I have completed research and community projects, exploring their cultural characteristics from an anthropological perspective, and with ethnographic tools at hand. In Bulgaria, but also as far as I know in the rest of world, anthropology is not part of the core subjects studied in primary or high-school, and young people often have not even heard of the discipline until they reach university.

However, it is precisely anthropology, I would argue, that can help the young generations develop a wide, rich, open worldview, trying to understand with analytical tools and emotional intelligence the « Other » and embrace with joy that diversity from early age onward. A key distinctive component of the educational program and what makes it a *cross-sensorial learning* experience is the baking of traditional breads or pastries (and sometimes cooking) for the particular culture. The baking/cooking take place at the beginning of the lesson for about half an hour and then during the baking time the cultural information and exploration of the country and its people engage students to think and analyse, while the culminating *sharing* of the country meal enables students to taste, touch, and smell the culture and its people- and thus connect to them not only through mental but also emotional, sensorial, and bodily memory. At various levels, the participants in the learning process incorporate the information, and as such, it becomes personal.

It is important that the *cross-sensorial learning* and the *inter-cultural doing* dynamics are analysed with attention to the distinct and culturally-specific human perceptions, experiences, and reactions to distinct sensorial stimulations and situations. If research is done to analyse how artistic and out-doors education help children learn more and develop emotional intelligence, such studies involve only a certain age group – children and youth – and do not consider situations where such cultural, creative, and culinary activities could engage very different ages, professions, and ethnic groups, as well as mixed groups, as is the case of the Bread and Arts methods and their related *sensory houses* physical spaces.

I thus want to further contextualise the *cross-sensorial learning* processes and programs analysed in this auto-ethnography within the dynamics of the typically Latin-American cultural tradition and on-going movements fomenting community development through the arts, framed as "arts for social change" (*artes para la transformación social*). The innovative practices towards liberating and democratising education, both formal and informal, in Latin America were catalysed by Paulo Freire (1970), similar to the way John Dewey (1916) fomented new discourses in education in Europe and North America. Freire's last works gave birth to the concept of *Ecopedagogy*, developed as a project for new planetary values and eco-social civilization based on cooperation instead of competition, balance and harmony of human beings with themselves and with nature, towards a global culture of peace (Grigorov and Fleuri 2012). The baking-with-metaphors methods also evolved in the spirit of these global movements for social justice, and in 2012 were selected and included in the *International Handbook of Ecopedagogy* (Grigorov 2012).

The Latin American concept and movements of "arts for social change" find many modifications around countries and cultural institutions when it comes to link between arts and community development. The terms vary among CA (community arts), SAP (social art practice, focused on social change), Art Education, Applied Art, Amateur Art, Voluntary Arts, Public Art, Mainstream Art Outreach, Art therapy, Talent Development, etc., but all ultimately point to a shift in aesthetic thinking from "art for art's sake" to community-driven art (sometimes also created by professional artists but *with* communities) that emphasizes the *tools* and the *process* rather than the *form* and the *product*. However, the key problem in most community arts projects is the short-term duration and the project-based funding, which rarely allows for sustainability after the end of the project (examined in more depth by the research group at the Social Impact of the Arts project at University of Pennsylvania).

The need for locally-sensitive and long-term policies and approaches to secure any sustainable development project is what I have previously termed the *hand-shake policy* (Savova 2011a) approach, founded on long-term basic financial and methodological commitment on the part of the public authorities. The *hand-shake policy* approach applies to both formal educational and cultural institutions and informal community learning/cultural centers. Development funding institutions, whether governments, the UN and EU, or private foundations, are, however, often locally disdained for their strict requirements for "hard data" and "quantitative indicators" to "measure the outcomes" of the projects and policies, and such data is very hard to obtain particularly when it comes to soft community engagement and empowerment processes.

One conceptual framework I developed to critically analyse this outcome-measuring approach is what I define as the need for an *income-based approach* (Savova 2011b) in any development work. So-called personal "income" for people in these cases is measurable (always partially, of course) mainly through anthropological, ethnographic methods and this long-term engagement: qualitative methodologies grounded in one-on-one interviews, informal conversations, focus groups, and perhaps most importantly, keen observations of what people do not say but how they begin to interact with the situation and the community of practice in which they participate.

Rehearsals for Sustainability: Edible Public Spaces through the *Theatre of Crumbs*

Would you deny for others
What you demand for yourself?
Where you live should not decide
Whether you live or whether you die

(*U2's song "Crumbs from your table"*)

U2's song *Crumbs from your table* uses the image and metaphor of crumbs to call for equality. Bread crumbs have, in fact, long been employed in contexts of social injustice, rooted as a cultural sign back in Biblical times in the parable about poor Lazarus eating the crumbs off of the rich man's table. During the rising discourse around the economic crisis in Bulgaria and the world since the wars in Iraq and Afghanistan, I noticed how people in Bulgaria often started using the metaphor of the bread crumbs as the little, if anything, left over for the poor off of the rich ones' table – the politicians and the corporate oligarchs – after having appropriated most of the available "bread"/ "dough" (money, resources, power).

In the famous fairy tale of Hansel and Gretel, one of the key elements are the bread crumbs which the abandoned children keep shedding along their way through the forest so that they would not lose their path to return home. In this case, the semiotic aspect of the crumbs is linked not so much to social inequality (even if the children are abandoned, indeed, because of poverty) but more so to the second main association of crumbs – rooted in the symbolic connection between the signifier bread and the signified space of the home/the hearth. The association is deeply engrained in European cultures heavily dependent on wheat and bread as basic staple foods but also basic religious symbols in Christianity.

In the fairy tale, the simple bread crumbs end up having much greater importance than the whole house made of fancy sweets inhabited by the witch, since this space remains simply a house – even if unimaginably beautiful and delicious – but not a home. On the contrary, the sweet castle becomes a prison for the two siblings. What is key in the lesson the fairy tale strives to teach is that children – and in general humans – need emotional fulfillment and not simply visual (aesthetic) and material satisfactions to fill in the vacuum of intimacy. It is a vacuum that back then, but perhaps even more so now, is growing due to the decreasing role models of the parents and the disappearing sensation of home and safety.

Child psychologists have proven the crucial importance of early-age feelings of home warmth and safety for the future emotional and intellectual development of a person, and one key ritual that strengthens the experiences and memories of home is the ritual of family commensality (literally, "sharing the table", or eating together). Anthropologist Richard Wilk (2010) from Indiana University points out how the ever decreasing time spent together around the table has multiple negative and much broader social, cultural, and economic implications. He discovered how the gradual disappearance of the kitchen table is a phenomenon mostly observed among low-income and immigrant families, losing ties with their traditional cultural backgrounds and engulfed in the stress of providing for their extended families in the country of origin. Wilk observes how the lack of time to share a meal produces people who are unable to develop and sustain stable and meaningful social relations.

The same phenomenon of lack of time for commensality and thus growing alienation is growing in post-socialist Eastern Europe due to the imported forms of capitalism that imposed long working hours and high competitiveness in education and at work. It is in this socio-cultural context that the Bread House community spaces flourished in a few towns- precisely for they seem to help people rethink their life and their consumption habits (more on new consumption communities is examined in the work of Caroline Moraes, Isabelle Szmigin and Marylyn Carrigan, 2010). At the Bread Houses people often seemed to wake up- surprised at how easy it is to forget the important things in life when you are locked in the vicious cycle of work-home, and how in a third space like the Bread House, it was somehow easier to appreciate again the importance of home, sensed through the hearth and the hot bread, both as a tangible experience and as powerful symbols.

It is in this context that people started telling stories, which then also gave birth to improvised theatre plays. Similar to U2's song *Crumbs from your table*, people's discussions employed bread crumbs to signify the socio-economic inequalities in Bulgaria and these improvised "scenarios" born in the discussions around kneading inspired us to call this evolving method *Theatre of Crumbs*.

The *Theatre of Crumbs'* improvised scripts offered a fertile soil for observing and analyzing local meaning-making processes, as people discuss, enact, resolve, and digest (figuratively and literally) important issues in the politics of their daily lives and the life of the nation. The *Theatre of Crumbs* is an innovative, mixed-media theatre form, which spread from the Bread House in Gabrovo to other countries and continents as more and more got interested in being trained. The *Theatre of Crumbs* started at the round table inside the Bread House, and it later, exited in the public space outside the Bread House walls, evolving as an outdoor performance in various festivals and public events and celebrations, where the stage is a portable table. The communal table changes the public space and turns impersonal city places into personalized spaces, in particular due to its association with the private kitchen and the home. Other such "personalized spaces" are analysed by Michelle de Certeau in his « Spatial Stories » in *The Practice of Everyday Life* (1984). Intriguingly, people of all ages started taking part, and thus, animated the public spaces by making, performing and consuming these edible street puppet performances.

The dynamics of the street *Theatre of Crumbs* events is reminiscent of the processes in the trans-national project *City of Children* by Italian Francesco Tonucci. Tonucci engages children to design and present before municipalities- their visions for their city, and in particular, the needs of children for public playgrounds.

The *Theatre of Crumbs* method inspires all "spectators" to become "makers" of the dough puppets and the connected narrative. People often choose to address issues related to real-life cases – thus naturally evolving in the way Augusto Boal directed his *Theatre of the Oppressed* and the forum theatre methods. The bread puppets open the space for creative solutions and imaginings of alternative realities. Once the puppets are baked (in a small mobile electric oven), the actors arrange the breads into puppets on strings or simply hold them in their hands, and the table becomes the stage. The table itself is often covered in flour and the props or the setting of the play are depicted with fingers and wheat stalks in the flour to create a truly appealing vision. The table then becomes a stage for performances of struggles, identities, social negotiations and hopes, but it is also a stage and space of commensalities and rehearsals of coexistences as the puppet makers span all generations and socio-economic groups.

When the performances take place inside the Bread House Cultural Centre in Gabrovo, the fire in the oven is used as the background props and the bread puppets are brought to life by performing on the round table in front of the oven, through long strings that the actors control from above, where a few meters above the table is the location of the small stage perched on top of the beams holding the rooftop. This unique "flying stage" also transforms the table below into a stage around which the "spectactors", as Boal defines all improvised actors, are sitting and interactively directing the play.

The key participation of the senses of taste and smell in the *Theatre of Crumbs* performances produce a dynamic edible experience that has proven to help people open up and share problems as well as dreams, which assume a kind of material form in the performance and thus a much more tangible and achievable perspective for how they can happen in "real life". The important element of food in theatre where food is being prepared, shared, and/or related to the theme of the play adds the two additional senses of smell and taste, usually lacking in classical theatre, and thus enriching the actor-audience reciprocity.

In order to achieve maximum mobility of the community baking and *Theatre of Crumb's* events, the *Mobile Bread House* prototype was developed and built at Princeton University in the spring of 2013, using only recycled materials on a second-hand trailer. The MBH visits mainly low-income areas around Princeton (such as Trenton, NJ) and strives to engage local people in rethinking their daily lives and visions for the future.

Fig. 5-7. The Mobile Bread House built by students from Princeton University (NJ), regularly traveling to low-income neighborhoods to engage people in breaking bread and in talking about values and non-violence.

A powerful example of the particular environment conducive to peaceful dialogue that the mobile structure could inspire took place during the launching of the Mobile Bread House in Princeton in May 2013. The Princeton Mayor was invited to come, and instead of giving simply a speech, she liked the extraordinary space and the activity of bread-making so much that she sat at the table to knead dough together with anyone who happened to be there and pass by. The people ranged from Mexican immigrant janitors at Princeton University to professors and students, low-income African-Americans and prominent businessmen, children with autism and adults with physical disabilities. People were inspired to create out of the dough their visions of a better Princeton and the larger county, more inclusive, and less economically unequal and extreme in its divisions. People imagined new public buildings, parks, social institutions, services, and infrastructure that they wanted to have access to. In the words of the man who called this experience "high-touch", bread unites because "we all knead joy" – and that day with the Mayor- people of all walks of life could openly and directly voice what they needed for joy to rise.

Instead of voicing their complaints in a negative and conflictual manner, people somehow softened their voices around the dough and the fire oven, and spoke with calmness but also engaged in quite serious conversations about what has not been fulfilled and what needs to be done. The Mayor did make some concrete promises that day which those people would have probably never felt the courage or found the access to plead for, and would have never been able to be that unified and also multifaceted in their pleas – simply because there was a table around which to sit for hours and knead.

Conclusions: Breaking bread and boundaries for sustainable development

In March 2013, the President of Bulgaria, Mr. Rossen Plevneliev, visited the first Bread House community cultural centre in Gabrovo together with the Gabrovo Mayor to make bread with local people and discuss their vision of a better town and of a better country. What was intriguing to all of us is that the reason why the President came was not because I had some special high-level connections, but due to a simple invitation letter I had once sent to the Presidential cabinet, inspired to try (and having pretty much no faith that it would happen) to facilitate an informal meeting like the one with the Princeton Mayor so that the local people could voice directly their complaints, shared regularly around bread-making. The President liked the invitation and the idea so much -that he came- asking specifically that no media be invited or informed about the event. Again, bread must have spoken to the President in very personal ways – as it does for pretty much everyone.

People noted afterwards that, though they had previously not supported the President politically, on that occasion they *felt* they got to meet and know *the person* Rossen Plevneliev, not the "President", and that this gave them much more tangible sense of connection to the government and a certain self-confidence to continue voicing their needs – regardless of the fact that noting really changed after they voiced the pleas to the President. I point, in particular, to the aspect of "feeling", because people kept emphasising in their words the feelings and senses that inspired and empowered them, pointing at the shared hot tasty bread with someone they only saw on TV, at the welcoming and soothing aroma of fire, bread, and the roundtable that somewhat naturally created a sense of equality and cooperation, even if only imagined when it comes to shaping the national policies.

The shared sensorial experiences with the President, rather than a formal dry conversation which usually happens in formal public discussions with authorities, immediately made people feel empowered and much more conscious of their positions as citizens with value and also with rights. The shared senses created an experience of "affect" between those in power and those without, and at least for some time enabled people to gain a tangible sense of self-worth, of strength to strive and hope for change, no matter if concrete changes were to take place.

The complex, multi-faceted issue of sustainability addressed in this book embraces diverse and often seemingly disconnected challenges faced by people in various parts of the world, yet we can also note a connecting thread of shared questions, quests, and hopes. These quests go much beyond the standard political, ecological, and economic dimensions of the standard notions of sustainability. We note this very particularly at the local, communal and family level, and this is precisely the sphere where anthropological ethnographic research and approaches to people, data, and issues is so crucial to comprehending what sustainability *really* means to people.

As we observed in the Bread Houses and growth of the informal BREAD movement, and what is in fact evident in most social movements, both international and local, is that more and more people and communities develop new forms of consumer behaviors and structures of community organizing around a cause, usually mediated through powerful symbols and discourses.

In many ways, what this research shows is how community cultural centres and in particular, those spaces we referred to as *sensory houses,* can play important roles in local communities and serve many more purposes than informal education and artistic expression, in particular, when it comes to civil society activism and community development. Year-long director of arts centres across the UK, John English, is arguing in his *Case for the Arts* (1982:21) that "every neighborhood should have a community arts centre", with "broad programmes of socio-cultural education" to help nurture civic values and empower people as citizens. His claims and hopes are carried forward in Lane's *Arts Centres: Every town should have one* (1978), in the on-going (since 1994) Social Impact of the Arts research project at University of Pennsylvania, in Clover and Stalker (2007), and in reflected practice in the vibrant Latin American movement of arts for social transformation. As shown in this chapter with the case study of the Bread Houses, community cultural centers can vary in their activities across artistic genres, cultural traditions, social services, and mixed/inter-disciplinary activities, but the most important aspect of their work and mission is to attract and engage people across all walks of life.

When people have access to experiential learning – whether in leisure, education, or work - and importantly, within a group, a "community of practice" and wider community contexts that stimulate people's creativity and engage the senses, the *cross-sensorial learning* and inter-generational *doing* processes enable people to *feel* that the concepts and strategies of sustainable development are much more present, tangible, real, and plausible - and as such, the senses simply, one could argue, make them make much more sense.

References

Amit, Vered. Ed. *Constructing the field: Ethnographic fieldwork in the contemporary world*. London: Routledge, 2000.

Caroline Moraes, Isabelle Szmigin and Marylyn Carrigan. "Living production- engaged alternatives: An examination of new consumption communities". In *Consumption Markets & Culture* (2000)13 (3): 273-298.

Clover, D., and Joyce Stalker. *The Arts and Social Justice: Re-crafting Adult Education and Community Cultural Leadership*. Leicester: National Institute of Adult Continuing Education, 2007.

De Certeau, Michelle. *The Practice of Daily Life*. Berkeley: University of California Press, 2011(1984).

Dewey, John. *Democracy and Education. An Introduction to the Philosophy of Education*. New York: Macmillan, 1916.

English, John. *The Case for Arts Centres*. Eastbourne: John Oxford Publications, 1982.

Freire, Paulo. *Pedagogy of the Oppressed*. New York: Plenum, 1970.

Gibson-Graham, J.K. *A Postcapitalist Politics*. Minneapolis: University of Minnesota Press, 2006.

Grigorov, Stefan, and Reynaldo Fleuri. "Ecopedagogy: Educating for a New Eco-social Intercultural Perspective". In *Visão Global*, Joaçaba (2012) 15 (1-2): 433-454.

Grigorov, Stefan. ed. *International Handbook of Ecopedagogy for Students, Educators and Parents. A Project for a New Eco-Sustainable Civilization*. BCSLDE, Sofia, 2012. Accessed September 15, 2013. www.bcslde.org.

Lane, J. *Arts Centres: Every town should have one*. London: Paul Elek Press, 1978.

Lave, Jean. "A comparative approach to educational forms and learning processes". In *Anthropology and Education Quarterly* (1982*)* 13(2): 181-187.

Marcus, George E. "Ethnography in/of the world system: The emergence of multi-sited ethnography". In *Handbook on qualitative research,* edited by Norman K. Denzin and Yvonna.S. Lincoln, 383-407. London: Sage, 1995.

Savova, Nadezhda. "Bread and Home: Global Cultural Politics in the Tangible Places of Intangible Heritage." PhD diss., Princeton University, 2013.

—. "Heritage House-guarding as Sustainable Development: Community Arts and Architectures Within a World Cultural Net(work)". In *Reconstructing the House of Culture: Community, Self, and the Makings of Culture in Russia and Beyond,* edited by Brian Donahoe and Joachim Otto Habeck, 237-262. New York: Berghahn Publishers, 2011 c.

—. "The Living (Bread) Houses Network: (fish) nets, nodules, platforms". In *Networks: The Evolving Aspects of Culture in the 21st Century,* edited by Biserka Cvjeticanin, 229-247. Paris: UNESCO, 2011 b.

—. "Arm's Length and 'Hand-shake' Policies: Community Arts Alternatives to Outcome-based Development (Insights from Brazil, Bulgaria, and South Africa)". In *Culture and Local Governance* on "Culture and Sustainable Communities" (2011a) 3(1-2), guest editors Nancy Duxbury, Centre for Social Studies (CES), University of Coimbra, Portugal and M. Sharon Jeannotte, Centre on Governance, University of Ottawa, 29-41.

—. "Heritage Kinaesthetics: Local Constructivism and UNESCO's Intangible-Tangible Politics at a *Favela* Museum". In *Anthropological Quarterly,* (2009*)* 82 (2): 547–586.

—. "Community Creative Capital: UNESCO's Intangible Heritage Policy Revisited at the Bulgarian *chitalishte".* In *International Journal of the Arts in Society* (2007) (2), 193 – 203.

Smith, Mark. "The social/situational orientation to learning". In *The Encyclopedia of Informal Education,* 1999. Accessed on June 12, 2012. http://infed.org/mobi/the-socialsituational-orientation-to-learning/.

Torbert, William. "The Practice of Action Inquiry". In *Handbook of Action Research,* edited by Hilary Bradbury and Peter Reason. London: Sage, 2001.

Turner, Victor. "'Liminal' to 'Liminoid' in Play, Flow and Ritual". In *Process, Performance, and Pilgrimage: A Study in Comparative Symbology*. New Delhi: Concept Publishing Company, 1979.

Wenger, Etienne, Richard McDermott, and William Snyder. *Cultivating communities of practice: a guide to managing knowledge*. Cambridge, Mass.: Harvard Business School Press, 2002.

Wilk, Richard. "Power at the Table: Food Fights and Happy Meals". In *Cultural Studies ↔ Critical Methodologies* (2010) 10: 428-436.

Notes

[1] See more at <www.international3c.org>.

[2] "Culture (Not) for Everyone", European ShortCut Meeting of the European Network for Cultural Centers. Warsaw, Poland. November 16, 2011. Interview conducted by Dr. Nadezhda Savova-Grigorova.

[3] See more at http://www.infed.org/biblio/communities_of_practice.htm.

CHAPTER SIX

THE ADEQUATE RESPONSE TO A DISASTER: EU REGULATIONS AND TRADITIONAL ECOLOGICAL KNOWLEDGE IN HARMONY AND IN CONFLICT

ELYA TZANEVA

"Anthropology of Disasters" is a relatively new domain of anthropological research, especially in national anthropological and ethnological schools that have just recently opened research towards general international subjects. Until recently, the Bulgarian scholarly tradition neglected disasters as a major area of study, and even now the research on hazards, calamities and critical situations is still considered an emerging field. Among the first bibliographical impulses for the development of this field were the observations followed by analysis of a small group of disaster researchers established among the American ethnologists and social anthropologists in the mid-1980s. Their studies have been recently revealed in two model books edited by the founders of this research subject, A. Oliver-Smith and S. M. Hoffman (1999), A. Oliver-Smith (1996), S. M. Hoffman and A. Oliver-Smith (2002) which, have all been well received in professional Bulgarian circles. The specialised and the more general anthropological journals with international reputations, such as *Disasters, Anthropology Today* and *Annual Review of Anthropology*, with their growing interest in this research field, also serve as guiding lights.

The ethnological study of crises and disasters began developing within Bulgarian post socialist anthropology mainly as a result of some dramatic natural, bio and technological catastrophes at the beginning of the new millennium; this forced ethnologists to collect and study numerous examples of the ways in which crises, disasters and extreme situations manifest themselves in individuals' and collectives' lives. In Bulgarian society, social crises are more visible than natural and biological ones. They appear to derive from the new stage in the country's development— the post socialist period and country's transition into European democratic institutions, signifying that for all EU members the measures to be taken in similar cases were predetermined, and the reaction especially of the new members was closely monitored. In addition, the last decade's earthquakes, floods, droughts, extreme snowfalls, the Bird-Flu threat in 2006, and especially the Foot-and-Mouth Disease outbreak in 2011, and cattle-measles in 2013, have caused high anxiety and asked for maximum mobilization of physical and cultural resources throughout society. Statistical data has established that handling the consequences of disasters is more likely to be successful when there is greater consideration of the specifics of the ethno and national characteristics of the population concerned. It became obvious for the Bulgarian social sciences that ethnologists should have a legitimate place among the researchers of crises, at least, insofar as they study the psychological, cultural and historical prerequisites for overcoming a crisis.

In the view of Bulgarian ethno-ecologists, this new field of anthropological study involves theorizing on disasters, building possible models of their genesis, development, prevention, reaction and consequences. These scholarly efforts should point at effective mechanisms developed in human history and culture which have to be studied, improved and encouraged with the purpose of guaranteeing individuals' and groups' survival. Most frequent crises are those of natural, biological and technological characters and their study from a historical and anthropological point of view infers the extent to which people are capable of combating them and overcoming their consequences. The crises have their causes and often, even explanations held within the parameters of their geneses, fitting in suitable social niches, opened by the vulnerability of the society. Therefore, these parameters are part of the history, culture and mentality of a society and their study, aimed in the final count, at building protective mechanisms, is a serious and topical scholarly challenge for the Bulgarian ethnologists involved.

When striking, disasters form a more or less defined "critical situation"— a phenomenon resembling a wave that embodies a large scale of factors, consequences, cataclysms and social change. This is true because a 'single disaster' that culminates into a solitary event does not exist. Heavy precipitations (rainfall, snowfall, hailstorms) always cause the death of livestock and force population and livestock movement, earthquakes bring about tsunamis and nuclear catastrophes, droughts are usually followed by famine, landslides by massive destruction; epidemics and pandemics, during demographic crises, could result in the serious displacement of people and working forces, etc. Some contemporary disasters have a longer life-cycle than others. They develop and act gradually, such as climate and bio-disasters, and present complex problems associated with the arid areas as well as the spread of diseases. Because of their longer presence in a population's life they are often documented in verbal forms or narratives of different kinds, and they appear in traditional culture and provoke rational or irrational prevention and coping strategies for future disasters.

In the case of Bulgaria, the character of the traditional culture—complex, mainly agrarian and self-sufficient—enables the country to indirectly develop a well-preserved system for keeping balance and sustainability during long periods of disaster. Troubles that mostly affect a community life are diseases that strike livestock. The recent appearance of such diseases, and the dubious ability to successfully cope with them, is the reason why Bulgarian ethnologists have turned to this theme. When constituting the initial group for disaster study, the Bulgarian ethnologists chose to interpret the disaster as a, "process/event involving the combination of a potentially destructive agent(s) from the natural and/or technological environment and a population in socially and technologically produced conditions of vulnerability" (Smith 1996: 303-328). In the first two co-published volumes on disasters with fellows-ethnologists from China, Russia and the USA (Tzaneva, Fang and Liu 2009; Tzaneva, Fang and Schmitt 2012), each author applied this definition to their own disaster-situation, presenting its social context.

My field-work on the subject was associated with the cases of livestock epidemics in Bulgaria in 2011 (on FMD: Tzaneva 2012: 139-161), and in 2013 (on cattle-measles: fakti.bg/bulgaria). Both situations occurred in the south-east of the country, and presented serious challenges to local sustainability. It was broadly announced that the animals were to be *"humanely euthanized"* (sofiaecho.com). The villagers gathered and requested a vaccine but were, however, told that the EU regulations prohibit the export of meat from vaccinated cattle. In the first mass case, more than 7000 animals, including cows, bulls, sheep and goats, were slaughtered, whereas in the other (which was a single and isolated case in the villages of Stoilovo and Kochan) more than one hundred sheep and goats were destroyed. The ethnological investigation was made about six months after the outbreak, and some results are described and analysed in a quoted thematic volume.[1] One of the conclusions was that two opposing groups were visible among the 'actors' in the events: the proponents of slaughter of the livestock (central officials), and the victims of these measures (the villagers, owners of domestic stock). Local officials are subjectively sympathetic to the second group, although they have rationally supported the decision of the officials. During the first crisis, proponents of the slaughter emphasized its capacity to eliminate the disease from the area, and claimed that it was the only effective way to achieve this. Alternative policies of isolation and vaccination were not considered at any stage of the crisis. No discussion regarding whether the slaughter, isolation of infected animals or vaccination represented the more appropriate response for Bulgaria's previous 2001 outbreak was considered—and the animals were killed in some of the villages on one of the most celebrated days in winter, the Day of St. Ivan, January 7th. The villagers experienced a traumatic loss because they were convinced the stock was healthy, "We were not sure that all the animals were sick"; "only the feet were damaged; it has happened before and it is curable, we know how to heal this" (AIEFEM, 931—III: 23). Two years later, in the fall of 2013, the villages of Stoilovo and Kochan in the area had their *"Black Saturday"*, September 21st, and again the breeders and owners were convinced that the stock was healthy, and quarantined it for a few days to treat the infected animals with their traditional means. The reaction from the breeders was identical as before—cries and suffering, *"What should I do now?"* asked an elderly man. "I was selling milk, until yesterday I've cared for 40 animals; today I am empty-handed and have nothing. How will I cope?" In the whole area, the plea of the population for a vaccine and time for application of traditional practices was not taken into account, which caused sorrowful moments and situations, widely described and discussed in the media. In both cases, lessons from the past and the suggestions from the culture—both from the sphere of traditional ecological knowledge and from the traditional beliefs—rational or not, were ignored.[2] Similar to cases in the UK during the 2001 outbreak of the epidemic, a symbolic line was drawn around the affected community, creating a zone that made the people in it feel confused and different from the people outside.

   This chapter is an attempt to look at the FMD and cattle-measles situation in south-east Bulgaria, a collection of information encoded in the traditional culture, and to answer the question of whether it is possible to develop a model for successful behaviour for coping with disasters based on cultural traditions whilst leaving the political aspect behind (i.e. relations with Turkey as a believed centre of infection). This study is more empirically (or ethnographically) driven, and some guiding lights from the rich UK literature on the subject of the FMD epidemic in 2001, and its investigation, have been used (Mort et al. 2004; 2005). It provides contextual understanding of the meaning and importance of these epidemics to Bulgarian local breeders. Structurally, the paper is based on a follow up to the 'three-step' process leading to a formation of traditional ecological knowledge—observations-practices-beliefs/rituals. Therefore, within the scholarly discipline, it investigates the impact of anthropologies of sustainability on environmental injustices. A significant part comprises the Bulgarian calendric rituals and cultural practices of everyday life associated with livestock, particularly with prevention and healing of diseases, and the traditional ecological knowledge embedded in them. Not surprisingly, these rituals and practices are largely presented in the culture because of the importance of stockbreeding as one of the major economic forms in Bulgarian traditional society besides agriculture.

Stockbreeding was the main economic activity for those that lived in proximity of the country's many mountains - in the Balkan Mountain Range, the Rhodopes, Mount Pirin and Strandja. In reality, stockbreeding as a supporting and alternative economic form besides agriculture is as old as human life in these areas. Homer called this region *"a Mother of sheep."* During the past number of centuries, the central subdivisions of stockbreeding gradually developed, mainly cattle breeding (including horse breeding, buffalo breeding), sheep breeding (including goat breeding), and poultry. For centuries, the villagers produced meat, wool and dairy products. The households were organized into nomadic and settled farms, with the stock also being used in the households for work on the fields.[3] A significant part of the male population in the area formed a stable community of quasi-nomadic cattle-breeders. Their lives followed the nomadic seasonal cycle of raising the herds in high mountain pastures during the winter, and the low plain pastures during summer, in conformity with the life cycle of the animals. "Winter" on the plain, both for the nomads and for quasi-nomads, covers the period between the feast day of St Demetrius (October 26th), and the feast day of St George (May 6th), when sheep are impregnated, and offspring are born and grow strong, whereas 'the summer', from the feast day of St George, the Assumption of the Holy Virgin, August 15th, to the feast of the field workday of St Demetrius, is the time for breeding the stock and production of dairy produce in high mountain pastures. Spending almost the whole year with the stock in close proximity and relationships of mutual dependence, the breeders, "had a chance to observe and experience all possible troubles that occurred with the animals" (Boneva 2009: 129-130). These observations and experiences have accompanied efforts to preserve herds and livestock during dangerous epidemics, and include detailed knowledge about the behaviour of the livestock, the anatomy and physiology of the animals, and methods of treating broken legs and other troubles, diseases and epidemics, etc. Many so-called "shepherds' stories" documented in the nineteenth and early twentieth centuries, contain records of such knowledge (Shishkov 1912: 4-10). Similar practices were developed within the local communities. It was only a matter of time before the practices accumulated into a logical and subordinated rational system- that turned out to be an adaptive response to the critical situation, which was later transmitted to subsequent generations.

This recent field-work presents the following state of ecological knowledge regarding the livestock's disease situation in the researched area.

Observations: The local breeders are well aware that the massive dying out of domestic life in the past was caused by epidemic diseases, indicated in the traditional culture of the Bulgarians as a pestilence [*"mor"*]. The pestilence in livestock is mentioned in many ancient soothsaying-books after the ninth century, and relevant ritual practices were presented in traditional customs. Foot-and-Mouth disease (known by the local name of *"Shap"* in Bulgarian) is known in the culture of the population in Strandja (as well as in the whole ethnic territory) as an infectious disease which spreads very quickly especially in rainy weather, and can easily turn into *"mor"* (considered a deadly epidemic). The symptoms are recognized from a wounded mouth and drooling when the animal cannot eat, and subsequently, weakens within a couple of days. Wounds appear on its ankles, becoming infected, and any movement is often impossible. The animal cannot move its extremities even after the disease alleviates, and may become lame. Field materials indicate that today the majority of breeders are aware that FMD is highly contagious, but that it cannot harm people. They believe that it now has mainly economic consequences:

> It mostly affects the cattle: pigs get free from this virus on the 21st day of the infection, but the cows, goats and sheep are weak and they die of it; although some stay alive and carry the virus, having for a longer time inflammations and drooling, blisters and mouth wounds, also nail dropping. It destroys the livestock, and the economy suffers. (AIEFEM 931—III: 39)

The breeders in the village of Kosti, where all livestock was killed, did not avoid any initial signs of the disease. They had a sharp eye on the stock and immediately noticed the first symptoms:

> We are well aware that drooling can be caused by other diseases, they are there all the time, and we know this from the past. FMD was fabricated by

the concessioners—they are Bulgarians from a Turkish background who come here during the weekends for hunting (AIEFEM 931—III: 51).

In the neighbouring village of Brodilovo, the FMD recalls memories of a different form:

> Shap came in 1939, remembers an older breeder. Then we had about 200 pairs of oxen for the fields. When the disease appeared, the vets came and ordered vaccination. Nobody killed an animal, and in each house we kept and healed the animals because they fed the children (AIEFEM, 931—III: 10).

My impression is that those memories are very exact because they are all personal:

> I remember my grandpa Assen, who had 2 oxen who got sick—it was Shap, a disease on the legs when their hooves were dropping, the only thing he knew was the so-called "blue stone". He used it and one of the oxen was cured, the other died, and we bought another one to make a pair. After this, my grandpa always prepared money for a vaccine, and had no problems. Also, about 15 years ago, in the democracy, again from Turkey another disease was transmitted—we called it "a blue tongue", affecting the sheep. The vets then killed the infected sheep, but all the other livestock was vaccinated and the problem went away. My father was a breeder. I know from him, if *Shap* comes, separate the sick animal, and watch it. In most cases this cures it, if not, only then you kill it, but never the healthy stock (AIEFEM 931—III: 11-16).

A woman, the daughter of a breeder, and a mother of a young man, who had the biggest herd in the village purchased with the help of European funding and developed by EU-regulations, shared that the first treatment for a lame sheep was to put the leg in a jar with a "blue stone" and bandage it, even without a vaccine. She recognizes the new requirements, however, insisting that, "our region will die without the breeding. And if we don't have the vaccine allowed, it is lost" (AIEFEM 931—III: 19-26).

The stories are the same in the whole area, and the conclusion is identical:

> In 1955 my grandfather had two small cows. One day my father, who fed them, said to him: 'Daddy, the cow's nail has fallen.' We did not do anything, but we knew it might be this disease … Then we used a vaccine. In a short time, the cow was cured. This is the problem: not all the animals were sick. We should have used a vaccine before killing them all
> (AIEFEM, 931—III: 16-17).

Similar knowledge was present in the villages with the spread of cattle-measles (locally known as: *"Sipanitza"* or *"Tzveteto"*) in 2013. Memories of the disease and how to avoid or cure it are also registered. The breeders recognize the disease as highly contagious-one that can kill the whole herd. Its' well-known symptoms are the following: red buds appear on the naked parts inside the legs and the belly of the sheep, as big as a lentils grain (Kolev 2005). Stressed by the official reaction, the people from the affected villages, Stoilovo and Kochan, are afraid the disease will come back that, and the actions will be the same:

> We don't want compensations, we want livestock, and permission to vaccinate it as in the past… Also, we were told the stock was not killed, it was deadened. I don't want to debate with people who do not understand the problem and only stick to documents and hide behind bureaucratic paragraphs missed by them when they signed the rules with the EU, and now don't know how to get rid of the situation (news.burgas24.bg).

Understandably, FMD and cattle-measles were not unfamiliar to the population. In the past, many of the ways of dealing with and explaining the diseases developed through both mythology and rationale. The more recent 'modern' response consists of regular vaccinations, separation and careful observation of the cattle. What is noticeable is that people actually did recognize both the FMD and the cattle-measles as costly and dangerous plagues. The reason they do not agree with the slaughter is their conviction that the majority of the animals have been healthy. "Stop killing the stock, heal it or let us heal it," was the appeal of the breeders. A possible conclusion here is the need for detailed explanatory work among the breeders. The officials who conducted the killings still owe the villagers in Strandja an explanation as to why vaccination was not preferred as a more civilized and economically beneficial policy. They also have to try to understand the prevailing perception of the affected people that slaughter is a backward and unethical method supported by a minority of official representatives, who sought to advance their own interests at the expense of villagers and the stockbreeding community as a whole.

Traditional practices: The breeders shared their experience in interviews after the epidemics.[4] The diseases are fought by treating the mouth and the tongue of the sick animal with infusions of a common balm; the whole mouth cavity is spread with warm honey, often mixed with alum. Special herbs—one known as *"shapiche"* (after the name of the disease), the other a special mushroom *"chanterelle"*—are put into the food or the hooves are washed. These herbs are collected through a particular ritual on St. George's Day (May 6th) and Midsummer's Day

(June 24th), and are kept for healing and prevention purposes for both animals and people for the whole year (Bulgarska 2013: 1077). Fire is a constant way of healing. Also, animal's legs are washed with cold water and then tarred, or smeared with *"blue stone"* or a mixture of tar and lard, and the ankles and legs are sprinkled with live coals and hot ashes to *"singe the disease."* The explanation is that the animal is *"startled"* by the fire, and the disease *"burns low."* The sick animal is fed with bran soaked in water and sea salt. With the idea of prevention perhaps, the saliva of the sick animal is smeared on healthy animals' mouths (AIEFEM 931—III: 20-25). In the case of cattle-measles, the first measure is to sprinkle the sick animal with an infusion of tobacco leaves, and to feed it with oat straw and bran. If the sheep is still healthy, to prevent the disease a silk thread covered in the blood of an infected animal is passed through its tail and/or ears. The breeder does this in a complete silence. In other parts of the country, the first dead sheep should be buried in the soil of the neighbouring village, as it is believed that the disease will also go to the neighbours (Bulgarska 2013: 1079).

The traditional knowledge of the breeders offers alternative ways of treatment and perspectives based on their own locally developed practices of resource use. This knowledge concerns a small segment of practical issues but is formed within the process of monitoring, responding and managing ecosystem processes and functions, with special attention to ecological resilience. Both FMD and cattle-measles studies revealed that there exists a diversity of local traditional practices for ecosystem management. These practices are not only part of the acclaimed "intangible cultural heritage," but also valuable data needed to ensure the survival of people and their environments. They include observations and experiences- that in time turned into adaptations for the generation, accumulation and transmission of knowledge. Nevertheless, the social mechanisms behind these processes for each discrete group, including the cattle breeding community in Strandja, are a specific combination of knowledge, belief, cultural value and action. So, there is a component of local observational knowledge, a component of practice in a way people carry out their resource use activities, and further, a component of belief regarding how people fit into or relate to the prevailing eco-system. In short, in this case traditional knowledge is a knowledge-practice-belief complex (Berkes, Colding and Folke 2000). These three sides are embodied/encoded in the ritual.

The Ritual: As revealed in the literature- sick animals were also treated with sorcery. Before sunrise, the breeder takes the sick animal to a river or the water source of another village. The sorcerer finds three leaves, three willow sticks and three blades of grass, dips them in the water and touches the animal's mouth with them, saying special words. Many different rituals with special requirements for the participants in the ceremony are remembered. In some cases, they were gypsies, who were naked while making fire by rubbing together two sticks; then they forged a metal stick and an old man from the village ticked off the sick livestock with it (Bulgarska 2013: 602). The whole village celebrated the next day by organizing a sacrificial *"kurban"* (an offering of ritual food), sharing it with the animals. The sacrificial offerings included a male lamb or an ox and the cooking of a common feast out of the village or in a certain place (such as a Christian temple, at some central place). Another practice, meant to protect and heal, involves putting crushed apple into cattle's food.

In some areas of South Bulgaria, a prevention ritual was performed on the night of a full moon, referred to as treatment by *"Live"* or *"God's Fire."* Two stacks were lit and the sheep were squeezed between them, being carefully watched (Bulgarska 2013: 1076). With a healing and protective purpose, cattle were drawn between the two shores of a river and taken through glowing embers. When *"Mor"* happened the cattle were driven through a hole that was dug under the root of a solitary tree- or at the border of a neighbouring village, wide enough to score the fattest animal. During this ritual, all home fires in the houses were doused, and a *"New Fire"* was produced in a village by two left-handed men or by two children with the same name- by rubbing together two sticks of hazel bush. With this *"New Fire" or "God's Fire,"* a stake for each home was lit. Animals were pushed through the hole one after another towards the *"foreign land."* The persons who lit the fire passed their hands over the animals—across their tails, ears and heads, or smeared their backs with tarred staffs. At the end, all participants in the ritual also squeezed through the hole, and fed the animals with salt in the borders of the *"foreign land,"* after which all returned home with new firebrands and made a *"New Fire"* there (Shishkov 1909-1910: 5-11).

In the second decade of the twenty-first century, the breeders in Strandja, have recollections of the role of this "Live/God's/New Fire":

> We also have it. I know from my parents that Live Fire was lit during the "Spanish War"—it happened on the place by the village with the same name. Some men from the village lit it. The Live Fire was "caught" by rubbing two pieces of wood together, after which the whole village together with the livestock passed through the fire, and the sickness was stopped (AIEFEM, 931—III: 23-26).

The practice is widely considered useful in the contemporary crisis as well: *"But now, with the Shap, they did not give us time to do the Live Fire."*

To prevent disease, ritual acts were performed throughout the calendar and business holiday cycle. The fertility and good health of the animals were achieved in the area by the stockbreeders through cults for certain saints—St Vlas, St George, St Haralampy, St Modest, St Petka, St Todor and others (Etnografia 1985: 222-224). Together with these specialized days for celebrating the health of the livestock, on many other days this idea was indirectly celebrated, such as on the days of St Ignatius (December 20th), or Marta (March 1st). In the villages struck by the recent epidemics, some special patrons of the stock are celebrated with particular festivities.

St Modest, or *Modesti,* is considered a patron and protector of cattle and other domestic animals. His cult is wide spread in Romania and Greece as well, and he is venerated in Strandja- where cattle breeding is the major means of livelihood. His day is celebrated by giving out small bread for cattle's health. The cattle are not set to work on this day (Bulgarska 2013: 596). In the research site-Kosti, most severely affected by the slaughter in 2011, there is an icon of the saint located in the old church. The icon represents a pastoral scene of St. Modest with typical features and vestments, including a richly decorated golden omophorion and epigonation, holding a Gospel in his hand. The saint is painted with the scattered figures of domestic animals as a background. His position in the church's interior is close to the main locally celebrated saints St. George, St. Demetrius, St. Constantin and St. Elena. In their search for help and solutions, the villagers have often returned to their religious traditions. In accordance with a long-existing tradition, they celebrate the Day of St. Modest on December 18, believed until now that he is a protector of the livestock (Grebenarova 1996: 312-320). The last celebration of the Day of St. Modest, called *Modesti* by the villagers, was in the 1980s. An elderly woman of Kosti remembers that this last celebration was devoted to the livestock's health. In almost every home, ritual bread called *"arto"* (consisting of five small round breads) was baked. The women brought it into the church, lit candles in front of the icon of the saint and placed the bread together with boiled wheat and wine. After the liturgy all the food was given out to the villagers and *"the stock were healthy."* The same women now think that the villagers are not true believers and that this is the reason for the disease. They claim that, "we didn't save the old church bell [which was stolen] and we don't follow Christian rules strictly … also some of our priests are greedy" (AIEFEM

931—III: 23—24). They want to *"make things right,"* which includes their intention to *"make a kurban,"* a ritual sacrifice, usually involving a domestic animal. They are also ready to make a *"Live Fire"* in a ritualistic way by observing the special rules from old times. They believe- that because in the winter of 2011- the disaster spread very quickly, they did not have the opportunity to organize such a protective ritual. In the villages of Kosti, Brodilovo, Stoilovo and others, the constant observation of religious practices for the livestock's health is considered a condition for revival of the cattle breeding in the region (AIEFEM 931, III: 23-25).

The materials presented show the existence of a present-day combination of observations, practices and rituals which is generally consistent with adaptive management as an integrated method for dealing with the diseases. It is adaptive because it acknowledges that environmental conditions that produce the diseases' conditions change, requiring the breeders to respond by adjusting and evolving. In this process, they chose to engage their inherited experience and are willing to synchronize it with the modern level of social management.

With respect to the population in Strandja, the conclusion must be made that that people actually did recognize both diseases as being dangerous. They did not try to avoid the seriousness of the case, and were ready to organize themselves in order to deal with it. They were aware that the situation would endanger the Bulgarian reputation on the European market, and were patriotic enough not to contribute to it. The reason they contradicted the slaughter policy was their conviction that the majority of the animals were healthy. Therefore, the official response to the disease reflects in this case the governing style of Bulgarian leaders, particularly in their relation to the EU, by obeying its directives and rules rapidly and categorically, without considering the uniqueness of the situation affecting traditional values. In fact, measures should also have been selected regarding broader social, economic, political, cultural and geographical concerns. If, on economic and scientific grounds, the central authorities had a strong case for using the prescribed *"slaughter-policy"*, their choice should also have been underpinned by the moral, cultural and ethno-historical convictions of the population affected.

As the crisis deepened in each village in the area, people prayed for a return to earlier, well-known traditions, related to memories passed down through the generations. Such traditions included methods of isolating sick animals, observing them, and deciding their fate accordingly. These calls and prayers were never taken into account. This negligence indicates a lack of understanding that there is a social mechanism behind those traditional practices and experiences, which includes a number of successful adaptations for the generation, accumulation and transmission of useful knowledge. Therefore, the local communities (e.g. the stockbreeding community) can provide the Bulgarian policymakers with adequate rules for social regulation based upon traditional cultural values in a more successful combination with the requirements of the recently established political responsibilities.

The 2011 FMD disaster unfolded within a landscape and century-old culture of the peasant population in Strandja. The scale of memories of the disease evidences the importance of this mass cultural experience for the population. Through this experience, people understand how their lifestyle impacts the elements of the environment and, in turn, how the environment (even a very small part of it concerning the domestic livestock) impacts health and prosperity. This experience is significant because it derives from practice (observations), is embodied in mythological-ritualistic forms (beliefs, symbols, rites and ceremonies) and ends up in the practice again (re-establishment of a healthy life-cycle). Contemporary reactions to the FMD epidemic developed in partial conformity with the cultural knowledge of the affected communities-which focuses on people, on who they are, what they do and the reasons for their actions. People are seen, in this interpretation, as key factors for sustainable solutions, which is the core of anthropological understandings of environmental issues.

In the case discussed, the government handling, and the overall public face of the epidemic (moulded by the official reports), overexposed the events where infection was confirmed, and livestock had to be killed. The official statistics and discussions left behind the huge unpublished numbers of culls, which took place because of proximity or dangerous contact. This study shows that the disaster's impact brings up not only practical (political and economic), but also ethical dilemmas. This serious amount of presumably healthy livestock must be treated with sensitivity and respect regarding the knowledge and practices accumulated from the past and proven to work during the years. If such a situation appears in Bulgaria in the future, local talks should be held before culling to avoid the reported frustration of the affected community, and to provide feedback to all sides of participants, i.e. breeders/practitioners and policymakers/executing administration. In similar cases, anthropological investigation is helpful because it may offer a real-life tool for a more adequate exploration of mandatory reactions as prescribed. This reaction should be equally suitable for the politicians and those who had to carry out the consequences of the prescribed policy. Therefore, a further (possibly funded) research study into the social consequences of the epidemic is needed, with a special accent on its human impact. Such studies will contribute to developing a holistic understanding of how the Bulgarians interact with their environment, and how they did so in the past and explore the concept of resilience in their society and culture in its continuity.

References

Berkes, Fikret, Johan Colding, and Carl Folke. "Rediscovery of Traditional Ecological Knowledge as Adaptive Management." *Ecological Adaptations* 10 (5) (2000): 1251–1262.
Boneva, Tanya. "Bulgarian Traditional Ecology." In *Disasters, Culture, Politics: Chinese-Bulgarian Anthropological Contribution to the Study of Critical Situations*, edited by Elya Tzaneva, Fang Sumei, and Liu Mingxin. 123–148. Newcastle: Cambridge Scholars Publishing, 2009.
Bulgarska, *Bulgarska narodna medizina. Encyclopedia.* [Bulgarian Folk Medicine. Encyclopaedia]. Sofia. 2013. Etnografia, *Etnografia na Bulgaria* [Ethnography of Bulgaria], Vol. III, Sofia, 1985.
Grebenarova, Slava. "Kalendarni obichai I obredi" ["Calendar Rites and Customs"]. In *Strandja. Materialna I Duhovna Kultura.* [*Strandja Material and Spiritual Culture*], 305–361. Academic Publ. House. Sofia. 1996.
Hoffman, Susanna & Anthony Oliver-Smith (eds.). Catastrophe and Culture: The Anthropology of Disaster. Santa Fe, School of American Research Press, 2002.
Kolev, Nicolay. *Kritichni situacii, svetogled I povedenie na bulgarite* [*Critical Situations, Worldview and Behaviour of the Bulgarians*]. Veliko Turnovo, Faber, 2005.
McConnell, Allan and Alastair Stark. "Foot-and-Mouth 2001: The Politics of Crisis Management." *Parliamentary Affairs* 55 (4) (2002): 664–681.
Mepham, Ben "Foot and Mouth Disease and British Agriculture: Ethics in a Crisis." *Journal of Agricultural and Environmental Ethics* 14 (2001): 339–347.
Mort, Maggie, Ian Convery, Cathy Bailey, and Josephine Baxter. The Health and Social Consequences of the 2001 Foot & Mouth Disease Epidemic in North Cumbria. *Report to the Department of Health, Lancaster University.* Report Ref: 121|7499(2004).
Mort, Maggie, Ian Convery, Josephine Baxter, and Cathy Bailey. "Psychosocial effects of the 2001 UK foot and mouth disease epidemic in a rural population: qualitative diary based study." *British Medical Journal* 31:1234 (26 November), doi:10.1136/bmj.38603.375856.68 (published 7 October 2005)

Mort, Maggie, Ian Convery, Josephine Baxter, and Cathy Bailey. "Psychosocial effects of the 2001 UK foot and mouth disease epidemic in a rural population: qualitative diary based study." *British Medical Journal* 31:1234 (26 November), doi:10.1136/bmj.38603.375856.68 (published 7 October 2005)

Oliver-Smith, Anthony. "Anthropological Research on Hazards and Disasters." *Annual Review of Anthropology* 25 (1996): 303–328.

Oliver-Smith, Anthony and Susanna Hoffman (eds.). *The Angry Earth: Disaster in Anthropological Perspective.* New York: Routledge. 1999.

Shishkov, Stoyu. "Sledi ot kulta na oganya v Rodopite" ["Traces of the Cult of Fire in the Rhodopes"]. *Rodopski napredak* [*Rhodope Advancement*] 5 (1909–1910): 5–11.

Shishkov, Stoyu. "Zhivotnite v svetogleda na rodopskite poseleniya" ["Animals in the World Outlook of the Rhodope Settlements"]. *Rodopski napredak* [*Rhodope Advancement*] 4, 5, 7, 10 (1912).

Tzaneva, Elya. "Responding to Food-and-Mouth-Disease in Bulgaria in 2011." In Tzaneva E., Fang S. and E. Schmit (eds.), *Disasters and Cultural Stereotypes.* Newcastle: Cambridge Scholars Publishing, 2012: 142–164.

Tzaneva Elya., Fang Sumei and Liu Mingxin. (eds.). *Disasters, Culture, Politics: Chinese-Bulgarian Anthropological Contribution to the Study of Critical Situations.* Newcastle: Cambridge Scholars Publishing, 2009.

Tzaneva Elya, Fang Sumei and Edwin Schmitt (eds.). *Disasters and Cultural Stereotypes.* Newcastle: Cambridge Scholars Publishing, Newcastle, 2012.

Archives

AIEFEM, 931–III "Foot-and-Mouth-Disease in Southeastern Bulgaria 2011." Collected by E.Tzaneva in July 2011, 102 p.

Official documents

Council Directive 2003/85/EC of September 29, 2003 on Community measures for the control of foot-and-mouth disease repealing Directive 85/511/EEC and Decisions 89/531/EEC and 91/665/EEC and amending Directive 92/46/EEC (1). November 22, 2003 EN Official Journal of the European Union L 306/1. http://eur-lex.europa.eu/

European Parliament, Conclusions of the rapporteur, Temporary Committee on Foot-and-Mouth Disease (2002). Available from:

http://www. europarl.eu.int/meetdocs/committees/fiap.

Internet Resources

http://eu.vlex.com/vid/foot-mouth-disease-repealing-decisions-
37788088http://news.burgas24.bg/464399.html

Notes

[1] It is the author's conviction that comparative analysis between settlements with a different degree of loss as a result of the disease can provide useful considerations about the effectiveness of the measures taken. Therefore, applying the anthropological idea of centre-periphery research, three villages within a close proximity to each other but with rather different fates in regard to the disaster were picked. The village of Kosti was directly hit and suffered severe losses. The village of Brodilovo neighbours Kosti, but was only partly affected. The village of Bulgari is located further away and was left untouched by FMD. Each settlement reacted differently to the disease, and these reactions reveal important characteristics of human adaptation to crisis, strategies of overcoming it and further survival (Tzaneva 2012: 139-161).

[2] By this time the Bulgarian administration was extremely sensitive to the EU's opinion in the context of its recently granted membership (at the beginning of 2007). For all EU members, the measures to be taken in similar cases were predetermined (eur-lex.europa.eu; europarl.eu.int). They haven't changed even after some "classical" EU countries (as the UK) expressed dissatisfaction with regulations concerning the severe measures regarding sick livestock (McConnell & Stark 2002: 664—681; Mepham 2001). These regulations say that in the event of an outbreak of FMD, the affected Member State must immediately put in place the measures laid down in EU Directive 2003/85/EC of September 29, 2003. This includes the culling and destroying of all susceptible livestock on the infected holding, tracing and destroying meat and other products from the infected holding, placing strong restrictions on the movement of people, vehicles or other animals in the area surrounding the infection, and cleansing and disinfecting the affected holding and any vehicles or equipment which entered that holding (eu.vlex.com 2003).

[3] In the area of Strandja mountain as part of the Balkan nomadic stockbreeding, seasonal migration of the herds of cattle, sheep and goats between the summertime and wintertime pastures was a long existing practice, the population been migrating with their herds along established routes (Boneva 2009: 128-129).

[4] These interviews have been conducted and archived in conformity with the specifics of field-work done in other countries by anthropological investigation of similar situations (Mort et al 2004, 2005).

PART III:

TOWARDS AN URBAN SUSTAINABILITY

CHAPTER SEVEN

RESTORING NATURE, RENEWING THE CITY: LOCAL NARRATIVES AND GLOBAL PERSPECTIVES ON URBAN SUSTAINABILITY

REBEKAH MCCABE

Introduction

Urban sustainability is in the spotlight. That the greater portion of the world's human population now live in cities is a fact widely repeated, underlining growing concern over the impact of urbanization on the natural environment. In the city, as in other arenas, the term sustainability references a diverse range of activities, from the management of urban infrastructure and shifting consumption habits, to the redesign of urban space and demands for environmental justice. Sustainability is pursued on two fronts: as a practical endeavour, invoking bio-scientific expertise to overcome the limits placed on humans by finite natural resources, and as an object of social reform, imploring people to question how they regard those limits and to shift their behaviour to lessen negative impact on the world.

There are obvious differences between these two field sites that need to be acknowledged. New York, on the one hand, is a global metropolis with a diverse population of nine million people. Belfast, on the other, is a small, regional Capital with a population of less than 300,000. Despite these differences, there are important connections. Since 2008, as will be outlined below, there has been a casual partnership between neighbourhoods in East Belfast and the South Bronx, involving mutual site visits, and references in text[1] and media[2]. Through these means, participants have emphasized their neighbourhoods' similarities. Both places have similar status as low income and socially marginalized areas, both projects are focused on the revitalization of neglected rivers, and both have adopted a similar rhetoric of participatory development.

The two projects are also examples of the tendency to think of urban sustainability as a spatial practice; the deployment of nature as a design principle in urban planning combines an ecological understanding of green urban infrastructure with a belief in the potency of green spaces as a force for civic transformation and economic recovery[3]. However, in both neighbourhoods, varying degrees of local support and ambivalence to these projects highlights the propensity for urban sustainability to succumb to existing forms of spatial contestation and conflicting voices within environmental politics.

This sharing of experience provides an example of urban sustainability's global reach and its local nuances. Within each community, we see a refraction of the idea of sustainability through a lens constructed from local meaning, history and social relations. In the South Bronx, urban sustainability represents mobilization for environmental justice and highlights tensions around race, displacement, and the politics of representation. In East Belfast, urban sustainability is understood in the context of emergent and contested post-conflict identity and underlines tensions around place and territory.

However, despite these divergences, it is possible to trace common themes. Sustainability, across global and local scales, has many interlocutors, ranging from techno-scientific experts whose opinions transcend local experience, to community representatives who speak with authority and credibility from direct personal experience intimately tied to place. These voices are diverse and often conflicting and contradictory, and they play out in multiple ways in the practice of urban sustainability.

Despite the ambitions of sustainability to produce social change alongside environmental reform, the appropriation of the discourse of sustainability by dominant ideologies can lead to a reproduction of existing social inequalities, injustices and exclusions. The shared vocabulary, enabled through the problematic catch-all quality of the language of sustainability (as other contributors to this volume also suggest), belies the tension and competition between forms of urban sustainability playing out in local contexts around the world. In many ways, the globalised discourse of urban sustainability reflects the wider global trend towards homogeneity in urban spatial practice- that began in the modernist period. Other global trends such as a resurgence in demand for city centre residential development, neo-liberal privatisation, and growing securitisation of urban space transcend local or regional contexts (Checker 2011; Newman 2011).

From the South Bronx to East Belfast:
shared experiences and parallel visions

In early October 2008, around a table in a sun-dappled conference room off Lafayette Avenue in the South Bronx, sat Majora Carter - a local urban sustainability activist of national reputation, her husband and business partner, three representatives of the Northern Ireland Bureau in Washington DC, and Margaret Ritchie, then Minister for Social Development in the devolved Northern Ireland Assembly. The purpose of the meeting was to share experiences and expertise in using the concept of sustainability to regenerate neighbourhoods that suffer major social deprivation.

The conversation turned to traits shared by low-income communities in New York and Northern Ireland. Ritchie and Carter talked about the frustration felt when efforts to improve the built environment are met with vandalism and destruction. They empathised over the struggle of trying to get people who are caught in cycles of poverty to see beyond what they think their future should be, and the ill-advised tendency for development to be something that happens to, rather than for, the community. In fact, it was such challenges that first brought Ritchie to this forgotten part of New York City: she wanted to hear about the work of Sustainable South Bronx, the organization Carter had founded in 2001- and from which she had recently resigned to pursue a new venture.

Sustainable South Bronx had been involved - as community consultants - in the development of a multi-million dollar scheme to construct a linear park that would connect residential streets in one of the poorest congressional districts in the United States with their long-forgotten waterfront. In Northern Ireland, the East Belfast Partnership Board had recently secured Big Lottery Funding to construct a linear park that would connect the historic shipyards on Belfast Lough with the hills and glens to the south-east of the city, passing through one of Belfast's most deprived and divided neighbourhoods along the way.

Two impoverished and stigmatized neighbourhoods, two urban sustainability initiatives that promise to restore the economy, ecology, and collective self-esteem of the communities around them. The organizations involved in the respective greenway projects were eager to promote similarities between their communities and the causes of their contemporary problems. Both saw once-robust local manufacturing economies go into steep decline; middle-class flight and disinvestment had gutted their residential communities; both had high unemployment and low educational achievement among those who remained; both endured the blight of poorly-planned infrastructure and resultant spatial severance; and both could attest to the alienation of the local population from nature[4].

"Greening the Ghetto"[5]: environmental justice and sustainability in the South Bronx

The area of New York City in which I carried out my ethnographic fieldwork comprises three neighbourhoods:- to the south west of the borough of the Bronx – Port Morris, Mott Haven, and the peninsular neighbourhood of Hunts Point. Formerly vibrant working class areas, they have been greatly affected by the combined mid-20th century forces that ravaged cities across the industrialised world: decline in manufacturing, disinvestment, large-scale highway building, and population displacement to the suburbs. In addition, New York's zoning practices, changes to welfare policy, financial red-lining, and a protracted city-wide fiscal crisis exacerbated the situation, concentrating poverty side by side with noxious industry in neighbourhoods with poor and minority populations. With the collapse of the real estate industry in the 1970s, arson attacks became widespread, and a smouldering South Bronx became synonymous in the United States' national imagination with urban desolation, lawlessness, and poverty. Zoning policy throughout the 1960s and 1970s designated much of the South Bronx, and almost all of Hunts Point, as a manufacturing area, leading to a concentration of polluting facilities and heavy industry, as well as a 329-acre food distribution centre that draws thousands of diesel trucks to the peninsula's southern tip daily (Mantaay 2001 cited in Sze 2007).

When I began my fieldwork there, late in the summer of 2008, I was advised that the best way to get to know the area and understand the issues faced by the community was to take a "toxic tour"[6]. The toxic tour was guided by Camila[7], who co-ordinated community outreach for Sustainable South Bronx. She told me, as we walked, how popular the tour had become – people had come from all over the world to find out about the challenges faced by residents of the South Bronx. The walk took in much of the peninsula of Hunts Point, stopping at a juvenile detention centre, at an 800-bed prison barge, at the New York Organic Fertilizer Company - with its brightly painted chimney stacks and vile smell. It took us past the marine transfer stations and the Hunts Point Water Treatment Plant, with scores of heavy trucks rattling by all the while. The tour also brought us to vacant land, spaces that were actively in contestation, such as the site adjacent to the Baretto Point Park, where the city was proposing the location of towering 130-foot anaerobic digesters, a plan that was currently being opposed by the community. Together, these locations highlight the number and scope of issues faced by local residents. Though seemingly disparate, the stops on the toxic tour are all connected in a history of neglect and discrimination in the South Bronx, summarised by the activists who oppose them under the term environmental justice.

Environmental justice is best understood as a movement that seeks to challenge the unfair distribution of environmental benefits and burdens, drawing attention to the inordinate siting of harmful, toxic, and dangerous industries in communities of colour -where environmental amenities such as parks and walkable infrastructures are also lacking (Bullard 2001; Checker 2011). In its historical genesis and its contemporary framing of the issues, it is more closely aligned with social justice and civil rights than with traditional environmentalism. Environmental justice campaigns typically call for improvements to the immediate environment, emphasising access to physical amenities such as parks at the same time as it seeks the removal or mitigation of dirty, polluting, and stigmatising facilities. The "environment" with which environmental justice is concerned extends beyond nature: it is the physical environment in its entirety, including the uneven social, political, and economic processes through which it is produced. By connecting pollution and environmental degradation with issues such as access to education, physical health, and nutrition, environmental justice activists see themselves as challenging the eco-centrism and social elitism of traditional environmentalism.

The contemporary environmental justice movement in the South Bronx began in the summer of 1999, when a loose coalition of community and special interest groups, staged a series of protests against a proposed expansion of the already extensive waste transfer stations lining the waterfront of the South Bronx. Mayor Rudolph Giuliani had promised the people of Staten Island that the hated Fresh Kills landfill site would close by 2001 and be transformed into a 2000-acre park and wetland. The waste transfer stations in the South Bronx would be crucial in moving the 10,000 daily tons of garbage onto trains to be taken to Virginia for dumping in landfill (Sugarman 1999). For people in the South Bronx, this was akin to adding insult to injury; their community had already borne an inordinate share of noxious municipal services, with 25 existing stations, alongside water treatment plants, a sewage sludge plant, and the daily inundation of diesel fumes from the food service trucks rattling down their streets and idling by their sidewalks. In addition, there was an under-provision of benefits: few parks or play areas, poor pedestrian infrastructure within and between neighbourhoods, and no safe access to the waterfront.

It was this period of intense activism that led to the founding, in 2001, of the non-profit organization Sustainable South Bronx by Majora Carter, in order to continue campaigning for environmental justice in the area. The beginning of my fieldwork in 2008 coincided with significant upheaval within that organisation, as Carter resigned her position as Executive Director of Sustainable South Bronx. Charismatic and engaging, as an individual she had come to be synonymous with urban sustainability and revitalization, taking on a demanding schedule of lectures and key-note addresses at events across the country, and receiving numerous personal awards and acknowledgements, as well as a TV show on the Sundance Network and a syndicated radio show. Feeling she was no longer able to fulfil her duties as director of her organization, she left, establishing a new enterprise - the homonymous Majora Carter Group. Sustainable South Bronx continues to exist, having gone through leadership changes since Carter's departure, and it was this organisation that became the anchor of my research in the South Bronx.

While Sustainable South Bronx is just one of several organisations working under the banner of environmental justice in that part of the city, I focus on it herein because of its high profile on a national and international stage. Its local advocacy work represents a significant point of tension in urban sustainability generally. Furthermore, despite Carters' formal disassociation from the organisation, her history with it had a significant impact on the organisation during the period when I was carrying out fieldwork. In addition, as a public figure, Carter, and by proxy Sustainable South Bronx, is often a point of reference for otherwise unarticulated conflicts around representation and authenticity in the environmental justice movement. By framing the campaigns in the South Bronx as urban sustainability, Carter found a way to bridge the gap between environmental justice and traditional environmentalism. By framing environmental justice as a means to achieve multiple benefits, she increased its appeal to a wider audience.

The environmental justice movement has made significant gains in the South Bronx. Campaigning led to the increased monitoring and eventual closure of the New York Organic Fertilizer Corporation sludge processing plant. Campaigning also led to the decision by the city to rehabilitate existing infrastructure rather than construct those towering anaerobic digesters. Sustainable South Bronx ran a successful opposition to the locating of another correctional facility in the area and the construction for the South Bronx Greenway and its related infrastructure is, at the time of writing, underway.

However, I found significant contrast to the large-scale urban restoration championed by Sustainable South Bronx in a group of activists loosely organised around a Mott Haven community garden. The group came to be key antagonists during the development of the South Bronx Greenway during the period when I was carrying out fieldwork. For example, they were critical of the section of the Greenway that would extend across the narrow strait of the Bronx Kill- and on to Randall's Island. Proponents of human-powered boating on the rivers, their objections were based on the navigability of the Kill at high tide, which is blocked by the presence of an electrical cable conduit owned by the electricity supply firm ConEd. The group pressed for the city to insist on the removal of the conduit as a condition for the Greenway connector onto Randall's Island – the negotiation of which would protract the construction of the Greenway and possibly threaten to derail the plan for it to extend across the Kill into the extensive parkland on Randall's Island. Discussing this opposition with a senior staff member of Sustainable South Bronx, she described the demands as needlessly ideological. It was, from her perspective, based on the needs of the very few people who access the Bronx waterways by canoe or kayak and "just to make a point."[8]

Both groups are also at the centre of the debate and growing concern over the threat of gentrification in the South Bronx. The gardeners regard the projects supported by Sustainable South Bronx, such as the Greenway, as regeneration and beautification activities that will open up the South Bronx waterfront to commercial development and escalating real estate values. They fear that this will reproduce and heighten, rather than challenge, the same inequalities that exist now; a concern that is echoed in my interviews with residents. Sustainable South Bronx responds to these criticisms and fears by emphasizing the potential for these projects to become a component of the green economy, which local people can access by participating in their heavily subsidized green collar training programmes.

One of the paradoxes of environmental justice is that an improved neighbourhood is a more attractive neighbourhood. As documented by Dooling (2009) and Checker (2011), urban sustainability and gentrification often go hand in hand. Compared with low-income neighbourhoods in Manhattan and Brooklyn, the South Bronx has been relatively resistant to gentrification. Despite this, there is a consistent feeling among residents of the threat of displacement, and it is an issue that was raised in many of the conversations that I had with activists in the area. The connection between greening and gentrification puts environmental justice activists in a difficult double bind, where the fight for fair distribution of environmental benefits and burdens comes with the threat of being priced out of their neighbourhoods, or having freedom and access to space curtailed in other ways.

The two groups – Sustainable South Bronx on the one hand, and the gardener/activists on the other, both espouse a goal of urban sustainability and the need for neighbourhood infrastructure that integrates and restores nature, and to increase green spaces in the South Bronx. The conflict between the two groups appears to centre on competing moral geographies, where inconsistencies in how urban sustainability is pursued in different ways by different parties are expressed in moral rather than technical or political terms. As Macnaghten and Urry (1999:99) describe, the multiple framing of environmental risks by different actors, has serious implications for people living with the reality of those risks. Inconsistency and conflict in how environmental issues are framed creates an even greater sense of risk and anxiety over whom to believe and what the risks actually are. Concerns over issues of representation and authenticity, of who really has the best interests of the people of the South Bronx at heart, were frequently expressed by my respondents and in media commentary. These concerns show a significant point of intersection between urban sustainability discourse and issues of race and class. Whereas the gardening group draw their battle lines by emphasizing personal agency, direct action, and a spiritual reconnection with nature through locally-grown food, and self-governance, Sustainable South Bronx emphasize the need to affect change on the policy level, through devising solutions and encouraging sustainability in communities through the creation of green jobs. The gardeners/activists see Sustainable South Bronx as acting disingenuously in the service of capital, and "selling out" the people of the South Bronx. Sustainable South Bronx, on the other hand, see the gardeners/activists – many of whom are White – as speaking from a place of privilege that is broadly ignorant of the needs of residents of the South Bronx. Much of my fieldwork in the South Bronx has been oriented around these two groups in an attempt to understand the nuances of their conflicting ideologies. In many ways, they embody the friction between two versions of environmentalism, one well-worn and based in a very peculiarly American discourse of the human-nature relationship, and one that is emergent and divergent, that intersects with other forms of social activism that has often been at cross-purposes with mainstream environmentalism, such as workers' and civil rights.

Their activism, protests, and day-to-day activities have proven rich ground to understand what is meant by sustainability, and local efforts to achieve it. For Sustainable South Bronx and its supporters, sustainability can be achieved through working within the framework of capitalism - the development of a green, inclusive, economy through philanthropic investment and capital programs for urban regeneration such as the South Bronx Greenway. For the activists who oppose this model, sustainability is achieved only through a radical rethinking of power relationships in society as well as the human/nature relationship. Combined, they reflect the growing complexity of environmental discourse, where the expression of moral values intersects with spatial contestation.

East Belfast – sustainability and post conflict urban space

In East Belfast too, the construction of the Greenway has been beset by problems and, nearly five years on, construction has yet to begin. Like the South Bronx Greenway it exists as a symbolic landscape for the East Belfast Partnership and other organisational stakeholders in the city for whom regeneration is a concern. However, it lacks the charismatic character of the South Bronx Greenway, and there has been little community mobilisation for or against it.

In spite of nearly five years of outreach efforts and community consultation, there is very little awareness of the project. I conducted street-intercept interviews at intervals throughout 2011 and 2012 in the area adjacent to the greenway, in which I approached adults on street, and, after establishing that they lived in the area, proceeded to ask them semi-structured questions about the greenway to test awareness of the project and opinions towards it. During these interviews, there was frequent confusion with a similar local project – a railway track that was turned into a cycle path, a greenway of much more modest ambition that opened in 2008[9]. Among those I interviewed who had heard of it, I was told many times that it was a waste of money, that it would attract violent and anti-social behaviour, that it would be taken over by young people so that nobody else would feel safe there, and that it was diverting funds from more worthy investments, such as sports facilities. This negative response from the community presented a major obstacle to the Greenway's outreach efforts and impacted on the desired-for "community buy-in". It was a source of frustration for the Greenway outreach staff. In an interview with an officer in July 2011, he told me how, after three years of press coverage, opening information points around the neighbourhood[10], and numerous stakeholder events, "there is still only a 52% awareness of the project in East Belfast" (Brannigan, interview, 2011).

Encountering apathy, disinterest, and boredom among respondents presents unforeseen challenges for researchers of urban transformation, predisposed to look for things that happen, for activity, mobilization and conflict. The languor with which local communities responded to the Greenway in East Belfast was partly understood by the group doing the outreach as an issue of visibility – people so used to disappointment and negativity would not risk optimism until they could *see* the Greenway take shape. Brannigan (interview 2011) told me:

> I actually think it's because there's nothing really happening, with them not seeing anything happening. [...] whenever you go out and do presentations and go out and talk to people they get really excited and think it' s brilliant, but then you get this...people saying, it's brilliant, can't wait to see it, but will it really happen? Where's the money? A lot of people are cynical that the money is somehow going to disappear and that in the current economic climate they just find it hard to believe. We need a section done that we can take people to and show them and say this is it, this is what it's going to look like. People can't really picture what we're doing.

Another explanation offered was that most people were unaware that there was a river there in the first place. In the process of exploring these themes, attempting to understand the existing relationship between the community and the river, I became aware of an emergent spatial discourse in the city that was concerned with the high incidence of vacancy in Belfast. The vacant and overgrown areas that pepper East Belfast amplify the partial and incomplete nature of urban transformation. In the context of a post-conflict city, these vacant spaces have particular resonance[11]. Hope for a sustained peace is inscribed in new places as visible evidence of regeneration and renewal, and vacant spaces are dangerously in-between zones, full of the promise of development while serving as a reminder that progress has stalled.

Vacant and derelict sites in cities, as spaces that are up for grabs, often become sites of negotiation around the meaning and intention of urban development, and are discursively deployed by different groups to communicate ideological positions and forms of agency. McDonogh (1993:7), conceptualises urban emptiness as "complex social space [...] defined by conflict among groups with distinct visions of the city and presences in its society". For my respondents in East Belfast, empty spaces convey poverty, loss, and social exclusion; missing out on the so-called peace dividend that was promised at the end of the sectarian conflict and that is becoming physically manifest elsewhere in the city.

Urban space has always been a key protagonist in the conflict in Belfast (Shirlow and Murtagh 2006: 18). Social division as a result of ethno-sectarian identity was galvanised during the years of conflict by spatial divisions. The conflict drove people further apart and deeper into territorial enclaves. Traditionally neutral spaces, such as the city centre - as the hub of administration for the province - became paramilitary targets and were heavily securitised during the conflict and, for many people, remain stigmatised as dangerous places to live, work, or visit. Post-conflict division in work, education, and housing maintains the apartness of daily life, and constricts the extent to which people feel able to move through the city. It is not unusual to hear people speak casually about the anxiety with which they enter neighbourhoods that are unfamiliar to them, a narrative borne out in surveys carried out in 2004 (Shirlow and Murtagh 2006:85-94). As Shirlow and Murtagh observe in their study of post-conflict Belfast, it is common for cities emerging from long periods of sectarian unrest to present the future as "utopian, shared and equal", an optimism that is often undermined by the reluctance of groups to part with their separateness, and for difference to reassert itself in new ways (2006:2).

Environmental improvement in Belfast has been a priority for a number of years, an element in the agenda of securing investment in the city and increasing tourism by expunging un-savoury reminders of the past from the urban landscape. It can mean anything from planting street trees to the replacement of sectarian symbols with imagery that "reflects Belfast's aspirations" (Arts Council of Northern Ireland 2009). Neighbourhood renewal as a policy was developed in 2003 under a Department for Social Development document called *People and Place*, the purpose of which was to "bring a focus to government departments and other statutory agencies to work together on area-based regeneration strategies."[12] Part of its remit is to "work with local people to see how contested places might be better used" (Department for Social Development 2003). Key to this plan are partnership arrangements between local community representatives and statutory agencies that are together given responsibility for delivering on local needs through the design of an action plan. The resulting projects then fall under the headings of physical, social, economic, and community regeneration. It was from within this general framework for renewal that the idea of bringing the two communities together through consultation on local environmental issues, particularly with regard to green space, emerged. It was, to use the words of Shirlow and Murtagh, "a common agreeable agenda around which communities could negotiate with minimum risk" (2006:161).[13]

The residential area directly adjacent to the Greenway continues to be deeply divided along sectarian lines and the Lower Newtownards Road remains a volatile interface area between Loyalist Ballymacarrett and Republican Short Strand. The division is palpable and starkly visible in the territorial markings, such as aggressive murals depicting armed paramilitary fighters and statements of allegiance to one side or the other, which are continually refreshed. Many of the formerly vibrant terraced streets and shop-fronts lie in enduring, dilapidated, vacancy. In working class residential areas, like this one, that bound the centre of the city, the ideal of shared space is trickier to deliver, but no less symbolically powerful. The intertwined nature of ethno-sectarian difference and spatial contestation in Belfast reinforces the sense of difference and strengthens the territoriality of urban space. As Shirlow and Murtagh (2006:16) argue:

> [S]egregation in Belfast is not based upon an ethno-sectarian standstill [...] but upon the need to re-deliver the meaning of separated living through novel, as well as rehearsed, narratives of inclusion, practice and belief.

In this context, the Greenway, as space that is imagined as shared, neutral, and safe in an otherwise deeply divided part of the city, is seen as both integral to a sustained peace, and yet impossibly optimistic.

As with the South Bronx Greenway, the contradictions inherent in the construction of the Connswater Community Greenway involve a negotiation of space on moral as well as political terms. In East Belfast, the Greenway, as an idea, is tightly intertwined with a post-conflict discourse of blame, authenticity, and contestation. Terms such as "maturity" and "normality" are applied in the parlance of local politics, and where communities index the degree to which they have let go of the past. There is a clear moral dimension in this choice of language, implying direct agency to choose between right and wrong, between division and violence or harmony and peace. As observed by Rallings (2014:434), the assertion that space in Belfast:

> [C]an be made a "shared space" by the neutralisation or restriction of symbolic displays reveals a tendency of policy (and of discourse more generally) to [...] discount these more complex factors affecting experiences of space.

The apparent or supposed failure of communities to embrace a non-sectarian future, often understood through a non-observance of the neutrality of "shared" space is framed as a deviant or corrupting act. For example, in December 2012, violence spilled over from its usual location in 'hotspot' interface areas into the city centre during protests over the flying of the Union Flag at Belfast City Hall. Despite the widespread and enduring nature of division in the city, there followed vociferous condemnation of the disruption caused to the civic and commercial life of the city, invoking a "real" people of Belfast who wished to distance themselves from the dispute. Similarly, when riots on the East Belfast interface in 2011 coincided with a competitive victory of Northern Irish golfer Rory McIlroy, media commentators were keen to point out that it was McIlroy, and not the rioters who represented the real Northern Ireland.

In the years since the Good Friday Agreement, the re-imagining of space in Belfast has been central to the process of social normalization and the ability of Belfast to emerge from its troubled past (Connolly and Bryan 2009; Neill 2010; Rallings 2014). The idea of shared space, and its connection with progress and sustainability, has been a powerful political motivation driving the commercial redevelopment of the blighted city centre, and behind the construction of iconic new urban spaces, such as Laganside and Titanic Quarter – spaces that represent Belfast's best face: cosmopolitan, modern, and utterly normal. The Greenway is seen as a project of similar ambition – intended to redefine the identity of East Belfast: the physical enactment of a shared future.

Conclusion: Sustainability and Moral Geography

I conclude this chapter with an attempt to bring these two divergent local narratives of urban sustainability back into alignment. The central research question that shaped my approach to data collection in both field sites was to understand the way urban sustainability is enacted on a local level through competing definitions of nature and moral geography. Western ideas of space and landscape are entangled with notions about the natural world. Environmental discourse has shifted from its preoccupation with conservation and the need to protect nature from the effects of human industry and settlement. However, there is evidence in environmental discourse of a lingering fear that urban populations' disengagement from the natural world will limit their environmental literacy and deaden their propensity to act on nature's behalf. Popular books like Richard Louv's *Last Child Left in the Woods: Saving Our Children from Nature-Deficit Disorder* exemplify this fear that cultural shifts, enabled by technology and urbanisation, are severing our connection to the natural world. According to this growing body of literature, not only are we losing experientially-gained knowledge about our surroundings, but we are also missing out on the positive effects of nature on our health and moral fibre. It is an idea that resonates with the early years of the wilderness movement in the United States, a belief that emphasised the value of spaces uncorrupted by civilisation that was, partially at least, fed by rapid urbanisation (Nash 2001). The importance of natural spaces in cities, introduced in the Victorian era and solidified through subsequent trends in urban planning, articulate cultural assumptions about the needs of citizens to connect with nature as a condition for health and wellbeing.

However, as Kate Soper (2004:183) points out, conceptions of the "naturality" of space are more complex than the binary distinction between built and unbuilt, or rural and urban environments. Instead, the naturality of space is a judgement of the quality of its temporal as well as its spatial characteristics. Soper argues;

> [N]ature, in this conception is both a present space and an absent – already lost – time/space: a retreat or a place of return, to which we "go" or "get" back" and which represents the idealised version of pastoral life that has been a mainstay of romantic environmentalism (2004: 187).

This temporal quality is evident in the case studies presented herein through the deployment of the language of restoration and reconnection, which implies reverting to an earlier, and therefore more natural, state. Within the discourse of sustainability, cities represent a paradox. They epitomise the human-made world, they absorb the bulk of the world's resources and produce vast quantities of waste. They are the antithesis of natural landscapes, those time/spaces often invoked in environmental discourse. However, with their high-density populations, sharing of mass infrastructure, and association with progressive politics and social change, they also represent an environmental ideal defined by a techno-scientific emphasis on efficiency, information transfer, and green consumption. The growing movement for environmental justice in urban areas like the South Bronx reframes the subject of concern from vulnerable wild spaces or endangered species to injustices faced by vulnerable human populations. However, there is still a persistent focus on the power of reconnecting to nature. As presented here in the two case studies, urban sustainability often involves the creation of new urban spaces, or the redefinition of existing ones, using language of restoration that extends to the human communities that will be its benefactors. These spaces are sites of social production; they are given meaning by the discourse that both constitutes and is constituted by them. In his study of the Toronto Waterfront, Matthew Cooper (2002: 377) argues that "focusing on changing forms of discourse opens a window on the historical processes through which spatial meanings and the experience of space change". Elaborating on how this discourse is formulated, he describes a process whereby:

[U]sing ideologies of place, people describe the kinds of places that exist, explain their nature, evaluate them (employing cognitively and emotionally salient imagery to create a symbolic landscape), identify with them, and imagine places as they ought to be (thus creating moral landscapes) (2002: 378).

In both the South Bronx and East Belfast, ideologies of space are used to describe places that exist. Those spaces are socially marginalised and physically run-down. In other words, the spaces that exist are also the problem to be addressed. They are explained and evaluated as places of unmet need (the absence of natural space) and action is mobilised around the creation of new spaces that will meet that need (the Greenways). In imagining the spaces as they ought to be, a moral landscape is produced that solidifies ideals of urban life: healthful, peaceful, and affluent.

As Cresswell points out, "space and place are used to structure a normative landscape" (1996:8). This normative landscape is what informs our notions of propriety and transgression, what is and is not, who is and is not, appropriate to a given place. Though often taken for granted, the idea of appropriateness, and its counterpoint, transgression, are not inherent or constant. They are in an ongoing process of negotiation and contestation. It is during periods when the meaning of space is undergoing change, as is the case with the urban developments described herein, that these negotiations are most explicit.

Urban sustainability stands at the intersection of elemental forces, socio-economic pressures, and cultural meaning. It often involves the creation of new spaces, or their redesign, and therefore, redefinition of existing spaces. In low income or marginalised neighbourhoods, sustainability is framed as a goal that intersects with other kinds of social change – job creation, lifestyle change, improved health, lower crime, better neighbourhoods and better neighbours. Many of these transformations are understood through the way they will transform, not just the material, physical reality of the neighbourhood and its appearance but also, by proxy, the individual behaviour and collective lives of the people who live there, often implicitly in terms of moral improvement. So, in the South Bronx, the symbolic importance of the Greenway is in its promise of improved health, escape from poverty, general community wellbeing, and an improved perception of the neighbourhood in the eyes of outsiders. Likewise, in Belfast, the Greenway there is a symbol of moving on, of putting distance between the present and a violent, shameful past. Its importance is as shared space, the most vaunted and elusive type of space in post-conflict Northern Ireland. Through contestation around these new spaces, activists, planners, the media, and other interlocutors are expressing implicit ideologies of space - competing moral geographies - that articulate what is good and appropriate within the ephemeral realm of urban transformation.

While sustainability is a loose and tricky concept, it does provide a vocabulary within environmental discourse with which to draw together previously discordant elements; it integrates a concern for the natural environment with a concern for human welfare, and acknowledges, to some extent at least, the interdependence of the two. However, the way in which urban space is configured, the connection between urban planning and flows of capital, and the complexity of ownership and belonging in urban space makes the enactment of sustainability in cities a highly mediated process.

Sustainability is an issue of global proportions; the image of the globe is an important symbol in environmental activism, and campaigners often invoke planetary systems in their framing of a looming global environmental crisis. But, as Tim Ingold (2000:218) points out, the environment is much too big to live in. Instead, the environment we experience directly is of a much more intimate scale. Sustainability, as a practice, takes place – failing or succeeding – at the level of local action. The values and ideas that shape community spaces, from urban planning to environmental activism, are therefore, a negotiation between local and global forces. That local places are shaped by a discourse forged in the global arena does not diminish the distinctiveness of the local context, but global perspectives are inherently indifferent to place, privileging the universal as rational, standardized, and complete against the messy immediacy of the local (Ingold 2000). I chose my two field sites because they were self-consciously participating in a global conversation about urban sustainability, but in a context where it was possible to observe and participate with sustainability in action-in particular, at a more intimate scale.

In both places, plans were underway for community greenway projects that aimed not just to restore the ecosystems of the neighbourhoods in which they were being built but also to restore, through reconnection with the natural world, the neighbourhoods' disenfranchised, divided, and impoverished residents. Before the greenways become physically manifest, in the ephemeral worlds that come into existence around projects like these, the spaces are produced as symbolic, moral landscapes through which opposing values clash and the active, ideological construction of urban space becomes alien.

References

Anusas, Mike and Tim Ingold. "Designing Environmental Relations: From Opacity to Textility". *Massachusetts Institute of Technology Design Issues,* 29:4, pp.58-69 (2013): 58-69.

Arts Council of Northern Ireland. *Evaluation of the re-imaging communities programme: a report to the Arts Council of Northern Ireland,* Independent Research Solutions, 2009.

Bartlett, Peggy F. (Editor). *Urban Place: Reconnecting with the Natural World.* Cambridge: MIT Press, 2005.

Berman, Marshall. *All That Is Solid Melts Into Air: The Experience of Modernity.* London: Verso, 2010.

Birch, Eugenie. L. and Susan M. Wachter. (Editors). *Growing Greener Cities: Urban Sustainability in the Twenty-First Century.* University of Pennsylvania Press, 2010.

Boal, Frederick W. and Stephen A. Royle. (Editors). *Enduring City: Belfast in the Twentieth Century.* Belfast: Blackstaff, 2006.

Brannigan, Sean. *Personal communication with the author.* July 2011.

Bryan, Dominic and Clifford Stevenson. "Flagging Peace: Struggles over Symbolic Landscape in the New Northern Ireland". In *Culture and belonging in divided Societies: Contestation and Symbolic Landscapes,* edited by Marc H. Ross. Philadelphia: University of Pennsylvania Press, 2009.

Bryan, Dominic. "Belfast: Urban Space, 'Policing' and Sectarian Polarization". In *Wounded Cities: Destruction and Reconstruction in a Globalized World,* edited by Jane Schneider and Ida Susser. New York: Berg, 2003.

Bullard, Robert D. "Environmental Justice in the 21st Century: Race Still Matters". In *Phylon,* 49:3/4 (2001): 151-171.

Checker, Melissa. "Wiped Out by the "Greenwave": Environmental Gentrification and the Paradoxical Politics of Urban Sustainability". In *City & Society,* 23:2, (2011): 210-229.

Connolly, Sean and Dominic Bryan. "Identity, Social Action and Public Space: Defining Civic Space in Belfast". In *Theorizing Identities and Social Action* (Identity Studies in the Social Sciences), edited by Margaret Wetherell. Palgrave Macmillan, 2009.

Cooper, Matthew. "Spatial Discourses and Social Boundaries: Re-imagining the Toronto Waterfront". In *Theorizing the City: The New Urban Anthropology Reader,* edited by Setha Low. New Brunswick: Rutgers University Press, 2002: 377 – 399.

Cresswell, Tim. *In Place/Out of Place: Geography, Ideology, and Transgression.* Minneapolis: University of Minnesota Press, 1996.

Dale, A., Dushenko, W. T., and Robinson, P. (Editors). *Urban Sustainability: Reconnecting Space & Place.* University of Toronto Press. 2014.

Department for Social Development. *People and Place: a Strategy for Neighbourhood Renewal,* Belfast, DSD, 2003.

Dooling, Sarah. "Ecological Gentrification: A Research Agenda Exploring Justice in the City". In *International Journal of Urban and Regional Research,* 33:10 (2009): 621-639.

Fitzgerald, Joan. *Emerald Cities: Urban Sustainability and Economic Development.* New York: Oxford University Press, 2010.

Ingold, Tim. *The Perception of the Environment: Essays in Dwelling Livelihood and Skill.* London, UK: Taylor and Francis, 2000.

Jonnes, Jill. *We're Still Here: The Rise, Fall, and Resurrection of the South Bronx.* Atlantic Monthly Press, 1986.

Komarova, Milena and Dominic Bryan. "The Production of Shared Space in Northern Ireland. Part 1: Introduction. Beyond the Divided City: Policies and Practices of Shared Space". *City: analysis of urban trends, culture, theory, policy, action,* 18:4-5 (2014): 427-431.

McDonogh, Gary. "The Geography of Emptiness." In R. Rotenberg & G. McDonogh (eds), *The Cultural Meaning of Urban Space.* Westport: Bergin & Garvey, 1993.

Macnaghtan, Phil and John Urry. *Contested Natures.* London: Sage Publications, 1999.

Nash, Roderick. *Wilderness & the American Mind.* Yale University Press, 2001.

Neill, William. J. V. "The Debasing of Myth: The Privatisation of Titanic Memory in Designing the "Post-Conflict" City". *Journal of Urban Design,* 16:1 (2010): 67-86.

—. "Whose city? Can a place vision for Belfast avoid the issue of identity? *European Planning Studies,* 7:3 (1999): 269-281.

Newman, Andrew. "Contested Ecologies: Environmental Activism and Urban Space in Immigrant Paris". In *City & Society,* 33:2, (2011): 192-209.

Pezzullo, Phaedra C. *Toxic Tourism: Rhetorics of Pollution, Travel, and Environmental Justice.* Tuscaloosa: University of Alabama Press, 2009.

Rallings, Mary-Kathryn. "Shared Space as Symbolic Capital: Belfast and the "right to the city". *City: analysis of urban trends, culture, theory, policy, action* 18:4-5, (2014): 432-439.

Shirlow, Peter and Brendan Murtagh. *Belfast: Segregation, Violence, and the City.* London: Pluto Press, 2006.

Soper, Kate. "What is Nature: Culture, Politics, and the Non-Human." Oxford: Blackwell, 2004.

Sugarman, Raphael. Hunts Point Protest Trash Haul Plan. *New York Daily News , Suburban,* July 1999:1.

Sze, Julie. *Noxious New York: The Racial Politics of Urban Health and Environmental Justice.* Cambridge, United States: Massachusetts Institute of Technoloy Press, 2007.

Tsing, Anna L. *Friction: An Ethnography of Global Connection.* Woodstock, United Kingdom: Princeton University Press, 2005.

Willer, Kevin. W., Lora B. Wilder, Frances A. Stillman, F. A., & Diane M. Becker, "The Feasibility of a Street-Intercept Survey Method in an African American Community". In *American Journal of Public Health,* 87:4, (1997): 655-658.

Notes

[1] For example, the South Bronx Greenway was referenced in the funding bid for the Connswater Community Greenway as an example of best practice.

[2] The Connswater Community Greenway was the subject of an episode of Majora Carter's radio show "The Promised Land" on National Public Radio in the US.

[3] See Anusas and Ingold (2013) for further discussion of the potential for design to limit or enable a deepening of ecological awareness through making tangible, rather than hiding, the flows and transfers of material and energy through which people and environment are inextricably linked.

[4] For historical insight into the decline of the South Bronx, see Berman (2010), Jonnes (1986), and for discussion into the impact of zoning in the area, see Sze (2007).

For a history of Belfast in the 20th Century, see Boal and Royle (2006). For discussion of the spatial segregation of the city see Shirlow & Murtagh (2006), Bryan (2009 and 2003), and Komarova and Bryan (2014)

[5] "Green the Ghetto" was the slogan, coined by Majora Carter, of Sustainable South Bronx and title of her widely-shared 2006 TED talk (ted.com:2006)

[6] For detailed discussion of the strategic use of toxic tours as a tool for engagement, education, and solidarity-building in the environmental justice movement, see Pezzullo (2007).

[7] Not her real name.

[8] Since the initial period of fieldwork when this conflict was taking place, the group's objection to the conduit was successful and the infrastructure was raised in height, making the Kill navigable. In December 2013, NYCEDC issued a press release announcing the launch of construction of the pathway connecting the South Bronx with Randalls Island. Following personnel changes within SSBx, the

organisation had shifted their position to support the campaign for removal of the conduit.

[9] The name of this existing development is the Comber Greenway

[10] These information points consisted of boards showing maps of the route and artist's impressions of selected locations along the greenway, and included contact information for the project team. They were located in public libraries and community centres adjacent to the route of the greenway.

[11] For further discussion of post-conflict space in Belfast see Neill (1999), Neill (2010), and Rallings (2014).

[12] Joe Torney, Deputy Director, Belfast regeneration office, personal communication, January 2009.

CHAPTER EIGHT

RECONFIGURING "THE SOCIAL" IN SUSTAINABLE DEVELOPMENT: COMMUNITY, CITIZENSHIP AND INNOVATION IN NEW URBAN NEIGHBOURHOODS

SAFFRON WOODCRAFT

In April 2014, London's Royal Society of Arts (RSA), a 250-year old organization- that describes its purpose as finding innovation and practical solutions to today's social challenges, organized a conference entitled *"Developing Socially Productive Places"*. The event brought 100 delegates to the RSA's central London office to debate how investment in the built environment can strengthen local communities by contributing to economic and social productivity. Among the conference delegates were urban planners, architects, property developers, housing associations, local government officials, social enterprises, and a former housing minister. The RSA's Chief Executive, Matthew Taylor, introduced the conference by calling on delegates to consider the importance of gaining a deep understanding of how communities work and how people understand their own places in order to make investments in the built environment more effective. He invited delegates to collectively develop new approaches, policies, and potentially institutions, to make this happen.

The RSA's conference is one of a growing number of debates taking place in the UK advocating new approaches to urban development that pay greater attention to local understandings of place and to the social outcomes of change in the built environment. These debates take a variety of forms from online groups and blogs, often led by individuals with a personal and professional interest in progressive urbanism, to events, conference workshops and reports that present institutional perspectives on the need for change in built environment professions. For example, in 2011, the Berkeley Group, a major UK house-builder, hosted a debate and published a report titled *"Putting the S-Word back into sustainability: can we be more social?"* (Dixon 2011), argued that the social pillar of sustainability was in danger of dropping out of planning vocabulary in an era dominated by environmental concerns. In the same year, the Young Foundation, a social innovation centre in East London, published *"Design for Social Sustainability"* (Woodcraft et al. 2011), proposing that the social infrastructure in new communities should receive same attention as the physical infrastructure. In 2012, the architecture practice John Thomson and Partners, hosted a debate as part of London's Festival of Architecture about the role of design in supporting social sustainability. In 2013, Tina Saaby, Copenhagen's City Architect, addressed the Academy of Urbanism's *"Digital Urbanism"* conference with a call to "consider urban life before urban space; consider urban space before buildings".[1] There are, most certainly, many other examples of this debate 'in action' to be found in blogs, articles and events in and around the UK.

The language of these debates is fluid. Political concerns, policy issues and popular discourse are frequently re-assembled to frame arguments for changing the way people and places are understood in planning policy and in practice. For example, the challenge of meeting housing needs in an era of austerity and public sector spending cuts is cited as a reason to pay greater attention to the relationship between the physical and social fabric of the city (John Thompson and Partners 2013). Investments in the built environment are portrayed as needing to work harder (RSA 2014), and, in this context, previous mass-housing initiatives like the UK's suburban New Towns and urban Modernist council estates are cited as examples of where the planning and architecture professions have struggled, and sometimes failed, to fully understand the relationship between space, place and social experience, resulting in problems that range from social isolation to crime (The Berkeley Group 2012; John Thompson and Partners 2013). For a short while in 2011 and 2012, following riots in London, Birmingham and Manchester, the narrative was expanded to connect the potential for social unrest to urban inequality as materialised in London's affordable housing crisis and concerns about regeneration and the displacement of residents in low-income neighbourhoods (Space Syntax 2011; The Berkeley Group 2012).

Behind the fluid language there is a consistent narrative that planning and development processes do not adequately take account of the social dynamics, needs and experiences of urban neighbourhoods, and should, as one architect described, "be more social". Social sustainability, social productivity, social innovation or collaborative place-making are proposed as conceptual and practical frameworks to re-insert the social as an operational category in planning practice. In this sense, the debates and events taking place in London are connected to a wider critique of sustainable development, which is acknowledged both to have become the dominant discourse in city governance and urban planning (Castells 2002; Evans 2002; Bulkeley and Betsill 2005; Whitehead 2003; Brand and Thomas 2013) and to have made poor progress on addressing social issues (J. Agyeman and Evans 2004).

This chapter explores how planners, architects, property developers and policymakers who are engaged in these debates construct "the social" in sustainability debates, and how social sustainability as a discursive space frames professional practice, enabling the materialization of some imagined futures while limiting others. It attempts to offer an anthropological perspective on sustainability as a key dynamic in the social and political organization of urban space and social life, a field that is currently understudied by anthropologists. Arguably, anthropology remains on the periphery of urban studies in spite of significant theoretical and methodological works on urban social life and the processes of city-making, notably, work on urban space and place (S. Low 2001; S. M. Low and Altman 1992; S. Low 1996; S. M. Low 1999), architecture (Buchli 2000; Buchli 2006; Buchli 2007; Buchli and Lucas 2006; Yaneva 2012; Yaneva 2008; Yaneva, n.d.), urban planning (S. Abram 2011; S. Abram and Weszkalnys 2011), and urban social networks (Hannerz 2004; Hannerz 1980; Wallman 1984). Elsewhere, many anthropologists are engaged in work on climate change (Fiske 2009; Haenn and Wilk 2006; Crate and Nuttall 2009), but the two research agendas are yet to come together to offer a cohesive perspective on how sustainability policies and practice shape urban landscapes and social experience.

The chapter begins by, first, exploring social sustainability as an emerging discourse that seeks to materialize certain forms of urban space and sociality, and second, following the theme of this volume, discussing what anthropology can contribute to studies of sustainable development as part of a social science of sustainability. The observations and arguments put forward are based on data from 18-months of PhD fieldwork, primarily participant observation and semi-structured interviews, carried out in 2012-14. My research is concerned with what it means to plan, design and build a sustainable community in contemporary London and explores how sustainability discourse shapes planning and design processes to configure and embed ideas about social relationships in the urban landscape. My fieldwork focuses on a group of regeneration managers, planners, architects and property developers working on the new residential neighbourhoods being created in London's Queen Elizabeth Olympic Park

(QEOP). Creating sustainable communities has been identified as an important element of London's Olympic legacy (Olympic Park Legacy Company 2010; London 2012/LOCOG 2010; Mayor's Office 2011), and up to 10,000 new homes will be built by 2030. Following the planning and design process for QEOP's new neighbourhoods has involved multi-sited research: observing public consultation events, planning meetings, residents meetings and site visits in East London, and undertaking a series of interviews with regeneration officers, planners, architects and urban designers. Engaging with sustainability discourse - how it is constructed and how it shapes planning and design practice - has proven to be a more dispersed research process, which has involved engaging with a series of events and debates taking place across the city and online, and with the texts and policy documents that are shaping how my informants understand and operationalize sustainable communities. This chapter focuses on my experience of following, and sometimes actively participating in, the events and debates that are producing and shaping social sustainability discourse in London. My work engages with discourse as a form of social practice (Rydin 1999; Brand and Thomas 2013)- that expresses shared values and has material outcomes, and draws on work by Shove et al. (Shove, Pantzar, and Watson 2012) on the socio-material entanglements of practices to provide a theoretical framework.

Situating Social Sustainability

Cities have become key sites for political and social action on sustainability over the past 20 years (Rydin and Holman 2004; Meadowcroft 2000; Cook and Swyngedouw 2012; Brand and Thomas 2013; Evans 2002; Bulkeley and Betsill 2005) driven by urban population growth and concerns with 'liveability' and resource management. The idea that cities could and should be sustainable has become a new urban paradigm (Whitehead 2003; Brand and Thomas 2013), which has been widely adopted by governments in the developed and developing world, since it was first identified in the Brundtland Report (World Commission on Environment and Development 1987).[2] There is "near universal recognition" (Bulkeley and Betsill 2005) among city authorities, public agencies and other advocates of sustainable development that sustainable cities are desirable and are capable of generating positive social, economic and ecological outcomes. In this sense, sustainable development can be understood as a key dynamic in the social and political organization of urban space and social life.

As this edited collection shows, sustainability and sustainable development are essentially contested terms (Connelly 2007), which are widely acknowledged to be ambiguous, interchangeable and loosely applied to a variety of contexts (Vallance, Perkins, and Dixon 2011; Gunder and Hillier 2009; Davoudi et al. 2012; Rydin 1999). Critics of sustainable development describe it as a neoliberal project (Raco 2005; Brand and Thomas 2013; Evans 2002) that has succeeded in integrating environmental concerns with economic interests, thereby enabling a discourse of ecological entrepreneurialism, or economic growth and technological innovation in the name of environmentalism, to dominate policymaking and practice (While, Jonas, and Gibbs 2004). It is widely acknowledged that poor progress has been made on addressing the social dimensions of sustainable development - social equality, inclusion and poverty reduction - in many cities (Julian Agyeman, Bullard, and Evans 2003; Julian Agyeman 2005; Vallance, Perkins, and Dixon 2011; Brand and Thomas 2013). While this is recognized by some authors to undermine the concept of sustainable development, philosophically and practically, (Julian Agyeman 2008; Julian Agyeman, Bullard, and Evans 2003; Cook and Swyngedouw 2012) the power and reach of sustainable development discourse does not appear to be limited by the evident inconsistency between rhetoric, policy and lived experience (Brand and Thomas 2013).

One consequence of this tension is the emergence of social sustainability as a distinct concept concerned with the social aspects of sustainable development that have been marginalized in mainstream discourse, policy and research (McKenzie 2004; Murphy 2012; Vallance, Perkins, and Dixon 2011). A growing body of literature explores how social sustainability is broadly interpreted and operationalized. Some authors explore the multiple dimensions and definitions of social sustainability- Sachs (Sachs 1999) and Agyeman (Julian Agyeman 2008) argue that social sustainability must be grounded in equality, democracy and social justice; Barbier (Barbier 1987) and Koning (Koning 2002) focus on the preservation of social and cultural values and ways of life; Littig and Griessler (Littig and Griessler 2005) address relationships between society and nature; while Vallance et al. (Vallance, Perkins, and Dixon 2011) discuss the importance of meeting basic social needs such as water, food and housing, before wider issues of environmental sustainability can be addressed. Suzanne Hanchett, in this volume, also situates the development of social sustainability in this scholarly body of work. Other literature addresses the diversity of settings in which social sustainability is being applied including: fair trade certification and organic food (Casula Vifell and Thedvall 2012), forest management

(Boström 2011), organic farming (Shreck, Getz, and Feenstra 2006), public health (Hancock 2012), sustainable tourism (Klintman 2012), sustainable buildings (Ole Jensen et al. 2012), and participatory environmental monitoring of a Brazilian mining company (Devlin and Tubino 2012).

In the UK, a discourse of social sustainability is emerging in urban planning and development, that seeks to establish a relationship between processes of change in the built environment, specifically regeneration and new housing development, and the creation of wellbeing, social capital and certain practices of citizenship at the neighbourhood level (Colantonio and Dixon 2010; Dempsey et al. 2011; Weingaertner and Moberg 2011; Magee, Scerri, and James 2012; Murphy 2012). In this context, social sustainability is loosely defined as the capacity of places to provide residents with a good quality of life now and in the future (The Berkeley Group 2012; Colantonio and Dixon 2010).

A number of the architects and property developers involved in my research describe social sustainability as a new iteration of the sustainable communities' policy agenda, which was introduced by the New Labour government in 2003. The Sustainable Communities Plan (Office of the Deputy Prime Minister 2003) identified the renewal of urban neighbourhoods as a vital element in repopulating cities and stimulating economic growth. It recognized the need to pay attention to the nature of urban sociality, as well as the material infrastructure of cities, in response to a perceived crisis in urban social relations (Forrest and Kearns 2001). Social exclusion, in particular the marginalization of deprived neighbourhoods from mainstream society, rising anti-social behaviour and fear of crime, falling levels of democratic and civic participation, and anxiety about the impact of online social interaction on face-to-face social relationships, characterized political representations of social decline (Forrest and Kearns 2001) at the time. Urban neighbourhoods were prioritised for intervention because of the contextual effects of concentrating poverty and deprivation in certain areas of cities, primarily social housing estates, and political recognition that improving the built environment could address anti-social behaviour and increase social interaction at the neighbourhood level. Raco (2007) argues that New Labour's focus on increasing neighbourhood social interaction represents an adoption of the Communitarian idea that "communities represent the essential building-blocks of social harmony and progress" (Raco 2007).

The Sustainable Communities Plan introduced the sustainable community as a socio-material concept, defined as a place that provides good quality housing, infrastructure and public services; a thriving local economy; neighbourhoods that are safe, inclusive, cohesive and foster a sense of belonging and attachment; and local civic and democratic involvement in an area-based model (Department for Communities and Local 2004; Office of the Deputy Prime Minister 2003; Raco 2007). The Plan established housing development and the planning system as the main policy instruments for creating sustainable urban communities. Environmental concerns were also linked to housing development through discussion of sustainable construction methods, energy efficiency and sustainable transport networks.

Anthropological work on planning acknowledges it to be a bureaucratic and political process of ordering space and social relationships (S. A. Abram 2000; Epstein 1973; Holston 1989; S. Abram and Weszkalnys 2011; S. Abram 2011). The sustainable communities' policy agenda introduced two initiatives intended to reconfigure urban populations and create new citizen subjectivities. First, the Mixed Communities Initiative (MCI) was launched in 2005, with the goal of transforming deprived, mono-tenure, mainly inner-city neighbourhoods, by changing the housing stock to attract new populations to previously run-down areas (Lupton and Fuller 2009). The idea of mixed communities is not new in British urban planning; 'garden cities' and post-war housing estates were designed to house people from different class backgrounds. However, the MCI is acknowledged to be different because of the scale of tenure diversification it intended to achieve, and the reliance on partnerships with private sector house-builders to fund new social housing through the development and sale of private housing (Silverman et al. 2005; Tunstall and Lupton 2010; Lupton and Fuller 2009). Area effects theory, which puts forward the argument that day-to-day co-existence of people from different backgrounds can increase social interaction through use of shared services and spaces, underpins the mixed communities principle (Silverman et al. 2005). Social interaction in the neighbourhood is thought to lead to the development of local social relationships, thereby increasing the likelihood of low-income households to have access and exposure to "more advantaged and aspirational social networks" (Silverman et al. 2005) and creating a means of reducing distance and prejudice (Atkinson and Kintrea 2001; Allen et al. 2005).

Second, is the "creation, identification, and mobilization of active communities and citizens" (Raco 2007), understood as individuals involved in local volunteering and democratic participation, and strong social networks at neighbourhood level- to encourage community self-help (Seyfang 2003). Sometimes described as a post-welfare political ideology (McGuirk and Dowling 2011), active citizenship is intended to encourage citizens to take greater responsibility for their own welfare and that of their communities based on the logic that "more developed communities and communities with more capacity are safer and healthier places to live" (Kelly, Caputo, and Jamieson 2005). Sustainable communities policy, therefore, places significant emphasis on increasing social interaction in neighbourhoods, both informally, through casual day-to-day interactions, and formally, through civic and democratic participation, to build trust and foster the local social capital needed to underpin the goal of self-sufficient communities and to ward off the risks of social isolation and decline in urban neighbourhoods.

The built environment is understood, in policy and practice, to be constitutive of the everyday social interactions that are thought to be the basis for building local social networks. Significant emphasis is placed on the arrangement and design quality of public spaces in the neighbourhood, including streets, open spaces, local parks and informal, semi-public meeting places like shops, cafes and pubs, in order to encourage low-level social interaction (and inhibit anti-social behaviour) and create a sense of local identity. Streets, parks and local open spaces are ascribed an important role in social cohesion and promoted through government policy and planning documents, such as this report published by the Commission for Architecture and the Built Environment, a public body created in 1999:

> Public spaces are open to all, regardless of ethnic origin, age or gender, and as such they represent a democratic forum for citizens and society. When properly designed and cared for, they bring communities together, provide meeting places and foster social ties of a kind that have been disappearing in many urban areas. These spaces shape the cultural identity of an area, are part of its unique character and provide a sense of place for local communities. (CABE Space 2004)

The sustainable communities' policy agenda has received widespread criticism from urban studies and social policy scholars. The validity of area effects theory has been questioned in the UK where there is some evidence that cross-tenure social interaction does not occur in mixed income neighbourhoods (Lupton 2008). Some authors have argued the mixed communities principle is a form of state-led gentrification, which leads to the displacement of lower income households (Lees 2008; O'Hanlon and Hamnett 2009), while others claim the sustainable communities agenda problematizes deprived communities by seeking to establish a connection between social need and unsustainability (Raco 2007). Nevertheless, the sustainable communities concept, along with mixed tenure and active citizenship have become institutionalized in planning policy (Department for Communities and Local Government

2012; Greater London Authority 2011) and urban governance with significant impacts for the configuration of urban populations and the materiality of everyday spaces of the city, in particular residential housing and public spaces in the neighbourhood. In this sense, the sustainable communities' policy agenda has succeeded in naturalizing certain forms of citizen subjectivity and sociality- and in establishing a dominant language of community that prioritises a locally spatialized collectivity over other notions of belonging.

Throughout the 2000s, a number of government bodies were responsible for promoting the sustainable communities policy agenda on these terms- as well as attempting to develop the capacity of government planning officers to deliver on this new agenda. However, since the Conservative-Liberal Democrat government was elected in 2010, many of these government bodies, such as the Sustainable Development Commission and CABE, have been disbanded or downgraded, and the planning system has been streamlined. Although the concept of sustainable communities remains central to the government's sustainable development commitments, and this is evident in reformed planning policy, the property developers, architects and planners informing my research describe how the coalition government has withdrawn resources and practical support, in the form of policy guidance or best practice programmes, from this area. One property developer describes the result as:

A vacuum … we don't have standards on social so it's a grey area between policy and day-to-day business. Planning authorities don't have the capacity or the confidence to demand a coherent response from developers on social so it's up to us, to the better developers, to suggest what we think makes sense

The vacuum they describe has created space for a new discourse of social sustainability to emerge. While holism is an important characteristic of sustainable communities policy, (for example, the Sustainable Communities Plan (Office of the Deputy Prime Minister 2003) recognises that a community is more than housing by acknowledging the interaction of social, material and political factors), social sustainability discourse attempts to reconfigure "the social" as a separate domain. In the next section, I describe how my research has attempted to explore the purpose of this separation by engaging with social sustainability discourse- ethnographically- in order to understand the situated meanings and practices that are embedded in language, and thereby, enable certain futures and interventions to become thinkable and operational. This ethnographic approach is also extended to the notion of community, which is frequently invoked by my informants to describe real and imagined places, social practices and a state of being. Community is a problematic term for anthropologists. As Amit (Amit and Rapport 2002) identifies, it is highly contested and comes with the theoretical and methodological baggage of a discipline that has a history of conflating place, people, identity and culture. The view of community constructed in sustainable communities policy and discourse speaks directly to Tönnies' (Tonnies 1957) ideal of community as a traditional, face-to-face collectivity, in which the neighbourhood is the primary setting for social relationships and practices that support a collective sense of belonging and attachment. In this sense, the "sustainable community" as a policy construct and a planning goal can be seen to negate other forms of identity, such as race, ethnicity, culture and gender. My work suggests that in the context of urban planning, sustainable communities' policy imposes an imagined homogeneity on urban life and space that denies the contested nature of places and privileges the neighbourhood as a locus of identity and belonging. Yet, community is ever present in my fieldwork, and therefore, cannot be ignored in spite of the theoretical and methodological issues it raises.

What is the Point of Social Sustainability?

It is early spring 2014, and I am sitting with a group of architects, together we are discussing the model for a new urban neighbourhood in East London. The conversation turns to the question of what makes a sustainable community and one of the architects describes his relief that the "green bling is over" and that architecture practices are no longer competing on the grounds of environmental sustainability: "environmental can just be done now. Green is embedded in policy so it has to be embedded in design. It doesn't have to be a point of difference anymore," he adds.

This perspective arises frequently in my fieldwork encounters with property developers, planners and architects. Environmental sustainability has become highly institutionalized, and consequently, is described as a taken-for-granted element of planning and design practice. In this sense, it no longer offers organisations' a competitive advantage. Social sustainability, however, is seen as a new space for architects, planners and developers to differentiate themselves in a highly competitive market. Social sustainability is an "unclaimed territory", as one property developer describes:

> Environmental sustainability is a hygiene factor now everybody else is
> doing it. It doesn't mark you out at all and you have no choice anyway.
> Being sustainable ... in future, it won't be about environmental. That
> leaves economic: not easy to deliver but easy to define and count jobs,
> apprenticeships, and you have to do it. And social: hard to count, hard to
> define, not assumed to be our expertise.

In this context, social sustainability is a discursive space that signifies innovation. The debates described at the beginning of this chapter can be examined as one part of a process to construct "the social," as a domain that is not well understood and demands attention, and action, if wider sustainable development goals are to be achieved. Analysis of social sustainability discourse, in texts, events and day-to-day practice, reveals two distinct elements: first, an effort to problematize a lack of professional and practical knowledge about how the material and social dimensions of the city interact and shape local social experience. Second, to connect this lack of knowledge to the failure of previous housing initiatives to create safe and thriving urban neighbourhoods. The RSA frames the problem in relatively mild terms, "with some notable exceptions, the property and development industry has struggled to quantify the value of the relationship and the nature of interaction between the 'hardware' and 'software' of socially productive places." (RSA 2014)

Some of my informants are bolder in their assertions that planning and architecture professions still fail to fully appreciate the inter-dependency between the social and material dimensions of place. In the debates I attend, and in several conversations with my informants, post-war mass housing programmes are frequently cited as examples of where planned development has failed to create thriving new places because of the lack of understanding about, or attention paid to, how communities form. Both low-density suburban estates and high-rise Modernist towers are criticized as urban forms that do not support the kind of social interactions that create a sense of community; the former because of over-reliance on cars and inability to support neighbourhood services, and the latter, for claims of alienating architecture. Avoiding the failures of the past is an important characteristic of social sustainability discourse and can be found in texts (The Berkeley Group 2012; Woodcraft et al. 2011; John Thompson & Partners 2013) and in debates like the RSA's *Developing Socially Productive Places* conference, where Mark Prisk, former housing minister and keynote speaker, identifies the need to learn from past experience:

> Housing is going to be one of the top issues at the next election ... the need
> to build more homes has become sufficiently pressing it has become top

priority for all parties ... so this renewed political focus is welcome but I put alongside it a significant caveat ... in an election year there is the danger that the political parties seek to outbid each other in how many homes can we build in the next five years ... real prospect that we repeat the old mistakes of building quickly and cheaply and building without really understanding what it is that makes a community and what it is that people want.[3]

In these debates the "social" in social sustainability becomes a problem of knowledge and capacity – *What is the 'social' in sustainable development? How do changes in the built environment influence social experience? What makes an estate into a community?* - this can be addressed by developing new insights and emergent design practices grounded in a situated knowledge of local social experience. This framing provides a logic for seeking to separate and reinterpret the social dimensions of sustainable development as a distinct category that requires specific strategies and actions. Problematizing social sustainability enables proponents of the discourse to argue that development that pays attention to social need and supporting local social relationships will create social, as well as financial, value by producing places that can thrive and a healthier, happier citizenry. At a time of austerity and planning reform, this narrative has broad appeal to local authorities that are under increasing pressure to address London's housing shortage and cope with widespread budget cuts. In this sense, engaging with social sustainability discourse enables property developers, architects and planners to demonstrate innovation and to frame urban development as an intervention that supports wider social policy goals, such as public health and wellbeing.

Configuring social sustainability as a value-generating practice follows an established logic in sustainable development practices. Several authors (Cugurullo and Rapoport 2012; While, Jonas, and Gibbs 2004; Brand and Thomas 2013) describe the emergence of entrepreneurial modes of urban governance in the UK during the 1990s and 2000s, which have seen cities competing to attract investment. Urban sustainability projects have figured significantly in this space (While, Jonas, and Gibbs 2004), in particular landmark projects like eco-cities or sustainable architecture. Cugurullo and Rapoport's study of the ideological landscape of urban sustainability projects identifies that they offer a way of fitting environmental considerations into "a tool that is largely about property development" (Cugurullo and Rapoport 2012) and is grounded in the belief that sustainable development "can and should be a profit generating activity" (Cugurullo and Rapoport 2012).

For the architects, house builders and planners involved in my research, "the social" is seen as elusive and intangible, in the sense that it cannot be mapped following the rational logic of planning and does not have the solid materiality of a building or a street. They prompted me to explore what constitutes "the social" in this context? Where can the social be found and who decides what can become part of this category? This has become a central theme of enquiry in my research project, and herein, I will describe one of these exchanges with two architects and an urban designer. For this group, "the social" is understood as the forms of urban sociality found in "a proper community ... you know, like knowing your neighbours, maybe helping each other out sometimes, having a pint in a local pub". We compare the sociality of our own, primarily urban, neighbourhoods to the notion of "proper community" where people know and trust their neighbours, talk to each other on the street, and maybe even help each other out in times of need. This view of "the social" sphere of sustainability as a collection of locally spatialized social practices is widely held among the architects, property developers and planners that I met with, to the extent that it is felt to be self-evident and not really worth discussing. My enquiries about what is or isn't categorized as social are often brushed aside in favour of discussing the real problem, which is "how to do social sustainability". Considerable effort is dedicated to identifying interventions to encourage people to talk to their neighbours and feel like they belong to their neighbourhood. Timebanks, street parties and 'meanwhile' projects, temporary initiatives from pop-up cafes to mobile community gardens, are increasingly being incorporated into large-scale urban development projects to create a sense of community and foster the social ties that are much sought-after by policymakers.

Although it is presented as self-evident, social sustainability is highly mediated and relies on the selective inclusion of policy goals and professional practices to make it an operational category in urban planning and development. Work, employment and local economic development are not configured as part of the "social" in social sustainability discourse, for example, although they are acknowledged to be vital in creating functioning neighbourhoods. Similarly, other major policy goals, such as improving public health, improving educational outcomes or tackling spatialized poverty tend to be excluded. My informants describe how the regulation of economic and environmental categories in sustainable development enables these distinctions to be drawn, although this does not account for the exclusion of health and education from the social domain. Another, possibly more compelling, explanation is about where the responsibility for sustainable development lies. Government, in particular

local government, is widely perceived to have responsibility for the quality
of public services, opportunities, growth and development of local
communities. Austerity and government's reliance on private corporations
to drive urban development and provide housing has shifted the balance of
this responsibility and the relationship between the state and private sector.
In response, house builders are selecting some dimensions of social
experience that can be influenced by built environment interventions for
inclusion in social sustainability discourse and rejecting others; a process
of selective inclusion also applied to environmental sustainability goals
that While et al. describe as an "urban sustainability fix" (While, Jonas,
and Gibbs 2004). For example, some house builders have put forward the
argument that addressing health and social equity are beyond the control
and influence of developers and should be the responsibility of
government (The Berkeley Group 2012). While this may be the case, the
effect of this argument is to marginalize concerns with social equity in
social sustainability discourse and to legitimize social sustainability as an
emerging planning and design practice that privileges quality of place and
social capital over spatial justice. In this sense, social sustainability, which
theoretically is a concept about equity and fairness, has been made safe
through a discursive process of reinterpretation that allows it to be
accommodated in dominant political and economic structures.

The architects, planners and property developers involved in my
research almost all describe social sustainability as a fluid concept that is
not widely understood or operationalized in the UK, yet has broad appeal
because it succeeds in synthesizing an array of established and emerging
policy priorities. Rydin (Rydin 1999) writes about the language games of
sustainability politics in the context of climate change and environmental
policymaking. Ambiguity, she argues, arising from the loose language and
fuzzy boundaries of over-arching terms like sustainable development,
creates space for different actors to disguise conflicts of interest and
negotiate positions that enable concrete policies and interventions to come
to fruition. Green growth through technological innovation has neutralized
potentially threatening arguments for limiting consumption and growth-
and has thus legitimized environmental sustainability as a practice. Social
sustainability discourse is similarly controlled to limit what constitutes the
social as a category and field of action and in so doing, to "transform the
perceptible into non-obvious meanings" (Rydin 1999).

Conclusion

This chapter attempts to demonstrate how anthropology can bring a situated perspective to the analysis of sustainable development that reveals the tensions and disjunctures between rhetoric and practice. Analyzing social sustainability as an emergent discourse and practice from the perspective of a loose network of planners, architects and property developers working on large-scale urban development projects in London has highlighted the instability of categories like social and sustainability, which appear to be fixed yet are highly mediated and contextually specific. By focusing on the reconfigurations, slippages and ambiguity of sustainability language, this chapter has attempted to explore how social sustainability is constructed as a nuanced reinterpretation of an established policy agenda, and can be understood as part of an effort to create a new discursive space, and an emergent form of design practice, that signifies innovation, leadership and value and seeks to justify interventions in the built environment. The UK government's emphasis on housing development as a means to achieve the broader goals of thriving cities and economic growth, and in turn on private sector property developers to provide housing, gives rise to deeply unequal power relationships in urban neighbourhoods. Sustainable development can be understood as one of the "subtle forms of power that saturate everyday life, through experiences of time, space, and work" (Ortner 2005), in the sense that it is shaping the material spaces of the city and citizen subjectivities in ways that are not immediately evident.

Sustainable development practices in urban settings are understudied by anthropologists yet arguably require close attention. From an anthropological perspective, social sustainability can be interrogated as a socio-material practice, which seeks to bring about certain forms of urban space, sociality and subjectivity using a diverse array of discursive and material processes. It relies on the selective incorporation of policy goals and theoretical concepts to construct a dominant view of sustainable communities as socially cohesive, self- sufficient and safe, which conversely, structures need and deprivation as unsustainable. Anthropology can make an important contribution to a social science of sustainability by highlighting the political and institutional contexts that shape discourse, practice, policy and sustainable development as a field of knowledge. Anthropology's grounded research methods can illuminate the inconsistencies and uncertainties generated in the process of translating sustainability as a normative concept into everyday social and professional practices.

References

Abram, Simone. *Culture and Planning*. Ashgate Publishing, Ltd. 2011.

Abram, Simone. "Planning the Public: Some Comments on Empirical Problems for Planning Theory." *Journal of Planning Education and Research* 19 (4): 351–57. 2011.

Abram, Simone, and Weszkalnys. Gisa. "Introduction: Anthropologies of Planning, Temporality, Imagination, and Ethnography." *Focaal* (61): 3–18. 2011.

Agyeman, Julian, Bullard, Robert, and Evans, Bob. *Just Sustainabilities: Development in an Unequal World*. MIT Press. 2003.

Agyeman, J., and B. Evans. "'Just Sustainability': The Emerging Discourse of Environmental Justice in Britain?." *The Geographical Journal* 170 (2): 155–64. 2004.

Agyeman, Julian. *Sustainable Communities and the Challenge of Environmental Justice*. New York University Press. 2005

—. 2008. "Toward a 'Just' Sustainability?." *Continuum* 22 (6): 751–56.

Allen, Chris, Margaret Camina, Rionach Casey, Sarah Coward, and Martin Wood. *Mixed Tenure, Twenty Years on - Nothing out of the Ordinary*. York: Joseph Rowntree Foundation. 2005.

Amit, Vered, and Rapport, Nigel. *The Trouble with Community: Anthropological Reflections on Movement, Identity and Collectivity*. London ; Sterling, Va: Pluto Press. 2002.

Atkinson, Rowland, and Kintrea, Keith. "Disentangling Area Effects: Evidence from Deprived and Non-Deprived Neighbourhoods." *Urban Studies* 38 (12): 2277–98. 2001.

Barbier, Edward B. "The Concept of Sustainable Economic Development." *Environmental Conservation* 14 (02): 101–10. 1987.

Boström, Magnus. "The Problematic Social Dimension of Sustainable Development: The Case of the Forest Stewardship Council." *International Journal of Sustainable Development & World Ecology* 19 (1): 3–15. 2011.

Brand, Peter, and Thomas, Michael. *Urban Environmentalism: Global Change and the Mediation of Local Conflict*. Routledge. 2013.

Buchli, Victor. *An Archaeology of Socialism*. Berg. 2000.

—. "Architecture and Modernism." In *Handbook of Material Culture*, 254–66. London: SAGE Publications Ltd. 2006.

—. "ASTANA: Materiality and the City." In *Urban Life in Post-Soviet Asia*. UCL Press / Taylor & Francis Oxon. 2007.

Buchli, Victor, and Gavin Lucas. "The Archaeology of Alienation." In *Archaeologies of the Contemporary Past*. Oxon, New York: Routledge. 2006.

Bulkeley, Harriet, and Michele Betsill. "Rethinking Sustainable Cities: Multilevel Governance and the 'Urban' Politics of Climate Change." *Environmental Politics* 14 (1): 42–63. 2005.

CABE Space. *The Value of Public Space How High Quality Parks and Public Spaces Create Economic, Social and Environmental Value*. CABE Space. 2004.

Castells, Manuel. "Preface - Sustainable Cities: Structure and Agency." In *Livable Cities? Urban Struggles for Livelihood and Sustainability*, ix – xi. Berkeley and Los Angeles, California: University of California Press. 2002.

Casula Vifell, Åsa, and Renita Thedvall. "Organizing for Social Sustainability: Governance through Bureaucratization in Meta-Organizations." *Sustainability: Science, Practice, & Policy* 8 (1). 2012.

Colantonio, Andrea, and Tim Dixon. *Urban Regeneration & Social Sustainability: Best Practice from European Cities*. John Wiley & Sons. 2010.

Connelly, Steve. "Mapping Sustainable Development as a Contested Concept." *Local Environment* 12 (3): 259–78. 2007.

Cook, I. R., and E. Swyngedouw. "Cities, Social Cohesion and the Environment: Towards a Future Research Agenda." *Urban Studies* 49 (9): 1959–79. 2012.

Crate, Susan Alexandra, and Mark Nuttall, eds. *Anthropology and Climate Change: From Encounters to Actions*. Left Coast Press Inc. 2009.

Cugurullo, Federico, and Elizabeth Rapoport. "Between the Global and the Local: The Ideologies and Realities of Sustainable Urban Projects." In. UCL, London. 2012.

Davoudi, Simin, Keith Shaw, L. Jamila Haider, Allyson E. Quinlan, Garry D. Peterson, Cathy Wilkinson, Hartmut Fünfgeld, Darryn McEvoy, Libby Porter, and Simin Davoudi. "Resilience: A Bridging Concept or a Dead End? "." *Planning Theory & Practice* 13 (2): 299–333. 2012.

Dempsey, Nicola, Glen Bramley, Sinéad Power, and Caroline Brown. "The Social Dimension of Sustainable Development: Defining Urban Social Sustainability." *Sustainable Development* 19 (5): 289–300. 2011.

Department for Communities and Local. "The Egan Review: Skills for Sustainable Communities." Publication (Reports and summaries). April. 2004

Department for Communities and Local Government. "National Planning Policy Framework." Department for Communities and Local Government. 2012.

Devlin, John, and Denise Isabel Tubino. "Contention, Participation, and Mobilization in Environmental Assessment Follow-up: The Itabira Experience." *Sustainability: Science, Practice, & Policy* 8 (1): 106–15. 2012.

Dixon, Tim. *Putting the S-Word Back into Sustainability: Can We Be More "Social"?*. London: The Berkeley Group. 2011.

Epstein, David G. *Brasília, Plan and Reality: A Study of Planned and Spontaneous Urban Development*. University of California Press. 1973.

Evans, Peter B. *Livable Cities?: Urban Struggles for Livelihood and Sustainability*. University of California Press. 2002.

Fiske, Shirley, J. "Global Change Policymaking from Inside the Beltway: Engaging Anthropology." In *Anthropology & Climate Change: From Encounters to Actions*. California: Left Coast Press Inc. 2009.

Forrest, Ray, and Ade Kearns. "Social Cohesion, Social Capital and the Neighbourhood." *Urban Studies* 38 (12): 2125–43. 2001.

Greater London Authority. *The London Plan: Spatial Development Strategy for Greater London, July 2011*. London: Greater London Authority. 2011.

Gunder, Michael, and Jean Hillier. *Planning in Ten Words or Less: A Lacanian Entanglement with Spatial Planning*. Ashgate Publishing, Ltd. 2009.

Haenn, Nora, and Richard Wilk. *The Environment in Anthropology: A Reader in Ecology, Culture, and Sustainable Living*. New York and London: New York University Press. 2006.

Hancock, Trevor. "Social Sustainability the 'Soft Infrastructure' of a Healthy Community." 2012.

Hannerz, Ulf. *Exploring the City: Inquiries toward an Urban Anthropology*. 1980.

—. *Soulside: Inquiries into Ghetto Culture and Community*. Chicago; London: The University of Chicago Press. 2004.

Holston, James. *The Modernist City: An Anthropological Critique of Brasilia*. Chicago; London: The University of Chicago Press. 1989.

John Thompson & Partners. *Social Sustainability: Process, Place, People*. John Thompson & Partners. 2013.

Kelly, Katharine D., Tullio Caputo, and Wanda Jamieson. "Reconsidering Sustainability: Some Implications for Community-Based Crime Prevention." *Critical Social Policy* 25 (3): 306–24. 2005.

Klintman, Mikael. "Issues of scale in the global accreditation of sustainable tourism: schemes toward harmonized re-embeddedness?" *Sustainability: Science, Practice, & Policy* 8 (1): 106–15. 2012.2012.

Koning, Juliette. *Social Sustainability in a Globalizing World: Context, Theory and Methodology Explored.* More on MOST: Proceedings of an Expert Meeting. The Hague: UNESCO. 2002.

Lees, Loretta. "Gentrification and Social Mixing: Towards an Inclusive Urban Renaissance?" *Urban Studies* 45 (12): 2449–70. 2008.

Littig, Beate, and Erich Griessler. "Social Sustainability: A Catchword between Political Pragmatism and Social Theory." *International Journal of Sustainable Development* 8 (1): 65–79. 2005.

London 2012/LOCOG. *London 2012 Sustainability Plan.* London: London 2012/LOCOG. 2010.

Low, Setha. "The Anthropology of Cities: Imagining and Theorizing the City." *Annual Review of Anthropology* 25: 383–409. 1996.

—. *Theorizing the City: The New Urban Anthropology Reader.* Rutgers University Press. 1999.

—. "The Edge and the Center: Gated Communities and the Discourse of Urban Fear." *American Anthropologist* New Series (March): 44–58. 2001.

Low, Setha M., and Irwin Altman. "Place Attachment." In *Place Attachment*, edited by Irwin Altman and Setha M. Low, 1–12. Human Behavior and Environment. Springer US. 1992.

Lupton, Ruth. *Neighbourhood Effects: Can We Measure Them and Does It Matter?* SSRN Scholarly Paper ID 1158964. Rochester, NY: Social Science Research Network. 2008.

Lupton, Ruth, and Crispian Fuller. "Mixed Communities: A New Approach to Spatially Concentrated Poverty in England." *International Journal of Urban and Regional Research* 33 (4): 1014–28. 2009.

Magee, Liam, Andy Scerri, and Paul James. "Measuring Social Sustainability: A Community-Centred Approach." *Applied Research in Quality of Life* 7 (3): 239–61. 2012.

Mayor's Office. *Convergence Framework and Action Plan 2011-2015.* Six Host Boroughs, Mayor's Office. 2011.

McGuirk, Pauline, and Robyn Dowling. "Governing Social Reproduction in Masterplanned Estates Urban Politics and Everyday Life in Sydney." *Urban Studies* 48 (12): 2611–28. 2011.

McKenzie, Stephen. *Social Sustainability: Towards Some Definitions.* Working Paper 27. Magill, South Australia: Hawke Research Institute. 2004.

Meadowcroft, James. "Sustainable Development: A New(ish) Idea for a New Century?" *Political Studies* 48 (2): 370–87. 2000.

Murphy, Kevin. "The Social Pillar of Sustainable Development: A Literature Review and Framework for Policy Analysis." *Sustainability: Science, Practice, & Policy* 8 (1). 2012.

Office of the Deputy Prime Minister. "Sustainable Communities Plan." Office of the Deputy Prime Minister. 2003.

O'Hanlon, Seamus, and Chris Hamnett. "Deindustrialisation, Gentrification and the Re-Invention of the Inner City: London and Melbourne, c.1960-2008." *Urban Policy Research* 27 (3): 211–16. 2009.

Ole Jensen, Jesper, Michael Søgaard Jørgensen, Morten Elle, and Erik Hagelskjær Lauridsen. "Has Social Sustainability Left the Building? The Recent Conceptualization of 'sustainability' in Danish Buildings." *Sustainability: Science, Practice, & Policy* 8 (1). 2012.

Olympic Park Legacy Company. *A Walk around Queen Elizabeth Park.* Olympic Park Legacy Company. 2010.

Ortner, Sherry B. "Subjectivity and Cultural Critique." *Anthropological Theory* 5 (1): 31–52. 2005.

Raco, Mike. "Sustainable Development, Rolled-out Neoliberalism and Sustainable Communities." *Antipode* 37 (2): 324–47. 2005.

—. "Securing Sustainable Communities Citizenship, Safety and Sustainability in the New Urban Planning." *European Urban and Regional Studies* 14 (4): 305–20. 2007.

RSA. "Developing Socially Productive Places: Learning from What Works: Lessons from British Land - RSA Conference." RSA. 2014.

Rydin. "Can We Talk Ourselves into Sustainability? The Role of Discourse in the Environmental Policy Process." *Environmental Values* 8 (4): 467–84. 1999.

Rydin, Yvonne, and Nancy Holman. "Re-evaluating the Contribution of Social Capital in Achieving Sustainable Development." *Local Environment* 9 (2): 117–33. 2004.

Sachs, Ignacy. "Social Sustainability and Whole Development: Exploring the Dimensions of Sustainable Development." In *Sustainability and the Social Sciences.* London: Zed Books. 1999.

Seyfang, Gill. "Growing Cohesive Communities One Favour at a Time: Social Exclusion, Active Citizenship and Time Banks." *International Journal of Urban and Regional Research* 27 (3): 699–706. 2003.

Shove, Elizabeth, Mika Pantzar, and Matt Watson. *The Dynamics of Social Practice: Everyday Life and How It Changes.* SAGE. 2012.

Shreck, Aimee, Christy Getz, and Gail Feenstra. "Social Sustainability, Farm Labor, and Organic Agriculture: Findings from an Exploratory Analysis." *Agriculture and Human Values* 23 (4): 439–49. 2006.

Silverman, Emily, Ruth Lupton, Alex Fenton, Chartered Institute of Housing (Great Britain), and Joseph Rowntree Foundation. *A Good Place for Children: Attracting and Retaining Families in Inner Urban Mixed Income Communities*. Coventry; York: Chartered Institute of Housing ; Joseph Rowntree Foundation. 2005.

Space Syntax. *2011 London Riots Location Analysis Proximity to Town Centres and Large Post-War Housing Estates*. Space Syntax Ltd. 2011.

The Berkeley Group. *Creating Strong Communities: How to Measure the Social Sustainability of New Housing Developments*. London: The Berkeley Group. 2012.

Tonnies, Ferdinand. *Community and Society*. Courier Dover Publications. 1957.

Tunstall, Rebecca, and Ruth Lupton. *Mixed Communities Evidence Review*. London: Department of Communities and Local Government. 2010.

Vallance, Suzanne, Harvey C. Perkins, and Jennifer E. Dixon. "What Is Social Sustainability? A Clarification of Concepts." *Geoforum* 42: 342–248. 2011.

Wallman, Sandra. *Eight London Households*. London: Tavistock. 1984.

Weingaertner, Carina, and Åsa Moberg. "Exploring Social Sustainability: Learning from Perspectives on Urban Development and Companies and Products." *Sustainable Development*, October, n/a – n/a. 2011.

While, Aidan, Andrew E. G. Jonas, and David Gibbs. "The Environment and the Entrepreneurial City: Searching for the Urban 'sustainability; fix' in Manchester and Leeds." *International Journal of Urban and Regional Research* 28 (3): 549–69. 2004.

Whitehead, Mark. "(Re)Analysing the Sustainable City: Nature, Urbanisation and the Regulation of Socio-Environmental Relations in the UK." *Urban Studies* 40 (7): 1183–1206. 2003.

Woodcraft, S, Tricia Hackett, Lucia Caistor, and Nicola Bacon. *Design for Social Sustainability: A Framework for Creating Thriving Communities*. London: The Young Foundation. 2011.

World Commission on Environment and Development. "Our Common Future." Oxford University Press. 1987.

Yaneva, Alberta. "Understanding Architecture, Accounting Society." *Science Studies* Vol. 21 No. 2008.

—. "The Architectural as a Type of Connector." *Perspecta 42: The Yale Architectural Journal*: 138-143. 2010.
—. *MAPPING CONTROVERSIES IN ARCHITECTURE.* Surrey; Burlington: Ashgate Publishing, Ltd. 2012.

Notes

[1] From *"Urbanism and the Unlearning of Architecture"* lecture given by Professor Tina Saaby, Copenhagen City Architect at Academy of Urbanism *"Digital Urbanism"* conference in Bradford on Thursday 16 May 2013.
[2] See Chapter 9, The Urban Challenge, The Brundtland Report *(Our Common Future)* (World Commission on Environment and Development 1987)
[3] For a video of the keynote address see https://www.youtube.com/watch?v=U4Yd5n9y7eM (accessed January 2015)

Chapter Nine

Rure in Urbs: Exploring Governance and Policy Aspects of European Urban Agriculture in the Age of Austerity

Mary Corcoran

Urban agriculture: Introduction

The allotment in history has been both peasant and proletarian (Crouch and Ward 1997: 15). Plots have been provided, for the poor in England, since the eighteenth century mainly by the landed gentry and clergy (King 2006). Agitation in favour of the granting of allotments can be traced to 1765 when 'cow and cot schemes' were advocated for resettling the displaced poor (Crouch and Ward 1997: 46). The Enclosure Acts deprived the rural peasantry of access to land that was previously held in common. In the United Kingdom, the landed gentry were opposed to any attempts by parliament to regulate the provision of allotments. They preferred such provisioning to remain within the charitable realm.

While allotments were initially a rural phenomenon under a 1908 (U.K.) Act, county councils were given the remit to provide small holdings and allotments if there was demand for them in their borough, urban district or parish. The 1922 Act, which consolidated a number of earlier Acts, codified an allotment garden as an allocation of land 'not exceeding forty poles in extent which is wholly or mainly cultivated by the occupier for the production of vegetable or fruit crops for consumption by himself or his family.' This remains the definition that is used to the present day in both the United Kingdom and Ireland. There is a strict injunction against producing foodstuffs for commercial sale although this only applies to allotment holders on publicly-provided land.

Civil society groups were instrumental in setting up allotment garden movements across Europe in the nineteenth and twentieth century. There is a long European history of allotment gardening borne out of citizens' efforts to bring nature into the city (Meller 2005). In the nineteenth century, working class communities and new immigrants to European cities survived by growing their own food. Crucially, though land for cultivation was available only through grace and favour, and in general, a strict demarcation was maintained between what was considered urban and rural.

In South East Asia, in contrast, the model of planning allowed for green patches within urbanized settlements. Yokohari points out that in the nineteenth century when Tokyo had a population in excess of one million (larger at that time than Shanghai, London or Paris) there were one thousand gardens and forests inside the city boundary constituting 40% of the land designated for agricultural use. Paddy fields were located within a couple of kilometres of the city centre surrounded by dense residential development. These played an integral role in the provision of cereals and vegetables to the expanding urban population (Yokohari 2014).

In the United States and Europe, allotments flourished during wartime periods. Urban agriculture reached a high point during the Second World War when citizens in Germany and in Britain were urged to cultivate all available land in order to increase the food supply. Social change in the latter part of the twentieth century, in particular the improvement of working conditions, the decline in poverty and the rise in the consumption and leisure industries transformed the function of allotments from self-provisioning to a recreational pursuit (Crouch and Ward 1997). The long-term trend has been one of dramatic decline. Allotments in the United Kingdom and Ireland in particular, came increasingly to be viewed as anachronistic, the provenance of a hardy band of retired males.

Urban Agriculture and Sustainability

Is an industry located within (intraurban) or on the fringe (periurban) of a town, a city or a metropolis, which grows or raises, processes and distributes a diversity of food and non-food products, (re)-using largely human and material resource, produces and services found in and around that urban area, and in turn supplying human and material resources, produce and services largely to that urban area (Mougeot 2000: 10).

Research on urban agriculture has primarily focused on its contribution to urban bio-diversity, sustainability and socio-economic development

(Binns and Lynch 1998, Hampwaye et al. 2009). This is in keeping with what has been described as the 'green turn' or 'ecological turn' in urban policies and beyond (Tornaghi 2014). There is ample evidence of this turn in popular culture. For instance, the development of TV shows on allotments such as BBC2's *The Big Allotment Challenge* (2014) and the flourishing of an urban agriculture genre in self-help and coffee table books (e.g. Novella Carpenter, *Farm City: the education of an urban farmer* (2010); Novella Carpenter and Willow Rosenthal, *The essential urban farmer* (2011); Sarah Rich and Matthew Benson, *Urban Farm* (2012); Jennifer Cockrall-King, *Food and the City: urban agriculture and the new food revolution* (2012).

The academic literature on urban agriculture has been very much focused on the global south or the *developing world* (Mougeot, 2005, 2006), but increasingly, the discourse of sustainability is also being deployed in cities of the North, for instance, in the revival of allotment and community gardening, the rise of community supported agriculture, the growing focus on food sovereignty and security, and imaginative plans for eco villages and towns (Tornaghi 2014). Eric Olin Wright (2014) argues passionately for the building of real utopias - re-purposing space in a long-term process of transformation that can ameliorate the more pernicious effects of capitalism. In the same vein as Polyani (1944), Wright focuses on the limits of the market and the consequences that flow from an over-marketised society. He argues that key resources such as land should be taken out of the market so that they can be restored to the commons. This would create a more utopian form of capitalism that puts people and the social imperative at its core. In this, he echoes the work of other social scientists, who have argued the benefits of the commons (Ostrum 1991: McKibben 2007). From a more prosaic perspective, critics argue that the degree to which the sustainability agenda in the global North actually proffers solutions to food security and food self-sufficiency is debatable, given that they do not generally challenge the underlying logic of growth oriented neo-liberal capitalism (Tornaghi 2014).

While urban agriculture in the global North may lack a radical edge and a wider political agenda for reframing the way in which capitalism uses the planet's resources, its transformative potential has been more readily recognized in the global south. Cuba has, for a long time, been recognized as a leading proponent of alternative agriculture. According to Premat (2005), urban agriculture became particularly important in Cuba during the post-Soviet economic crisis- one consequence of which was greater food insecurity. The success of Cuban organic agriculture heralds not just the application of new agricultural technology- but the transformation of social and spatial relations on the land (Clausen 2007). Moreover, it offers an alternative model of food production and consumption-predicated on social justice and sustainability- to that offered by the industrialized model, which dominates elsewhere.

Creative mechanisms for promoting urban agriculture tend to flourish at times of crisis. In 2001, for instance, in the wake of a severe economic crisis, one innovative strategy pursued in the city of Rosario, Argentina was to turn over public land and offer tax breaks to owners of vacant lots to let poor residents grow organic produce on their properties. The local authority also supplied tools, seeds, and other supports to the amateur growers (Butler 2006). Although the numbers engaged in urban farming declined as the city began to recover economically, urban agriculture has transformed the formerly vacant lots and dumps into green and productive spaces. Crucially, the allotments' rise and fall mirrored the trajectory of the economic crisis: when the economy temporarily faltered, alternative forms of food production flourished, when the economic growth model reasserted itself, the allotments declined. This indicates the essentially contingent nature of urban gardening (within the current urban economic regime) and its failure to become embedded as a core, sustainable and sustaining element of urban and regional planning.

We can trace a direct link between crisis-ridden urban settlements and a new found interest in local food cultivation. An urban agriculture trend has been underway for some time in rustbelt cities such as Detroit, Michigan where a charitable organization, *Urban Farming* has been pioneering a programme of transforming waste ground into vegetable gardens that can help feed the local population. Recent research suggests that optimal usage of publicly owned vacant lots of land in Detroit could feasibly produce significant quantities of fresh produce for the local population (Colasanti and Hamm 2010). In New York City, community gardens, which date to the economic crisis of the 1970s, are viewed as an instance of counter hegemonic space that can arrest the decline of the commons implicit in the neo-liberal political project (Eizenberg 2012). As such community gardens, and indeed allotments, offer an alternative modality of social reproduction that takes after the model of 'the commons'. Land is held in common under a public tenure system which, is the opposite of speculative financialisation. The focus is largely on cultivation for the purpose of personal consumption (vegetable produce) or for aesthetic gratification (flower gardens). The mode of production is non-hierarchical and participatory and is not directed at generating profit. This kind of cultivation is popular among urbanites, and in particular, has undergone a renaissance in cities of the global North, as Eizenberg outlines in the context of New York City. In Berlin, 15 per cent of the city's land is used for urban agriculture. All 80,000 of Berlin's allotment gardens are in use with many people on a waiting list (Butler 2006).There are approximately 200,000 allotments in Britain. In 2009, a survey conducted by the National Society of Allotment and Leisure Gardeners (NSALG) recorded long waiting lists for allotment plots prompting one NSALG member to observe that in some parts of country one is more likely to secure a burial plot before securing an allotment (Quarmby 2010).

In recent years, and in response to food scandals and globalization of agriculture, growing numbers of urban farmers in Japan have attempted to enhance their own self sufficiency by turning to agri-activities (Yokohari et al. 2010: 226) Interestingly, this renewal of interest which is evidenced in both urban and suburban areas constitutes a restoration of traditional Japanese urban agricultural landscape, alluded to earlier. Nonetheless, the idea of green infrastructure provision in Asian cities remains secondary to the provision of grey infrastructure. Yokohari et al. believe this is particularly shortsighted- because urban residents are heavily reliant on functional units outside of the urban area for the supply of food and other resources. In the event of a natural disaster there is a risk of a breakdown of supply chains, something that could be avoided were cities to actively engage in securing a locally based system of food provisioning. Green infrastructure has much to offer in this context. For instance, researchers have found that top quality/highly fertile soils can be found in and around the centre of many Asian cities, providing a good case for maintaining urban agriculture in cities. Moreover, cultivated patches of land in the urban zone host a number of eco-systems including microclimate control which can play an important function in reducing the ambient temperature in cities such as Tokyo where residential density is very high. Researchers have demonstrated a two degree centigrade differential between measured air temperatures in urban paddy fields in Tokyo as compared to the air in the residential areas surrounding them (Yokohari 2014). Creating urban environments stocked with a variety of urban agri-greens has significant potential to advance a sustainability agenda in Asian cities, particularly in those that are a risk of natural disasters. Lessons currently being learned in Japan can also speak to the concerns of European urban populations. In recent years, the latter have had to contend with a new set of economic challenges, which require new forms of resilience. Urban agriculture offers one avenue for beleaguered citizens who seek to engage in self-provisioning to supplement declining incomes, who want to assert some autonomy in the face of the global agri-business sector or who desire to exercise skills of cultivation and creation which have been made redundant within a transformed labour market.

Urban Agriculture in the Age of Austerity

Since the economic crisis that began in 2008, a number of European countries have found themselves in serious economic straits. They have been facing massive budgetary deficits, enormous levels of debt, and have been subject to austerity programmes instigated by the EU/ECB/IMF, which have raised serious questions over their economic and political sovereignty. In effect, "the domestic economy in the countries affected has been put on a life support machine" (Rigney 2012: 10). In Ireland, massive speculation in the housing sector, and the over extension of the banks brought the country perilously close to financial ruin. Post-boom Ireland has been plunged into austerity as the country comes to terms with the economic and social costs of the profligacy of the past. Ireland has moved from having a low debt ratio to being one of the more heavily indebted economies in Europe. Domestic output has dropped dramatically, and 70 percentage points were added to the debt/GDP ratio- between the beginning of 2008 and the end of 2010 (Rigney 2012: 3) The social effects of unemployment are primarily seen in the high rates of youth and long term unemployment, both of which doubled in Ireland (and in Spain) during the crisis period (2007-2012). Unemployment (currently the rate is 9.7%) has been accompanied by the resumption of net outward migration, after almost a decade of unprecedented levels of immigration. In 2010, the deprivation rate (those experiencing two of more types of enforced deprivation) was almost 23% compared with just over 17.0% in 2009 (Rigney 2012:7).

As in Ireland, the anti-crisis measures in Spain have had as their primary focus the objective of reducing the public deficit, which has been accompanied by the destruction of jobs and a commensurate rise in the unemployment rate. The Spanish unemployment rate in 2012 stood at 22.9%, double the rate four years earlier (Grau and Parraga 2012). Some three million jobs disappeared between July 2008 and January 2012. Long term unemployment accounts for 40% of all the unemployed, the highest such proportion in the EU. Moreover, unemployment has had the greatest effect on young workers (Grau and Parraga 2012: 9). The impact of austerity is felt not just in terms of workers and their working conditions, but also in terms of the wider societal impact. According to a recent report, the years of austerity have driven rising poverty, deepening inequality, and a serious deterioration in a variety of economic and social rights in the country (CSER, 2014).

In Italy, we have seen ample evidence of such a political crisis, with several governments having been formed and dissolved since the advent of the economic downturn. With a debt-to-GDP ratio of 120% in 2011, Italy is one of the most indebted countries in the Euro area. The crisis is effectively increasing the risk of poverty, according to ISTAT figures, some 18.2% of residents in Italy are at risk of poverty, while 6.9% live in conditions of "severe material deprivation". Moreover, the incidence of poverty in Italy rose between 2007 and 2009 while remaining broadly stable in 2010. Further increases in the tax burden alongside cuts in public spending in the health and social arenas may increase the risk of poverty among Italian families (Borghi 2012). Unemployment figures rose in the first years of the crisis, and dropped in 2010, but have been on an upward gradient since then. Given the deteriorating labour market, activity rates have dropped, and a growing number of workers are disillusioned about their chances of securing work (Borghi 2012).

In Portugal too, the reduction of public debt has been foremost among the anti-crisis measures put in place since the advent of the recession in 2008. While public debt remains high, there are also growing levels of unemployment, an increase in the number of those denied access to social protection, a decline in public provision in various domains and deepening inequalities (Caldas 2012: 2). Caldas notes that the indicators at the end of 2011 pointed towards a worsening of these trends, exacerbated by a decrease in disposable income, and a corresponding squeeze on private consumption. He contends that unless public and private investment expands, and the country's balance of trade improves, the economic recession is likely to engender a social crisis (Caldas 2012: 2). Already, loss of confidence in the political system suggests a political crisis of democratic representation.

Right across Europe then, there is evidence of an economic crisis that has real consequences for European citizens in terms of their access to work, to welfare and to the means necessary to secure optimal life chances. How people respond to these challenges is a question beyond the scope of this chapter. Nevertheless, I want to suggest that one significant development (which if not caused by the economic downturn at least correlates with it) is the renewal of interest in urban agriculture taking place in Europe in the last decade. There is little doubt that the post 2007 crisis of capitalism has brought into sharp relief an emergent trend toward UA in developed countries. It may well be that this resurgence of interest in urban agriculture is in fact an unintended consequence of economic retrenchment, borne out of economic necessity, but also out of a desire to re-assert an unmediated relationship to the land, and to secure a sense of ontological security in a world that has become increasingly uncertain. As McClintock has observed "the popularity of UA in the global North has surged and the discourse surrounding it has shifted from one of recreation and leisure to one of urban sustainability and economic resilience" (2010: 192).

The focus of the remainder of this chapter is on the governance and policy context within which contemporary urban agriculture across Europe is located.[1] The chapter notes that, while UA is broadly approved at supra state level (the EU), in practice, support for UA is extremely uneven across the continent.

In practice, the success of UA is more attributable to bottom-up actions and initiatives that may or may not garner local and regional support. Bottom-up initiatives frequently model innovation, entrepreneurship and social inclusion strategies. Moreover, many UA initiatives are indirectly implicated in a range of local and regional policies, but are frequently not named as such. The chapter calls for a greater focus on the intersectional potential of UA within the policy and governance domains.

Governance

The concept of governance refers to collective activities, procedures and processes of -governing together – governing shared by different types of actors, belonging to different spheres of society. Governance can be seen not as an architecture or a rigid structure, but as a multi-level collective agency and socio-spatial process through which decisions are discussed, negotiated, taken and implemented (Adger et al. 2003; Swyngedouw 2005). Urban agriculture as a social process reflects both the complexity of the multi-level social relations in which it is embedded, and the particular dynamic which arises from the way it intersects with other policy domains.

The 'ecological turn' towards greening cities through initiatives such as urban agriculture creates new challenges for governance structures and local policies. The state, the market and civil society have key roles to play in conceiving, developing and articulating policy. In the last year, the European Union has issued a communication on Green Infrastructure, which specifically addresses concerns about the degradation of natural capital, the jeopardising of long-term sustainability and the undermining of resilience in the face of environmental shocks (COM 249 2013:2). The Communication calls for a commitment to Green Infrastructure that would ensure that protecting and enhancing nature and natural processes, and the many benefits human society gets from nature, are consciously integrated into spatial planning and territorial development (2013: 3).

The enhancement of Green Infrastructure is seen as contributing to better regional policy and sustainable growth in Europe, including the maintenance and creation of jobs. While the EU institutions may endorse green infrastructure, they are not in a position to implement them on the ground. Broad value based statements such as the Communication on Green Infrastructure are primarily of symbolic value. It is up to national, regional and local governments to implement them. It is, after all, generally government that:

> plays a vital role in shaping the cultural context within which individual choice is negotiated through [government's] influence on technology, infrastructure, market design, institutional structures, the media and the moral framing of social goods(Jackson and Michaelis 2003:60 cited in Pape et al. 2011: 26).

Social practices, in general, and urban agricultural practices, in particular, are likely to be shaped not just by formal state policies, but by a range of "complex interactions between non-state actors and institutions from the private sector, civil society as well as the actions of societal groups and individuals" (Davies et al. 2010: 60). The freedom of manoeuvre that localities have- varies across different cities, and depends very much on the institutional frames of reference, which constrain and enable options at different scalar levels (Kazepov 2005: 26). Below I illustrate elements of this complex mosaic with reference to a number of European case studies.

Farmers working in and serving the urban and peri-urban area, allotment plot holders, community garden volunteers, food entrepreneurs, people selling their produce through farmers markets in the city or schools 'grow it yourself projects' are all engaging in a form of urban agriculture. All of these practices when seen together present us with a picture of agriculture which is linked to concerns about food quality, traceability, sustainability, environmental awareness, consumer literacy, knowledge transfer, leisure gardening and sensitivity to nature. Furthermore, there are ancillary social benefits that indirectly are derived from UA; such as the promotion of social capital, enhancement of community solidarity, the redefinition of public space, rehabilitation for marginal groups, for example, the homeless, prisoners, travellers and the inculcation of an alternative developmental imaginary built around the principle of sustainability.

Table 9.1 Urban Agriculture by Policy by Selected Regions

Country	Reference region	Context	UA focus	Policy focus	Predominant governance strategy
ESP	Barcelona	Protection of agricultural land from urban expansion	Baix Llobregat Agricultural Park: promoting local agric and professional farming	Spatial planning at city level	Consortium dominated by statutory bodies and municipalities
ESP	Vitoria-Gasteiz (Basque country)	Create commercial periurban farming opportunities	Basaldea project: promote work for unemployed and professional training for farmers	Economic intervention	Private and public stakeholders
ESP	Vitoria-Gasteiz	Optimize use of public space	Zabalortu Project:revitalisation of neighbourhood public space through UA and related initiatives	Spatial planning at neighbourhood level	Lead partner and catalyst is Zabalgana Neighbourhood Association alongside municipality
FRA	Toulouse	To promote peri-urban commercial farming	Agricultural Park Project, commune of Pin Balma: for use of urbanites	Spatial planning; preservation of farm lands/avoidance land speculation	Municipal lead, contracted NGO to engage additional partners esp. farmers
GER	Rhur region	Re-utilisation of post-industrial landscape	Emscher Landscape Park: land art, productive landscape and environmental education	Special protected region for multi-functional usage	Public -private partnership

Rure in Urbs

ICE	Reykjavik	Development of city wide UA plan	Participatory municipal planning involving all citizens	Urban planning	Municipal lead, consultation with civil society groups and general public
ITA	Assisi	Protection of agricultural land as cultural heritage	San Francesco Forest: providing work in UA for jobseekers, promoting tourism	Environmental preservation	Project owned and managed by an Environmental Foundation (civil society)
IRE	Dublin	Promotion of food growing	Grow It Yourself: educational and support initiative to promote urban cultivation	Improve food knowledge and cultivation capacities	GIY is a civil society organisation founded by activists
NOR	Bergen	Preservation of outdoor life	Educating citizenry about "gifts of nature"- foraging has legal protection	Public health policy	Bottom- up rights claiming by citizens
SWE	Malmo	Use of public space as meeting point for diverse communities	Enskifteshagen Community garden: UA in a public space	Sustainable urban development	Lead by municipality, organisation and management contracted to NGO Mykorrhiza.

The kinds of issues, which informed the collation of data across Europe, included the following: To what extent do government and civil society acknowledge these linkages in terms of their policies and practices? Where and how is Urban Agriculture embedded in local, regional and national policy contexts? What kinds of advocacy groups exist or are emergent in relation to Urban Agriculture? Are such groups locally, nationally or transnationally based? What is the extent of networking between such civil society groups? What role do urban agriculture entrepreneurs play in advancing policy in this field?

Urban Agriculture and the Urban Regime

It seems that in all of the reference regions for which we have collated information there is no state or national level policy directed at UA. This appears to be a significant gap in the policy framework. Urban planning by definition has tended to see the city as separate to the countryside, and indeed, much planning and urban design is focused on managing urban growth so as to prevent spillover effects in the adjacent countryside. Yokohari (et al. 2010: 228) call for a re-examination of the dominant planning paradigm asserting that it is time to question the sacrosanct belief in the partitioning of the urban and the agricultural. Given the current planning challenge facing many countries in the global North- where many cities are facing ageing and declining populations, there is a pressing need "to plan for and utilise the emerging abandoned spaces left behind in the wake of shrinking cities". Interestingly, history teaches us that the separation of urban and agricultural is not inevitable. In fact, many European medieval cities were surrounded by cultivated agricultural land, which provided the city with food. Similarly, in Japan (alluded to earlier), urban development right through the nineteenth century retained farmland plots within the city limits (Yokohari et al. 2000). This mixing of farmland and urban tracts was both logical and efficient serving the resource needs of both the cultivating farmers and the consuming urbanites. However, in the modern European city, this idea of a symbiotic relationship between the urban and the rural has long since been fractured, with the result that the promotion of agriculture for its own sake within the urban domain is rare, and does not generally receive positive political support. Farmers are a key lobby group at national and supra-national level and it is their interests, as traditional custodians of the countryside, which have long dominated national and European agricultural policy-making.

There are many instances, however, of policy development and innovation at municipal level around UA, though frequently this *may be only indirectly* aimed at UA. For instance, urban planning includes attention to open and natural spaces and enhancing biodiversity (a project of planned open agricultural parkland in the city of Toulouse, France aims to preserve farm lands close to the metropolitan core to serve as a "green lung" for the whole urban area and limit continued urban development); the provision of public spaces (the municipality in Malmo, Sweden is committed to planning and designing places such as community gardens that can facilitate encounters between different social groups in an effort to build cross-community bridges) and active public participation in the planning process (widespread and meaningful consultation among the citizenry on the development of a first every Urban Agriculture policy in the city of Reykjavik, Iceland). In each case, these policies have implications for devising and implementing an UA policy, but this is not always straightforward. For instance, in the agricultural park project in Toulouse, there is no consensus on the type of agriculture that should be pursued in the park (and whether it should be an open park) among the stakeholders, which include landowners, farmers, elected bodies, NGOs and local people (Duvernoy 2012). Urban agricultural activities are often subsumed within the policy briefs of *other policy domains* such as environment, city planning, food security and architecture. For instance, in the metropole Rhur area in Germany, the concept of a regional park - the Emscher Landscape Park - was implemented and constructed to revalorize the post-industrial landscape, and to generate new initiatives for re-development (Kemper 2013; 2014). Within the European Union, the Rhur metropolitan region is the third largest urban and most populated area after London and Paris. It is not a traditional park, but an unconventional, polycentric park, involving a regional network of landscape and district parks. In terms of actual land practices, up to 41% (about 192km2) of the parkland is in agricultural use including farming, grassland, and specialised horticulture, areas of fallow land and allotment gardens. It is a co-operative venture involving 20 municipalities and several regional ministries including Climate Change, Environment, Agriculture and Nature and User conservation. A number of innovative policies have tried to integrate different park-based practices such as developing productive agriculture in combination with aesthetic land art design and other services (Mechtenberg-Essen); developing an educational centre in a disused farm building (Ingenhamshof, Dortmund), and establishing a certified organic meat cutting hall (Neulandbetrieb, Bergkamen) as part of generating a transparent agricultural value chain process, (Kemper 2014; 2013).

A similar initiative, involving multiple partners across a number of municipalities is also underway in the Barcelona region.[ii] Baix Llobregat

Agricultural Park is a protection and management project which promotes peri-urban farming. It involves 621 farmers in cultivation. The metropolitan region spatial plan protects the 'Baix Llobregat Agricultural Park' area as part of the 'open spaces system' and because of its agricultural interest. This plan protects agricultural land from urban encroachment and sets specific rules for the agricultural area. Some of the land is held in private ownership, but the space is open and is bisected by tracks designed to accommodate visitors. The project is mainly financed by the Provincial Council, and is aimed primarily at promoting professional farming, local agriculture, and by extension, local production and local consumption. Farmers can sell their produce directly to Barcelona citizens. The partnership governance model, includes connections to the School of Agriculture at the Polytechnic University of Catalonia/Barcelona tech, to all the local associations dealing with agricultural activities, to local schools and local enterprises. The park is managed by a consortium; made up of several public bodies (Regional Government, Provincial Council, County Council and the 14 municipalities within the area) and one private entity (Farmers' Union). While decisions are taken democratically, there are power differentials between the various stakeholders. The perspectives of all stakeholders are not the same: some view the Park through a primarily agricultural lens while others value it as a green landscape- while still others are more concerned with landscape design. In such multi-functional landscapes, with multiple stakeholders, the Urban Agriculture narratives can be easily obscured, and policies frequently only indirectly address issues of urban cultivation (for more information see Giachee and Toth 2013 and Carril 2013).

In Bergen, Norway the tradition of utilizing various wild foods, especially berries, edible mushrooms and fish, is embodied in the term *"matauk"* (literally "food increment"). In practice, the term refers to the harvesting of wild foods, which is widely socially accepted and seen as an integral part of leisure activities. Norway's Outdoor Recreation Act provides for free access to "outfield", non-cultivated areas including private grazing and forest areas, for everyone. This free access does also include the collection of nuts, plants, berries and mushrooms. But it is the importance of the outdoor life for public health that is stressed in public policy documents, not any sense of an *urbanite's right to cultivation* of land.[iii] Similarly, in the reference region of Umbria and Lombardia in Italy, case studies of Assisi and Milan demonstrate public policies on education and health care that indirectly support UA and can impact on the form it takes. Furthermore, there may be important inter-institutional linkages such as the local provisioning of schools (Milan) and the focus on the procurement of food from local suppliers in public canteens (Toulouse). These have a primarily educational and economic focus rather than a specific policy focus on the integration of agriculture into the urban domain. Thus, there is a degree of policy *intersectionality* at work but these policy linkages are not always explicit- and are not generally considered in a strategic way by municipalities. Different departments deal with issues such as health, education, land use, agriculture and heritage and we found few strategic links being made between these different policy domains. There is, therefore, much scope for developing a transversal policy analysis to illuminate the myriad ways in which concerns with cultivation and food production are implicated in a whole range of urban policies, but without directly alluding to urban agriculture as such.

The data we have gathered from the different reference regions all provide explicit examples of good practice in relation to the development and implementation of UA. The examples identified include: the multifunctional Emscher Landscape Park in the metropolitan Rhur area, the agreement between the Umbria region and the ANCI (National Association of Italian municipalities) to define appropriate guidelines for urban gardens-*ortiurbani* (Giachee et al. 2012), an agricultural park (that is still under discussion) in Toulouse, and the funding of garden facilitators to promote UA to strengthen social cohesion in Malmo, Sweden.

It seems, however, that there is frequently an '*ad hoc*' quality to UA policy. It is not envisioned as a policy field in its own right, but cross cuts a number of policy domains- including environmental and biodiversity policy, tourism, planning and development. Moreover, even despite the best efforts of stakeholders many planned projects are difficult to bring to fruition because of lack of funding. For instance, in the region of Victoria-Gasteiz in the Basque country of Spain the innovative Zabalortu Project which is aimed at optimizing green public space in a newly created residential area was blocked for some time because of lack of municipality funding arising from the economic crisis. The allotment gardens at Zabalortu finally got off the ground in 2014. The Vitoria-Gasteiz municipality´s legal department succeeded in finding a way to allow for self-management of the lot as the neighbours wished. Although it is a small lot in the middle of the Zabalgana neighbourhood, the innovative aspect of the initiative has to do with it being a bottom-up/top-down example of using urban agriculture as a way to recreate the urban fabric, creating social vitality and environmental quality.[iv] It could be argued that the potential of UA across Europe is not fully realized, because it is *viewed as marginal* both by the national and local state. Other policy goals appear to take precedence over ones that would directly address issues of innovation and sustainability in food production in and around cities.

Civil Society as a Conduit of Innovation in Urban Agriculture

We found many examples of bottom- up strategies emerging from civil society that are pushing for a greener city agenda and to have UA incorporated into the policy repertoire of the urban regime. These range from initiatives aimed at professional farmers to those aimed at gardening urbanites. In Vitoria-Gasteiz, Spain for instance, the Zabalgana Neighbourhood Association of committed neighbours, has led the social demand for integrated community gardens in a newly built peripheral neighbourhood (Verdaguer 2012).

In Toulouse, the municipality had contracted an NGO, *SaluTerre*, to organise local participation to create new community gardens. The municipality also provided direct support in identifying spaces, offering expertise and classes, providing plants, trees and water supply. There are numerous examples of networks of partners working together for UA. Malmo has a city urban agriculture network that includes municipal officials, NGOs, and local universities. The local Somali association, *Hidde Iyo Dhaqan*, has developed a social entrepreneur model for promoting UA (Delshammar 2012). In Granada citizen actors such as environmentalists, residents associations, farmers associations and committed consumers have formed a platform- *Plataforma Salvemos la Vega de Granada* (Coalition to Save the Agricultural Plain of Granada)- to confront and collaborate with local government to protect the urban and peri-urban landscape and promote UA. In Spain generally, and in La Vega (Granada), many of these groups have been linked in one way or another with *Ecologistas en Acción* (Environmentalist in Action) and their federations, which have been active in the defense of Urban Agriculture (for more information see Mataran 2013).

In the Dublin region, the *Grow It Yourself* organization actively aims to empower people to grow their own by bringing together community groups off and online to share tips, advice and expertise. The *Grow It Yourself* organization was started by concerned citizens and receives funding from the philanthropic sector. There is some evidence of the institutionalization of the UA sector with people moving from guerrilla gardening and informal initiatives to more permanent urban allotments and garden space (e.g. Malmo, Dublin and Vitoria-Gasteiz in Spain). In

Bergen, Norway, transition groups have been advocating for UA, and several of the activists are employees at the municipality or private consultancy firms involved in planning. Nevertheless, in some contexts, municipally supported initiatives continue to co-exist with illegal allotments (Milan). Reykjavik offers an important example of consultation with urban dwellers on how policy can be developed through neighbourhood committees, community requests, and public submissions made through a citizens website. The momentum built through these consultations has legitimated and provided a solid basis for the municipality to develop specific policy on UA.

Community supported agriculture (CSA) is prominent in a number of reference regions (Geneva, Milan and Clermont-Ferrand), for instance, a practice that is already well established in the United Kingdom. The goal is to recreate producer-consumer links, to support agriculture that is not fully embedded in the market and to promote food sovereignty. Solidarity purchase groups (GAS) in Milan are consumer networks collectively organised to make purchases direct from selected manufacturers based on quality and ethical criteria. *Agriclocal 63* is a tool of the Department du Puy-de-Dome at the provincial level in the Clermont-Ferrand region, France to 'geo-localise' the food chain linking local producers to public procurement (schools, colleges, etc). This constitutes an innovative example of how an internet platform can be used to link consumers and producers directly within a locality. The initiative is now being extended to connect to restaurants and has been recognized by the French Ministry of Agriculture and disseminated in other provinces (Loudiyi et al. 2012).

The municipality of Vitoria-Gasteiz along with other institutional and non-institutional bodies has developed the *Basaldea project*- the objective of which is to generate employment and businesses related to the sector of ecological production and distribution of farming products. Located in the Basque country, which has a strong national identity, this public-private initiative is aimed at driving commercial agriculture in the peri-urban area, through a business nursery or incubator structure as a starting point. Two groups are targeted: agricultural training of fifteen unemployed persons and the training in ecological practices of 20 professional farmers. A General Collaboration Agreement has been signed by the involved private and public stakeholders (Verdaguer 2012). Such examples show us that, in Europe, UA can be both innovative and entrepreneurial, can involve multiple and diverse partners and can be oriented to both community and market-focused ends. UA is highly versatile and has a role to play in the development of urban 'sustainabilities' in the twenty-first century.

The Sustainability Agenda and the Social Sciences

Interest in sustainability has broadened the terms of reference of analysts to the extent that a wider range of disciplines from within and outside of the traditional social sciences are now being called upon to contribute to envisioning sustainabilities. Returning to the EU communication on Green Infrastructure, we note that it explicitly links natural capital depletion to social capital depletion, if more emphasis is not placed on sustainability in planning futures (COM 249 2013: 2). This communication represents a significant advance at policy level even if it is largely discursive rather than substantive in linking society and nature, affording them co-equal concern. Promoting the wellbeing of its citizens is a primary objective of the European Union (Article. 3 (1) of the Treaty), but how we define well-being has to be linked to wider social, political and environmental contexts of sustainability. In practice, most cross national comparisons have been based almost exclusively on economic variables. GDP growth and GDP per capita are the key measures to rank countries, regions and cities (Ottaviano and Pinelli 2006). However, a wider concept of growth is emerging in policy and research debates and this reflects the impact of the growing body of work on sustainability by social scientists. Numerous efforts have been made to go beyond GDP as the only criterion for measuring economic performance and social progress. Increasingly, growth is not understood only under the restrictive terms of income- but also with reference to all aspects of an individual's well-being. The report by the Stiglitz-Sen-Fitoussi Commission (2009) represents a milestone for recommendations on how to find a more comprehensive approach toward gauging human progress. The goals of promoting urban sustainability operationalized through fostering social cohesion and minimizing social polarization are predicated on enhancing the capacity of people to participate fully in the life of their society, and this is central to quality of life. Socio-economic security and a sense of empowerment and personal capacity foment collective social capital and enhance the collective lifeworld. Parra and Moulaert (2012) advocate a perspective in which 'the social' is primarily seen as a socio-political process that dialogically reveals the essential multi-partner and multi-scalar nature of sustainable development and its governance process.

Pathways to urban sustainability, especially as articulated at policy level, are frequently aspirational with little practical guidance on substantive content or guides to strategic implementation. By focusing on real practices of urban sustainability, such as those outlined in this chapter and in the wider volume, social scientists can make the connections between sustainability goals (articulated from above) and the life world of real European citizens (articulated from below) who through practices such as Urban Agriculture, in all its myriad manifestations, are contributing to urban sustainability. Bradley (2009) suggests that we need to adapt urban sustainability policies to the growing diversity of urban populations, and to develop more scepticism about the prevalent discourse on sustainability which especially reflects middle class values. Social science is well placed to interrogate the grassroots experiences of actors on the ground, and to mediate those experiences to relevant policy makers. Social science can also uncover the rich and textured nature of urban sustainability across Europe as it is nurtured and cultivated literally from the ground up.

Conclusion

Urban agriculture is often juxtaposed to the global agri-food industry, which has brought with it industrialization, intensification and commodification of food production. Joanna Blythman, author of *Bad Food Britain*, argues that:

> if we want our food to be truly safe, we must recognize that this can only be delivered by a radically different model of food and agriculture, one that is based on the largely untapped potential of *small scale, much more regional production and distribution,*" (*The Guardian*, 5 June 2011). (My emphasis)

Friedmann (2010) has argued for a re-embedding of food systems in overlapping ecosystems, human settlements and cultures. She observes that in a highly urbanized and multicultural region such as Southern Ontario (Canada) a vibrant 'food shed' has emerged in which a community of food practice links land use, social justice, and cultural creativity. In a similar vein, McClintock argues that UA can be understood as an attempt to overcome the metabolic rift- ecological (environmental degradation), social (commodification) and individual (alienation) - that is at the core of capitalism in general, and the modern agri-food system, in particular. According to McClintock, it is an ethos of agricultural sustainability that informs UA practice. UA is viewed as 'restitutive' agriculture because of its attempts to mend the metabolic rift. Furthermore, as a protective counter-movement, UA attempts to mitigate social rift by de-commodifying land, labour and food itself. Finally, alienation or individual rift can be addressed by re-engaging the individual in non-exploitative relations with his or her labour and nature.

Our preliminary exploration of urban agricultural activity across contemporary Europe indicates evidence of the emergence of an ecological turn (both at the supra-state level and on the ground); the flourishing of a range of different agriculture-related initiatives that have the potential to transform European citizens' relationship to food, and food production systems; and the potential for a much greater embedding of agricultural initiatives within the urban domain. The strengths of European Urban Agriculture include increasing interest in civic agriculture (DeLind 2002) and alternative agri-food initiatives (Jarosz 2008) particularly in light of the economic downturn that has negatively impacted many European cities; urban gardening as a multi-beneficial activity for regenerating derelict plots; promoting the values of sharing, creativity and *integration;* re-acquaintanceship with land and respect for the environment and indirect promotion of *social inclusion.*

On the other hand, we can identify clear weaknesses particularly in relation to the governance and policy context of UA. The national state is more or less absent from the UA agenda playing no major role; municipalities only partially engage with UA, often indirectly rather than directly; many municipalities see UA as a marginal, leisure time activity; and many regions lack adequate mechanisms for getting citizens involved in planning for and implementing a UA strategy. Overall, there are many opportunities that can be built upon: crisis can be seen as an opportunity-the decline in real estate values, vacant lots, disused urban buildings create possibilities for greening initiatives; citizens may be more motivated to grow their own, given the new focus on food security, sustainability and traceability. Further, there is potential for diverse *entrepreneurial* approaches; and a growing interest in UA as an integral part of public spaces; media attention is significant. UA holds out the enticing potential to reverse urban sprawl, re-green the city and suburbs; it also affords the opportunity to rekindle dialogue between urban and suburban, built up areas, open spaces and daily leisure and create *innovation* in the urban food chain. These opportunities must be placed against the continued threats posed by: pressure on land for development purposes; inexorable urban sprawl; the decline of agriculture generally in peri-urban areas; the dominance of consumerist culture and the further aesthetisisation of countryside for tourist purposes.

Following Yokohari et al. (2010:22), this chapter argues for the re-establishment of garden zones both in and around cities. Such mixed land-use zones are conceptualized as "spaces where urban residents can craft their own local food cultures and agro-biographics in response to the globalization of agriculture and food consumption". The promotion of a 'middle landscape'- integrating both *the urbs* and *the rure* could form a central strategy within the sustainable cities agenda. The benefits of a re-integration of cultivation into city life have already been highlighted in terms of public health, cultural connection, human interaction and community development (Howard 1965; Moselle 1995; Crouch 1989; Smit and Nasr 1992). Other studies suggest that UA practices are an important means of self-expression, help migrants maintain cultural identities, contribute to the enhancement of health and well-being for urbanites, and constitute landscapes which cement relationships within communities (Warner 1987). As European urbanites come to terms with the current age of austerity, Urban Agriculture offers a multi-faceted means of re-engaging with food, with the land, with each individual's own human creativity and ingenuity and with the generalized other.

References

Adger, W. Neil. "Adaptation to climate change and the developing world." *Progress in Development Studies*, Vol, 3, No. 3 (2009): 1179-195.

Allen Patricia, Margaret Fitzsimon, Michael K. Goodman, Keith Warner. "Shifting plates in the agrifood landscape: the tectonics of alternative agrifood initiatives in California." *Journal of Rural Studies* 19 (2003): 61-75.

Borghi, Elisa. The impact of anti-crisis measures and the social and employment situation in Italy. European Economic and Social Committee's Workers Group. (2012) http://www.eesc.europa.eu/resources/docs/qe-32-12-542-en-c.pdf Accessed March 5, 2014).

Binns, Tony and Kevin Lynch. "Feeding Africa's Growing Cities into the 21st Century: The potential of Urban Agriculture." *Journal of International Development*, 10 (1998): 777-793.

Blythman, Joanne. *Bad Food Britain*. London: Fourth Estate, 2006.

Bradley, Karin. "Planning for eco-friendly living in diverse societies." *Local Environment: the International Journal of Justice and Sustainability* 14, 4 (2009): 347-363.

Butler, Don. "A growing opportunity: urban agriculture takes root in empty lots and abandoned spaces" *The Ottawa Citizen*, June 18, 2006.

Caldas, José Castro. The impact of anti-crisis measures and the social and employment situation, Portugal European Economic and Social Committee's Workers Group. (2012) www.ictu.ie (accessed March 5, 2014).

Carpenter, Novella. *Farm City. The education of an urban farmer.* New York: Penguin, 2009.

Carpenter, Novella and Willow Rosenthal. *The essential urban farmer.* New York: Penguin, 2011.

Carril, Valiera Paul. "Agriculture in the Metropolitan Area of Barcelona: A key issue, multiple landscapes and various solutions" in COST Urban Agriculture Europe, Documentation of 2nd Working Group Meeting, Barcelona, ed. Luis Maldonado , Castelldefels, Barcelona: Polytechnic University of Catalonia/Barcelonatech, 2013 http://www.urbanagricultureeurope.la.rwth-aachen.de/files/131008_cost_uae_barcelona_2013_standard.Accessed June 29, 2015.

Clausen, Rebecca. "Healing the rift" *Monthly Review,* Vol. 59, Issue 1 (May 2007) no page numbers.

Cockrall-King, Jennifer. *Food and the city: urban agriculture and the new food revolution.* Amherst, New York: Prometheus books, 2012.

Colasanti, Kathryn .J.A. and Michael.W. Hamm. "Assessing the local food supply capacity of Detroit, Michigan." *Journal of Agriculture, Food Systems and Community Development*, Vol. 1, Issue 2, 2010: 41-58. Accessed online www.agdevjournal.com, March 31, 2011.

COM (2013) 249 final Communication from the Commission to the European Parliament, the Council, the European Economic and Social Committee and the Committee of the Regions: Green infrastructure (GI)-Enhancing Europe's Natural Capital. Brussels: European Commission 6.5.2013.

Commission on the measurement of Economic Performance and Social Progress.Also known as the Stiglitz-Sen-Fitoussi Commission. Government of France: Paris,France, 2009 http://www.urbanagricultureeurope.la.rwth-aachen.de/files/131008_cost_uae_barcelona_2013_standard.pdf.

Crouch, David. "The allotment: its landscape, and locality: ways of seeing landscape and culture." *Area* 21 (1989): 261–267.

Crouch, David and Colin Ward. *The Allotment: its landscape and culture.* Nottingham, U.K: Five Leaves Publications, 1997.

CSER. Spain Fact Sheet No. 14. Center for Economic and Social Rights. Brooklyn, NY: CSER, 2014. http://www.cesr.org/article.php?id=1285 Accessed June 26, 2015

Davies, Anna, Frances Fahy, Henrike Rau, Jessica Pape. "Sustainable consumption and governance: reflecting on a research agenda for Ireland." *Irish Geography*, Vol. 43, No. 1, March (2010): 59-79.

DeLind, Laura. "Place, work, and civic agriculture: Common fields for cultivation." *Agriculture and Human Values* 19 (2002): 217–224.

Delshammar, Tim. Malmo, Sweden http://www.urbanagricultureeurope.la.rwth-aachen.de/action/working-groups/wg-2-ua-and-governance/pdf-papers-of-reference-regions/t-delshammer_malmoe-sweden_-2012.html Accessed 23 November 2014.

Duvernoy, Isabel. Toulouse, France http://www.urbanagricultureeurope.la.rwth-aachen.de/action/working-groups/wg-2-ua-and-governance/pdf-papers-of-reference-regions/iduvernoy_toulouse-france-_2012.html Accessed 24 November, 2014.

Eizenberg, Efrat. "Actually Existing Commons: three Moments of Space of Community Gardens in New York City." *Antipode*, Vol. 44, 3 (2012): 764-782.

Friedmann, Harriet. "Changing Food Systems, Two Futures." Abstract of paper delivered at Bitish Sociological Association Food Study Group Food Society and Public Health, London, 5-6 July, 2010. http://www.britsoc.co.uk/events/food.aspx. Accessed December 15, 2010.

Giachee, Giulia, Paola Branduini, Biancamaria Torquati, Lionella Scazzosi, Assisi and Milan, Italy http://www.urbanagricultureeurope.la.rwth-aachen.de/action/working-groups/wg-2-ua-and-governance/pdf-papers-of-reference-regions/ggiacch-pbranduini-btorquati-lscazzosi-assisi-und-milan-italy-2012.html Accessed January 17, 2015.

Giachee, Giulia and Attila Toth. UA *in the Barcelona Metropolitan Region. Short Term Scientific Mission.* Castelldefels, Barcelona: Polytechnic University of Catalonia/BarcelonaTech, 2013 http://www.urbanagricultureeurope.la.rwth-aachen.de/files/130319_stsmreport_barcelona.pdf Accessed June 20, 2015.

Grau, Antonio B. and Francesco.T. Párraga The impact of anti-crisis measures and the social and emplymnet situation in Spain, European Economic and Social Committee's Workers Group. ICTU: Dublin, 2012 http://www.ictu.ie/download/pdf/espagneen.pdf Accessed March 5, 2014).

Hampwaye., Godfrey, Etienne Nel, Lutango Ingombe. "The role of urban agriculture in addressing household poverty and food security: the case of Zambia." GND Working Paper Series, FANRPAN, 2009. http://www.gdnet.org Accessed 8 Jan 2014.

Howard, Ebenezer. *Garden Cities of Tomorrow.* Cambridge, Massachusetts: The M.I.T. Press, 1965.
Jackson, Tim and Laurie Michaelis. *Sustainable consumption and production, economic regeneration: policies for sustainable consumption.* London: Sustainable Development Commission, 2003.
Jarosz, Lucy. "The city in the country: Growing alternative food networks in Metropolitan areas." *Journal of Rural Studies,* Vol. 24 3 (2008): 231-244
Jonsdottir, Salvor. Reykjavik, Iceland
http://www.urbanagricultureeurope.la.rwth-aachen.de/action/working-groups/wg-2-ua-and-governance/pdf-papers-of-reference-regions/s-jonsdottir_reykjavik-iceland_2012.htmlAccessed December 12, 2014
Kazepov, Yuri. "Cities of Europe. Changing Contexts, local arrangements and the challenge to social cohesion." In *Cities of Europe. Changing contexts, local arrangements and the challenge to urban cohesion.* Ed, Yuri Kazepov 1-42. New York: Blackwell Publishing, 2005.
Kemper, Denise. Emscher-landscaftspark, Germany. 2013
http://www.urbanagricultureeurope.la.rwth-aachen.de/action/working-groups/wg-2-ua-and-governance/pdf-papers-of-reference-regions/d-kemper_emscher-landschaftspark-germany_2013.html,
Accessed December 5, 2014.
—. 2014. *The Emscher Landscape Park.* In *Urban Agriculture Europe. Report on Third Working Group Meeting, Dublin/Maynooth.* Ed Mary P. Corcoran and Patricia Kettle,
www.urbanagricultureeurope.la.rwth-aachen.de/.
King, B., 2006. *A short history of allotments in England and Wales.* Available from:
http://www.b.king.dsl.pipex.com/ShortHistoryOfAllotments.pdf
(accessed May 30, 2011).
Loudiyi, Salma, Giulia giacche, Sylvie Lardon, Clermont-Ferrand, France, 2012
http://www.urbanagricultureeurope.la.rwth-aachen.de/action/working-groups/wg-2-ua-and-governance/pdf-papers-of-reference-regions/sloudiyi-ggiacch-slardon_clermont-ferrand-france_2012.html.
Accessed June 29, 2015
McClintock, Nathan. " Why farm the city? Theorizing urban agriculture through a lens of metabolic rift." *Cambridge Journal of Regions, Economy and Society,* 3, (2), (2010): 191-207.
McKibben, Bill. *Deep economy: the wealth of communities and the durable future.* Oxford, UK: Oneworld, 2007.
Mataran, Alberto Vega de Granda, Spain, 2013

http://www.urbanagricultureeurope.la.rwth-aachen.de/action/working-groups/wg-2-ua-and-governance/pdf-papers-of-reference-regions/a-mataran_vegadegranada-spain_2013.html Accessed November 25, 2014

Meller, Helen. "Citizens in pursuit of nature: gardens, allotments and private spaces in European cities 1850-2000." *Resources of the city: contribution to an environmental history of modern Europe.* Ed. Dieter Schott, Bill Luckin, Genevieve Massad-Guilbaud 80-96.Aldershot: Ashgate, 2005.

Moselle, Boaz." Allotments, Enclosure and Proletarianization in Early nineteenth century England." *The Economic History Review*, New Series, 48 (3), (1995):482-500.

Mougeot, Luc, J. A. Urban Agriculture: definition, presence, potential and risks in *Growing Cities, growing food: urban agriculture on the policy agenda. A reader on Urban agriculture.* Ed. Nico Bakker, Marelle Dubbeling, Sabine Gundel, Ulrich Sabel, Koschella, Henk De Zeeuw. 1-42. Feldafing, Germany: German Foundation for International Development (DSE), 2000.

—. 2006. In *focus: growing better cities. Urban agriculture for sustainable development.* Canada, IDRC.

—. 2005. *Agropolis: the social political and environmental dimensions of urban agriculture.* Earthscan/IDRC.

Ostrum, Elinor. *Governing the Commons.* Cambridge, UK: Cambridge University Press, 1991.

Ottaviano Gianmarco I P and Dino Pinelli,"Market potential and productivity: evidence from the Finnish region." *Journal of Science and Urban Economics*, 36,(2006): 636-57.

Pahl, Raymond.E. *Urbs* in *rure:* the metropolitan fringe in Hertfordshire, London School of Economics and Political Science Geography Paper, No. 2, 1965.

Pape, Jessica, Henrike Rau, Frances Fahy and Anna Davis "Developing policies and instruments for sustainable household consumption: Irish experiences and futures." *Journal of Consumer Policy*, 34 (2011): 25-42.

Parra, Constanza and Frank Moulaert, "The governance of the nature-culture nexus: literature and lessons to learn from the San Pedro de Atacama case", *Paper presented at the International Workshop Beyond Utopia: Crisis, values and the socialities of nature*, University of California Santa Barbara, USA, 2012.

Polyani, Karl. *The Great Transformation.* New York: Beacon Press, 1944.

Premat, Adriana. 2005. "Moving between the plan and the ground: shifting perspectives on urban agriculture in Havana, Cuba." In *Agropolis: the social and environmental dimensions of urban agriculture*. Ed Luc Mougeot 153-186 Earthscan/IDRC, 2005.

Quarmby Katharine. "Growing Pains." *Prospect* Magazine, July, 2010.

Rich, Sarah and Matthew Benson. *Urban Farms*. New York: Abrams, 2012.

Rigney, Peter. The Impact of Anti-crisis measures and the social and employment situation: Ireland, Dublin: Irish Congress of Trade Unions European Economic and Social Committee Workers' Group, 2012 http://www.ictu.ie/download/pdf/impact_of_austerity_on_ireland_eesc_paper.pdf Accessed March 5, 2014.

Smit Jac and Joe Nasr, "Urban Agriculture for sustainable cities: using wastes and idle land and water bodies as resources." *Environment and Urbanisation*, 4, (1992): 141-152.

Swyngedouw, Eric. "Governance Innovation and the Citizen: The Janus Face of Governance-beyond-the-State" *Urban Studies*, Vol, 42, No. 11 (2005): 1991-2006.

Tornaghi, Chiara. "Critical Geography of urban agriculture" *Progress in Human Geography,* Vol 38, No 4 (2014): 551-567.

Tsui, Enid. High Rise to low rice. *Financial Times*, Sat/Sun 16-17 June, 2012.

Verdaguer, Carlos. Vitoria-Gasteiz, Spain, 2012 http://www.urbanagricultureeurope.la.rwth-aachen.de/action/working-groups/wg-2-ua-and-governance/pdf-papers-of-reference-regions/c-verdaguer_vitoria-gasteiz-spain-_2012.html Accessed January 16, 2015.

Warner, Sam B. Jr., *To Dwell is to Garden: A History of Boston's Community Gardens*. Boston: North Eastern University Press, 1987.

Wright, Eric Olin. "A sociology of real utopias. Second Presidential Plenary Alternatives to an Unequal World", International Sociological Association International Congress, Yokohama, Japan, July 18, 2014.

Yokohari, Makoto. "Agri-activities in Asian cities", paper presented at 3rd COST working group meeting, Dublin/Maynooth, September 11-14, 2013.

Yokohari, Makoto, Marco Amati, Jay Bolthouse, and Hideharu.Kurita. "Restoring agricultural landscapes in shrinking cities: reinventing traditional concepts in Japanese planning." In *Globalisation and Agricultural landscapes: change patterns and policy trends in developed countries*, (eds) Jorgen Primdahl and Simon Swaffield. 201-224 Cambridge, Cambridge University Press, 2010.

Yokohari, Makato, Kazuhiko Takeuci, Takashi Watanabe, Shigehiro Yokota. "Beyond greenbelts and zoning: a new planning concept for the environment of Asian mega-cities." in *Landscape and Urban Planning*. 47, (2000): 159-171.

Notes

[1]As a first step in developing a profile of UAE policies and governance contexts members of Working Group 2 of the COST ACTION Urban Agriculture Europe (TD 1106) set out to identify the key policy actors and stakeholders across eleven reference regions in Europe. We focused on collecting information on state, civil society and market actors. The aim was to identify city case studies, i.e. a city in each participating country which can be the focus of analysis, and then to explore how is urban agriculture defined (if at all) at municipal, regional and state levels and what is the remit adapted at each level in relation to urban agriculture; how coherence is the policy framework for managing urban agriculture, and what kinds of examples of good practice exist in the field. We also sought to identify key civil society actors in the field and examine what kinds of governance structures they had in place, what kinds of activities they engaged in, what policy innovations they practiced and their outcomes. Finally, we also explored the policy frameworks in place at urban, national and supranational level to promote urban agricultural entrepreneurs and urban agriculture as a sustainable economic activity. This work was undertaken mainly in 2012 and 2013. For more information see: http://www.urbanagricultureeurope.la.rwth-aachen.de/

[ii] Information on this case is based on a field visit to Barcelona, March 2013. I am grateful to Professor Luis Maldonado who organised the local presentations and site visits.

[iii] I am grateful to Hans Peter Andersen for providing this information in a presentation to the Working Group of UAE in Barcelona, March 2013

[iv] I am grateful to Carlos Verdaguer for this information.

AFTERWORD

A REFLECTION ON ENVISIONING SUSTAINABILITIES

PAT BRERETON

Sustainability as a concept has important implications as an interdisciplinary topic reflecting research within the social sciences, humanities and the arts, as this volume clearly testifies. The wide ranging and well-honed essays address the 'social side' of sustainability, which is often sidelined by the engineering/scientific and the more economic aspects of development. Hanchett and other writers in this volume, most effectively foreground the important role of anthropologists in developing this cross-disciplinary area of sustainability research.

In the 1980s, sustainability as a concept, though vaguely defined, gained new life and broad acceptance beyond more specific environmental circles. There continues to be considerable disagreement- nonetheless-with regards to how to achieve a sustainable way of life, or even what it might evolve into for the future. Scholars tend to fall back on and quote the 1987 Brundlandt report 'Our Common Future', but maybe this well-worn definition has reached its sell-by date.

The intrinsic character of the concept of sustainability itself – apart from being 'normative, ambiguous and subjective' (Kemp et al. 2006) – lies in its most prescient requirement to be lived and thus transformed into action. Most importantly putting 'the S (social) word back into sustainability' (Dixon 2011), according to many of the papers in this volume is essential, as the social pillar underpinning sustainability was in danger of dropping out of the planning vocabulary.

As an environmental communications scholar myself, I might take issue with an assertion that the 'environment' element has become dominant in the literature, much less in practice, nevertheless, I would certainly concede that 'social' values need to be more explicitly foregrounded in the matrix of influences and concerns around all aspects of sustainability.

Yet, in spite of a growing consensus, notions of sustainability and sustainable development remain at various levels a contested term and is widely acknowledged to be ambiguous, interchangeable and loosely applied to a variety of contexts. The most virulent critics of sustainable development describe it as a neoliberal project that has in turn succeeded in integrating environmental concerns with economic interests, thereby enabling a discourse of ecological entrepreneurialism, or economic growth and technological innovation in the name of environmentalism, to dominate policymaking and practice.

Meanwhile, anthropology as a broad based discipline and methodology remains a major feature and focus of this book, and is fruitfully read as a form of glue across such debates. Several chapters call for more engagement across different fields and disciplines, while actively framing perceptions of global change and sustainability, all the while mobilizing a wider social science community to take action in developing a more integrated and transformative global community to act more sustainably. Yet, while acknowledging that anthropologists have much to offer, sustainability related research and planning also should be fully inter-disciplinary and inclusive. For instance, the knowledge and skills of those with expertise and backgrounds in sociology, geography, environmental studies, public health, political science, public administration and economics (of the non-neoliberal varieties), and others including film and cultural studies, are badly needed to flesh out the full range of sustainability discourse, as a unifying template for action.

While accepting these caveats, anthropology, as a broad-based discipline and effective audience-centred methodology, can bring a 'situated perspective' to the analysis of sustainable development that, in turn, reveals the tensions and disjunctures between rhetoric and practice. In particular- anthropology can make an important contribution to the social science of sustainability- by highlighting the political and institutional contexts that shape discourse, practice, policy and sustainable development in the field of knowledge. Anthropology's grounded research methods can also illuminate the inconsistencies and uncertainties generated in the process of translating sustainability as a normative concept into everyday social and professional practices (see Woodcraft this volume).

This study most usefully throws up many fascinating and memorable case studies of sustainability in action across a range of chapters. For instance, recalling a cautionary tale of water usage in Bangladesh, and a UNICEF study of the public's reaction to the serious problem of arsenic in drinking water, together with the effectiveness of various mitigating efforts to solve the problem. Echoing the familiar 'care for future generations' theme spilling out from the sustainability discourse, one elderly African woman proudly announced that she had persuaded her husband to support this activity for the sake of the long-term health of their grandchildren. But returning to the same village three years later in 2009, the researchers alarmingly found the filters in total disrepair. The study's conclusions perceptively stated that technically oriented and science-driven donors and their local counterpoints need explicit and detailed social information, if their planned changes are to take root. This remains a useful cautionary tale, which should be taken to heart for future sustainable-driven projects across the world.

No more are crudely constructed binaries that polarise postcolonial/western; ideology/ecology, as simple uni-directional frames or debates helpful in articulating, much less constructing, and progressive forms of engagement. Instead, such binaries need to be re-appraised and re-coded, as world cinemas fluctuate across the three-dimensional nexus of local/global, Indigenous and trans-national polarities, and feed into more complex debates around the periphery/centre and across reductive divisions between Third, First and other world cinematic outputs. The crudely constituted shorthand of the West, as an imperialist colonizer, together with the even more restrictively constituted bulwark of the continent of Africa as a passive post-colonial space, as I suggest in a forthcoming monograph [*Environmental Ethics and Film*] needs to be re-appraised and re-constituted, so that scholars can approach very complex notions like sustainability and environmental ethics together with universal sustainability, through more considered and balanced evaluation of geo-political structures and systems.

In turn we can learn how such frames might be usefully re-constituted, re-articulated and re-politicised through a firm commitment to universal justice and global ethical responsibility. Furthermore, by developing a more productive and reflexive sense of place through civic identity and environmental connectivity, film as a fictional medium, in particular, can help re-imagine and promote a more benevolent co-operative series of protocols across our polarised planet earth.

Another very useful anthropological study in this volume examines the idea of shared space, and its connection with progress and sustainability. This has been a powerful political motivation driving the commercial redevelopment of two (blighted) city centres – namely Belfast in Northern Ireland and New York's Bronx areas. According to a growing body of literature, not only are we losing experientially gained knowledge about surroundings, but we are also missing out on the positive effects of nature on our health and moral fibre. The study also calls attention to the growing tension between greening and gentrification of city neighbourhoods, which in turn places environmental and sustainability activists in a double bind. Such pervasive notions of well-being resonate with the early years of the wilderness movement in America and demonstrates the need to marry environmental concerns with more prescient debates around sustainability.

Saffron Woodcraft's case study 'Reconfiguring 'the social' in sustainable development: Community, citizenship and innovation in new urban neighbourhoods' foregrounds research around what it means 'to plan, design and build a sustainable community in contemporary London' is also very pertinent in this regard. She explores how sustainability discourses shapes planning and 'design processes to configure and embed ideas about social relationships in the urban landscape.'

Meanwhile, Mary Corcoran sets up an extensive reading of 'urban agriculture' (UA), which for some might seem a contradiction in itself, noting that the post-2007 crisis of capitalism has brought into sharp relief an emergent trend towards UA in developing countries. 'It may be that this resurgence of interest in urban agriculture is in fact an unintended consequence of economic retrenchment, borne out of economic necessity but also out a desire to reassert an unmediated relationship to the land, and to secure a sense of ontological security in a world that has become increasingly uncertain' (Corcoran, this volume:12). Such astute and contextual explorations helps to break down crude binaries between urban and rural, which many environmental and sustainability experts seem to perpetuate almost unconsciously.

In research on environmental communication and film for instance, we strive to unpack so-called 'creative imaginaries' and narrative storylines which can help counter the dominant 'business as usual' growth models that by all accounts make sustainability and environmental concerns like climate change much worse. Geoff Mead in a review piece in *The Guardian* (30th April 2014) titled 'Sustainability needs new Narratives between Catastrophe and Utopia' is certainly apt in mentioning deep ecology scholar Thomas Berry- who affirms, '[I]t's all a question of story. We are in trouble just now because we do not have a good story. We are in between stories. The old story, the account of how we fit into the world, is no longer effective. Yet we have not learned the new story'. This new story, which anthropologists are also essential in developing and promoting, must involve connection with our fragile environment and looking beyond our own selfish desires for short term gain.

Corcoran and others speak of a wider concept of growth, which is emerging in policy and research debates, and this also reflects the impact of a growing body of work on sustainability by social scientists. Numerous efforts have been made to go beyond GDP as the only criterion for measuring economic performance and social progress. We urgently need to acquire new measures of wealth and profitability if the full impact and recuperative possibility of sustainable development is to be felt across the corporate political and social spheres.

By focusing on *real practices* of (urban and rural) sustainability, such as those outlined in Corcoran's chapter, and across the whole volume for that matter, social scientists can make the connection between sustainability goals (articulated from above), and the life world of real European citizens (articulated from below), who through practices such as Urban Agriculture in all its myriad manifestations, are contributing to urban sustainability.

The major question, however, is how can we motivate publics through effective actions- and promote all forms of sustainability? As Murray Bookchin puts it, 'Capitalism can no more be "persuaded" to limit growth than a human being can be "persuaded" to stop breathing' (Wilkinson and Picket 2009: 180). Economic sustainability remains- unfortunately- for the present at least locked into a conventional capitalist mindset. As Tim Jackson illustrates in his classic study, our current socio-economic thinking is locked into what he calls the 'iron cage' of consumerism, which is characterised by a severe lack of macro-economic models that do not rely on growth, but rather are designed for functioning at a steady state (Jackson 2009: 100). We certainly need every avenue possible to promote robust levels of sustainable literacy, as it applies both socially, politically, economically, and of course, environmentally.

Nonetheless, as environmental and sustainability scholars, including most explicitly, anthropologists, we need to constantly seek to explore and explain how such cultural artefacts and the various case studies examined in this excellent volume might encode various shades of 'progressive' versions of sustainability, while maintaining social justice in particular, together with other environmental concerns. Gauging mass psychological and cognitive responses to such global challenges is necessary, in framing and understanding the power and impact of such case studies and theoretical models, as they extend their reach and appreciation around broad-based sustainability issues.

he proposed solution of applying a 'Resource based economy' (Sando 2015), as explored in Chapter 2 by Gregor Claus, is certainly interesting. Jacque Fresco sees it as a rational system of arranging the economy, centred on the idea that the earth and its resources are a finite system. Market process do not measure externalities and companies can actually gain competitive advantage by externalising costs and passing them on to society in the form of pollution, increased job insecurity, potentially harmful products etc. The *real* costs, not in money but in the effect on individuals, society and environment, is *hidden* by the market price.

Furthermore, given the increasing privatization of Nature, through the so-called 'Tragedy of the Commons,' and other abuses of natural resources by industrial style farming and various national resource exploitation, John Bellamy Foster asks a particularly difficult but pertinent question; whether capitalism can ultimately be 'reshaped' to the demands of what environmentalists and others call sustainable development. One of course wonders and hopes that this left-leaning strategy does not remain an unrealizable utopian political dream. In any case, if only as a first step, constructing environmentally and socially aware individuals is an essential part of successful environmental citizenship and 'ecocentrism' and deep ecology do indeed have a role to play in this, although given their unwillingness to embrace anthropocentrism, it is necessary an incomplete role' (Gandhi 2008: 47).

At the same time many of these chapters recognise the dangers of 'greenwashing' in business terms and the legitimation of more shallow forms of corporate responsibility, evident in mainstream entrepreneurial culture, which in turn can be used to affirm a 'business as usual' strategy, while paying lip service to notions of universal sustainability and a range of deep environmental ethics. All of these loaded, discursive and contested terms are very much part of the lexicon of modern economic, cultural and political thinking and are also becoming infused within eco-critical cultural analysis.

Embracing this austere form of sustainability appears a long way for instance from the neoliberal mantra of conspicuous consumption, together with balancing all forms of capitalistic valuation and the pervasive fiction of ever increasing economic growth. While probably it is somewhat counter-intuitive to expect all forms of research, including mainstream (Hollywood) cinema for example, to promote such a puritanical form of sustainable values. Nonetheless, one can recognise the progressive and sometimes even radical evocations of environmental scenarios across a range of contemporary narratives like *Wall-E* (2008), which explicitly highlights the consequences of excessive waste and allegorically valorises the need for adapting more stoical and sustainable environmental values.

An ethical and environmental scholar Holmes Rolston III wonders out loud, can and should humans win or lose when they 'do the right thing', by for instance, caring for nature and the environment. Life is defined by many in the modern world as simply a utilitarian model of economics, foregrounding value gain and value loss. 'There must be winners and losers among the humans who are helped or hurt by the conditions of their environment'. Nevertheless, it can more fruitfully be suggested that a socially defined model that cares 'properly for the natural world can combine with a strategy for sustainability, a win-win solution. A bumper sticker reads: re-cycling, everyone wins. That is almost an aphoristic model for the whole human-nature relationship. If we are in harmony with nature, everyone wins' (Rolston 1994: 218). Of course, many sustainability critics, including some of the scholars cited in this volume, contest this somewhat simplistic and relatively easy and utilitarian correlation around use/benefit. Possible 'easy gains' ought to be highlighted, in the first instance, to gain traction, as like most things, once you go deeper, the problems and difficulties appear to proliferate and often serve to deaden any resolve to uncover clear systemic and effective solutions.

References

Brereton, Pat. *Environmental Ethics and Film.* London: Routledge, 2006.

Dixon, Tracey. Putting the S Word Back into Sustainability. 2011. Accessed July 18th, 2015. http://www.berkeleygroup.co.uk/media/pdf/1/f/Putting-the-S-word-back-into-sustainability-report.pdf

Kemp, Rene, Loorbach, Derk, and Jan, Rotmans. "Transition management as a model for managing processes of co-evolution." *International Journal of Sustainable Development and World Ecology* (2006): 14(1):78–91.

Gandhi, Devadatta. 'The Limits and Promise of Environmental Ethics: Eco-socialist thought and anthropocentrism's virtue'. University of California, Davis. Vol. 31: 1, 2008. Accessed July 18th, 2015. http://environs.law.ucdavis.edu/volumes/31/1/gandhi.pdf

Jackson, Tim. *Prosperity without Growth? Steps to a sustainable economy.* London: Sustainable Development Commission, 2009.

Rolsten, Holmes III "Winning and Losing in Environmental Ethics." In *Ethics and Environmental Policy: Theory meets Practice,* edited by Frederick Ferre and Peter Hartel, 217-234. Athens, GA: University of Georgia Press, 1994.

Wilkinson, Richard, and Pickett Kate. *The Spirit Level: Why more equal societies almost always do better.* London: Allen Lane, 2009.

CONTRIBUTORS

Pat Brereton is Professor of Media Studies in Dublin City University. Pat has an academic background in all aspects of film studies and new media literacies. His research focuses on representations of: ecology, science, war, religion and national identities among others. He was a previous Director of SIM and continues to be an active member while carrying out his duties as Associate Dean for Research in the Faculty of Humanities and Social Sciences. His research adapts a broad interdisciplinary approach to textual analysis, together with a growing involvement with reception study, as evidence of the symbiotic relationship between media texts and audiences.

Gregor Claus is a part-time PhD Politics student at Queen's University Belfast, whose current research focuses on the critical analysis of concepts and approaches for just and sustainable societies. He has a Masters in European Union Politics and a Bachelor Joint Honours in Philosophy and Politics from Queen's University Belfast.

Mary P. Corcoran is Professor of Sociology at Maynooth University (National University of Ireland Maynooth) where she is also a member of the University's Governing Authority. She is a graduate of the University of Dublin, Trinity College and Columbia University, New York. Her research and teaching interests lie primarily in the fields of urban sociology, public culture and the sociology of migration, and she has researched and published widely on these topics. She is a member of the COST ACTION Urban Agriculture Europe (2012-2016), and co-chair of its Working Group on Governance and local policy. Mary P. Corcoran was a Taoiseach's nominee to the National Economic and Social Forum (NESF) for five years. She has previously served on the Senate of the National University of Ireland, on the Social Science Committee of the Royal Irish Academy (RIA) and on the Expert Advisory Committee of the Childhood Development Initiative, where she is now a Board member. Her RIA Dublin Talk "Publi-City" is available at
https://www.ria.ie/events/dublin-talks.aspx

Susanne Elsen is professor of sociology and social development at the Free University Bozen-Bolzano. Currently, she is also vice dean for research and director of the PhD-program of the Faculty of Education of the Free University. She has studied social work, sociology, economics and educational sciences and has research- and development experiences in the fields of community development and local economy in Europe, Asia and Latin America. Her particular research interests are on social innovation, eco-social transformation, community work and development, social and solidarity economy, as well as sustainability and post-growth perspectives. Her interest and contribution in the project is the analysis of local conditions and actors and the development of specific strategies of participatory knowledge production and bottom-up solutions.

Marinus Gebhardt is a Geographer (Dipl.) focusing on the interrelation of land use and vegetation ecology in Caucasian Alpine grasslands. Prior to his PhD-studies in "Management of Mountain Environment" at the Free University of Bolzano, he was involved as a trainee and consultant in the field of nature conservation and pasture management. During the elaboration of his Diploma thesis in the Javakheti Highland, he realised that vegetation patterns can only be sufficiently explained by considering present and past land-use systems

Suzanne Hanchett is a social anthropologist with a doctorate from Columbia University. She is a Partner in the consulting firm, Planning Alternatives for Change LLC, and a Research Fellow at the Center for Political Ecology. She has done basic and applied research on social structure, gender, and poverty-related issues in Bangladesh, India, and several other countries. She is the author of *Coloured Rice; Symbolic Structure in Hindu Family Festivals* (1988), based on her research in Karnataka State, India, and a co-author of *Water Culture in South Asia: Bangladesh Perspectives* (2014). Since 1997, she has been working primarily on water and sanitation programs, arsenic mitigation projects, and gender issues in water resources management. She has served as Team Leader for baseline and evaluation studies for organisations such as UNICEF, CARE, WaterAid, and the World Bank.

Alex Koensler is a social anthropologist working in the Institute for the Study of Conflict Transformation and Social Justice in Queens University Belfast. Alexander received a PhD in "Methodologies of Socio-Anthropological Research" (University of Siena 2009). Before joining ISCTSJ, he held postdoctoral and teaching positions at the University of

Perugia (Italy), the University of Muenster (Germany) and the Blaustein Institutes for Desert Research at Ben-Gurion University of the Negev (Israel). He also coordinates with Elena Apostoli Cappello the network "Anthropology and Social Movements" of the *European Association of Social Anthropologists* (EASA).

Rebekah McCabe is a Belfast-based PhD Candidate at the Department of Anthropology in Maynooth University. Her primary research interests include environmentalism, sustainability, urban space, social conflict, social exclusion, and neighbourhood regeneration. From 2008-2012, she carried out fieldwork for her PhD dissertation in the South Bronx and East Belfast. Since 2012, Rebekah has worked as Creative Producer for Northern Irish built environment non-profit PLACE, on an interdisciplinary team developing projects that look critically and creatively at urban challenges.

Pierre McDonagh BSocSc. MBA (QUB) (PhD, Cardiff) is Professor of Marketing in the University of Bath. He has worked at Universities in Ireland, Scotland, Wales, England & the US since he began in academia in 1987 at QUB. Since 1989 Pierre's research primarily focuses on the (im) possibility of sustainability within the prevailing order and oppositional counter culture. In 1997 he co-edited Green Management: A Reader with Andy Prothero. He has published widely and received awards for his work on the interactions among Markets, Marketing and Society; dark marketing; critical marketing; and transformative consumer research. One current research project considers the experiences of lead users of electric vehicles. Pierre has been published widely with articles in the Journal of Consumer Research, Journal of Business Research, European Journal of Marketing, Journal of Marketing Management and others. Guest Editing work includes the first double Special Issue of the Journal of Macromarketing (with Andy Prothero, University College Dublin) on 'Sustainability as Megatrend' (Sept 2014 and March 2015). Recently he Guest Edited a Journal of Marketing Management Special Issue on 'Sustainable Consumption, Activism, Innovation and Brands' (with Diane Martin, Aalto University). Previously he has Guest Edited special issues of Consumption Markets & Culture, European Journal of Marketing, Irish Marketing Review & Journal of Strategic Marketing. Pierre serves as Associate Editor for the Journal of Macromarketing (US), and has served on the Advisory Committee for Transformative Consumer Research for the American Association for Consumer Research 2009-15; he also serves on the editorial boards of the Journal of Marketing Management (UK),

Consumption Markets & Culture (US), Recherche et Applications en Marketing (FRA). He is married to the Welsh academic Andy Prothero with whom he has three wonderful sons Ethan, Cal & Dylan.

Fiona Murphy is a Queens University Belfast Research Fellow based in the Institute for the Study of Conflict Transformation and Social Justice. Fiona earned her doctorate in Anthropology in Maynooth University in 2009. Previously she has held Postdoctoral Research Posts in Maynooth University (2009-2011) and in the School of Business, Dublin City University (2012-2014). Fiona works across the disciplines of anthropology, sociology, literary studies and marketing. She specialises in Indigenous politics and movements, refugees and mobility studies, and sustainability in Australia and Ireland. The key thematics in her work include trauma, memory, reconciliation, mobility and integration. She has served as secretary of the Anthropological Association of Ireland (2013-2015), book review editor for the Irish Journal of Anthropology (2011-2014) and is a member of a number of Anthropology networks and associations, including the European Association of Anthropologists. Her current work focuses on both the politics of reparations in the context of the removal and institutionalisation of Aboriginal Australian children and sustainable consumption in the context of economic crisis in Ireland.

Nadezhda Savova-Grigorova, originally from Bulgaria, received her PhD in Cultural Anthropology from Princeton University, USA, alongside being a Research Fellow at the Princeton Center for Arts and Cultural Policy Studies. Nadezhda's research examined cultural policies and community development projects employing the arts with comparative studies of the community cultural centres networks in Bulgaria (*chitalishte*), Brazil (*pontos de cultura*) and Cuba (*casas de cultura*). As an academic and consultant to UNESCO's Intangible Heritage Section, Nadezhda founded and is currently the President of the International Council for Cultural Centers (I3C), www.international3c.org, based in Bulgaria and coordinating the global network of national networks and individual community cultural centers from around more than 50 countries. Nadezhda also founded an innovative community cultural center called a Bread House (translation of the name Bethlehem, envisioning bread as a symbol of peace and sharing among diverse people and cultures). The model inspired other organizations and individuals and spread into a network now called the Bread Houses Network, www.breadhousesnetwork.org, which evolved in some cases from community cultural centers into self-sustainable bakeries-social enterprises

employing people from disadvantaged groups and offering unique "bread therapy sessions". For this initiative and her travels researching local cultural and culinary traditions, Nadezhda was recognized as "Traveller with a Mission of the Year 2012" by the *National Geographic*. Nadezhda is currently developing a program "Cultural Anthropology for Children" in order to promote anthropology from early age on and among youth. She is also a guest lecturer in Sociology and Cultural Anthropology at different universities in Bulgaria and abroad.

Anja K. Salzer is a social anthropologist and geographer (M.A.) with focus on post-Soviet countries currently meandering between Bozen-Bolzano/Italy and Georgia/Caucasus. Prior to her PhD-studies at the Free University of Bolzano/Italy, she was working as a freelancer in the field of civil society engagement and environmental education, and as a coordinator of a university-network and a civil society platform. Further, she had worked as a consultant in the areas of nature conservation and natural resource management, and as a trainer for global education and development cooperation. During her practical experiences, she realized that core components of a sustainable future are to be found in the areas of civil society engagement and joint learning and thus require transdisciplinary approaches and action.

Elya Tzaneva is Assoc. Prof. and Head of Scholarly Council of the Institute for Ethnology and Folklore Studies of the Bulgarian Academy of Sciences. PhD in Ethnology (Moscow State University) and PhD in Sociology (University of New South Wales, Sydney). Her research interests are in Theory of Ethnicity and Nations, Ritual Kinship, and Critical Situations and Ethnic Culture. Her monographs include Interpreting *Ethnicity. Historiographical Overview and Assessment of Theoretical Discussions*. Sofia (2000); *Bulgarian Ethnography. Texbook for Students*. 3 editions: Sofia (2000, 2005, 2008); *Ethnoses, Regions, Cultures. Readings in non-European Ethnology*. Sofia, 2010; *Adoption in Bulgarian Cultural Tradition* (with A.Kirilova and V.Nikolova). Sofia (2010). Initiator of international projects on "Anthropology of Disasters", and editor-in-chief of two volumes on the subjects with participation of Bulgarian, Chinese, Russian and American anthropologists - *Disasters, Culture, Politics: Chinese-Bulgarian Anthropological Contribution to the Study of Critical Situations*. Edited by Elya Tzaneva (Editor-in-Chief), with Fang Sumei and Liu Mingxin. Cambridge Scholars Publishing, 2009; and *Disasters and Cultural Stereotypes*. Ed. by Elya Tzaneva (Editor-in-

Chief), with Fang Sumei and Edwin Schmitt. Cambridge Scholars Publishing, Newcastle, 2012.

Saffron Woodcraft is a PhD candidate in UCL's Anthropology Department. Her research is exploring sustainability cultures in urban planning from the perspective of planners, architects, housing providers and community activists. Her fieldwork focuses on the social and material processes of placemaking and community building in the new residential neighbourhoods being created in London's Olympic Park.

Stefan Zerbe is vegetation and landscape ecologist with a particular research focus on landscape history, sustainable land use, biodiversity research, biological invasions, urban ecology, and ecosystem restoration. He currently is affiliated at the Faculty of Science and Technology at the Free University of Bozen-Bolzano (N Italy). In research and teaching, he works in interdisciplinary groups in order to integrate key disciplines of the natural and social sciences for the development of sustainable land-use strategies. He established two international Master study programs on landscape ecology & nature conservation and environmental management in mountain areas, respectively, at the University of Greifswald (Germany) and the Free University of Bozen-Bolzano (Italy). He has published around 200 papers, book chapters, and monographs in the fields of vegetation ecology and interdisciplinary landscape ecology